# The Story of CHRISTMAS

Its growth and development from the earliest times

By

MICHAEL HARRISON

ODHAMS PRESS LIMITED
LONG ACRE, LONDON

Made and printed in Great Britain by
ODHAMS (WATFORD) LTD., WATFORD
T.1151.PQ

# THE STORY OF CHRISTMAS

THE NATIVITY, BY ALBRECHT DÜRER, 1504

## CONTENTS

# LIST OF PLATES

CHAPTER ONE

# FESTIVAL OF THE WINTER SOLSTICE

Customs and traditions survive longer than does a language. In Britain, for instance, the names of rivers show that the people of these islands once spoke a language allied to the tongues still spoken in North Africa. Then came the Celts in three great waves, and the original—if, indeed, it was original—African tongue disappeared, save for the names of some rivers, mountains and lakes and for the grammar with which the Welsh language uses its Celtic vocabulary. Then came the Romans to impose the Latin tongue on Britain, and when the Romans left, the Angles, Jutes and Saxons arrived, to impose a Teutonic speech on all those parts of Britain that they could occupy.

The Normans, too, though they did not succeed in changing the Anglo-Saxon speech of the country to Norman-French—except in the law-courts, in which pleadings had to be drawn up in Norman-French until the year 1729—fundamentally altered the original character of Anglo-Saxon, itself corrupted by the contact of the Saxon invaders with the Celtic and Latin speaking peoples whom they had conquered.

But we, whose history shows us to be the descendants of a people whose language has undergone many changes, still retain customs of immemorial usage; customs which were old before the monoliths of Stonehenge were raised or the Thames first received its name. And some of the very oldest of these customs are to be found associated with our Christmas rejoicings.

In primitive society, the year is full of festivals—all of them connected with the fertility of the earth, since primitive man is highly conscious of his dependence upon the earth, and upon the sun, whose warmth makes the earth to bring forth her fruits.

The words "civilized" and "polite" mean "according to the style of those who dwell in cities"—the first is derived from the Latin, the second from the Greek, language. And men who dwell in cities tend to forget, when they eat, that food comes from the earth: a fact that no countryman ever forgets—for if he did forget it, not only he but the whole world would soon starve to death.

We expect, then, to find that many of the feasts that country-folk celebrate throughout the year become neglected when men gather themselves in cities. But the greatest feast of all—the festival of the Winter Solstice, which celebrates the apparent rescue of the sun from a total disappearance beneath the dark horizon—this men have taken with them into their cities. Racial instinct, even more than racial memory, has made them hold on to this celebration even when all the other feasts of sowing and growth, of ripening and harvest, have been left to the country-folk.

Christmas is the one feast of the civilized world which still possesses that unifying quality implicit in the traditional message of the angels on the very first Christmas of all; and persons of Christian, Jewish, Moslem, Buddhist and many other faiths—and some of no particular religious faith at all—celebrate the feast, conscious or unconscious, as the case may be, of its original religious significance.

For though the celebration of the Winter Solstice dates from thousands of years before Christ, and was once celebrated with rites which had nothing to do with Christianity, a new significance was given to the ancient festival when the Church decided, in the earliest days of Christianity, to celebrate the birth of Christ on a date that ancient usage had made already one of universal respect.

First of all, it must be noted that, despite the efforts of innumerable scholars, it has not yet been proved upon what day—or even in which year—Christ was born. We reckon our dates "A.D."; that is, *Anno Domini*, "in the year of the Lord" just as the Jews reckon theirs from the Creation, the Moslems from the Hegira—or the flight of Mohammed from Medina to Mecca—in A.D. 622—and certain peoples of the ancient East reckoned their dates from the accession of Seleucus Nicator to the throne of Syria, in 312 B.C.

It was not, so far as we know, until the year A.D. 533 that the custom of reckoning dates from the birth of Christ came into use. Before that, all dates in the West had been reckoned from the foundation of Rome: a date corresponding to 753 B.C. in our time-reckoning. The introduction of our present system of chronology—used, incidentally, by many who are not Christians—we owe to a Russian monk, named Dionysius, nicknamed Exiguus, or "the Little."

It was he who first began to reckon dates from the birth of Christ, but he made the mistake of taking the year A.U.C. ("from the building of Rome") 753 as that of the birth of our Saviour, whereas the Gospels make it quite clear that Christ must have been born before that date, since St. Luke says that the birth took place "in Bethlehem of Judaea, in the days of Herod the King"—and we know that Herod died between 13 March and 29 March, in the year A.U.C. 750, so that Christ must have been born before that date—that is, *at least* three years before A.D. 1.

Though the error in Dionysius's reckoning was noticed very early in the Church's use of the new system of chronology (the wonder is that it was not noticed at the very beginning!) scholars have not yet been able to agree just how many years "B.C." we must put the birth of Christ.

Since Dionysius, in his *Cyclus Paschalis*—a treatise on the computation of Easter, written in the first half of the sixth century A.D.—introduced his new system of reckoning dates, many have tried to fix the definite year in which Christ was born in Bethlehem. Ewald, Petavius and Usher believe that the birth occurred in what we must call "5 B.C.," while Bengel, Anger and Winer think that it occurred in "4 B.C." Scaliger and St. Jerome place it in "3 B.C.," while Eusebius sets it at two years before the official beginning of our era, and Ideler goes so far as to set it not less than seven years before "A.D. 1."

Nor are the authorities agreed better upon the actual day of the year than they are upon the year itself. And there seems every reason to believe that the date, 25 December, was fixed arbitrarily by the Church because it was about that date when the pagan world celebrated a series of feasts connected with the Winter Solstice. It was the practice of the Church in early times to seek rather to give a sacred significance to established pagan festivals than to abolish them altogether.

St. Gregory, writing to St. Augustine regarding the best means of converting the Anglo-Saxons to Christianity, advises Augustine to accommodate the ceremonies of the Christian as much as possible to those of the heathen, and not to abolish the sacrifice of oxen, but to see that the converts sacrificed the beasts "to the glory of God, as they had formerly done to the honour of the Devil."

Now, the winter festival was celebrated in pagan Rome with great and extended rejoicing, the period beginning on 17 December and lasting into the New Year. The feast was called the *Saturnalia*, named supposedly after a primitive tribal god of the Roman people, Saturnus, whose name simply means "plenty" or "bounty," and who was obviously the personification of kindly Nature, which gave men enough—and that, the proverb holds, is a feast.

"At this festival," says an historian, "the utmost freedom of social intercourse was permitted to all classes; even slaves were allowed to come to the tables of their masters clothed in their apparel, and were waited on by those whom they were accustomed to serve. Feasting, gaming and revelry were enjoyed by all classes, without discrimination of age, or sex, or rank. Processions crowded the streets, boisterous with mirth: these illuminated the streets with lighted tapers of wax, which were also used as gifts between friends in the humbler walks of life. The season was one for the exchange of gifts of friendship, and especially of gifts to children."

As written, that description of the *Saturnalia* sounds not unlike our present Christmas—with the exception of the processions of taper-bearers through the streets. But the *Saturnalia* had its grosser side, and the excesses committed by too many—far too many—of the revellers caused the Church to wish to purge the celebrations of their baser elements.

Now, in the middle of this period of general gaiety, there was a day set aside for special reverence to the sun whose apparent rebirth on the Winter Solstice had originally provided the excuse for all these widespread pagan jollifications. This day was known as *Dies Solis Invicti Nati,* the Day of the Birth of the Unconquered Sun, and it fell on what corresponds to 25 *December* in our calendar.

It was, in particular, the greatest feast-day of the Mithraic religion, which appeared, for a time, to be rivalling the Christian faith as the state religion of the Roman Empire; for Mithraism enjoyed the enormous advantage of being the fashionable faith of the Roman soldiers. In the end Christianity triumphed over Mithraism, but the reverence that the Mithraists paid to 25 December certainly had its influence in deciding the Church authorities in fixing the official birthday of our Saviour on 25 December—a decision arrived at neither early in the Church's history, nor without considerable opposition from supporters of alternative dates.

If Mithraism was the chief rival of Christianity in the first centuries of our era, we must not forget the immense influence that Judaism had upon early Christian thought. The Apostles and the first disciples were all Jews, and the traditional ceremonies of the Jewish religion were practised by them.

Now, one of the principal feasts of the Jewish year was that of the Dedication of the Temple, which was established by Judas Maccabaeus, in commemoration of the cleansing of the Temple at Jerusalem in 164 B.C., six and a half years after its profanation by Antiochus Epiphanes. The learned German scholar, Dr. Cassel, upheld the theory that our Christmas owed its origin, especially with regard to its sacred character, to this great feast of the Jewish Church, since the Dedication of the Temple was always celebrated on 25 Kislev (corresponding to 20 or 21 December: and thus obviously establishing it as having been originally a feast connected with the Winter Solstice).

Deriving its spiritual authority from the sacred books of the Jews—known collectively as the Bible (which is the Greek word for "book")—the Christian Church, making its principal headquarters in the then capital of the world, Rome, was necessarily faced with the problem of converting, really as a prime factor in the Church's survival, the Roman pagan.

It was, therefore, inevitable that an attempt should have been made to avoid antagonizing the prospective Roman converts—who were also, let us not forget, the neighbours of the early Christians; the people among whom the Christians lived and worked.

What the Church, in those days, was seeking to do was this: to utilize, for her own purposes, the fund of reverence drawing its need from the popular festivals, which were essentially religious in origin, while purging those festivals of the grossly material features which had come, through the centuries, to obscure and alter their original character.

Thus the end-of-year celebrations to mark the "rebirth" of the sun could, by making the celebrants thank God for that rebirth, be brought into line with Christian practice; and by identifying God with Nature, pagan festivals could be—and were, as it turned out—transformed into Christian ones. And this policy it was, undoubtedly, which was responsible for the Church's making the principal festival of the Christian year to fall upon a day already greatly reverenced by Jews, pagans and—in short—the majority of dwellers in the then known world.

The Teutonic peoples, too, in common with the rest of mankind, celebrated the Winter Solstice under a name which still survives as the English word, Yule. The month of December, among the Anglo-Saxons, was known as *aerre-geola* ("ere Yule" or "before Yule") and January as *aeftera-geola* ("after Yule"). The derivation of the word *Yule* is obscure, but there is a word in old Norse, *jol,* which means feasting or revelry, and it may be from this word that our word *Yule* is derived.

Another etymological theory would seek to connect *Jol*—or *Yule*—with the same word-root which has given us "wheel"—on the assumption that "Yule-tide" celebrations marked one complete turn or revolution of the seasons.

Whatever the correct theory, it is certain that the word *jol—geola* in Anglo-Saxon—had a deep religious significance for our Teutonic ancestors. The twelfth title of Odin (or Woden), All-Father or Father of the Gods, is given as *Ialg* or *Ialkr* (pronounced *yolk* or *yulg*), while the Russians, who got their Christmas-tree from the Scandinavians, call it *yolka.*

The Anglo-Saxon conquerors of Britain celebrated the high feast of Odin, their All-Father, under the name of *Iálka tid*—or *Yule-tide*. Some say that *Iálka tid* was celebrated in mid-winter because it was at that time that the Vikings were unable to put to sea in their dragon-ships, and were able only to "assemble in their great halls and temples and drink to the gods they served so well." But it is beyond argument that at *Iálka tid* the Vikings were celebrating the "rebirth of the sun" at the Winter Solstice—a natural phenomenon, by the way, much more noticeable in the northern lands than in the regions farther south. Indeed, the Eddas—the old Norse sacred books—strangely mixing heroic legend and the crudely barbarous theology of the ancient Teutons—are full of references to the heavenly signs, and clearly indicate the consciousness that Northern Man had of the celestial bodies and their movements and changes.

To select 25 December, then, as the official date of the Nativity was to adapt, to the service of Christianity, a feast of immemorially ancient origins and world-wide observance.

But it was not selected altogether arbitrarily: the legend that Christ was born on 25 December arose, apparently, in the very earliest days of the Church, and Titus Flavius Clemens, generally known as Clement of Alexandria, refers to this belief in rather scornful manner. He says: "There are those who, with an over-busy curiosity, attempt to fix not only the year but the date of our Saviour's birth, Who, they say, was born in the twenty-eighth year of Augustus, on the 25th of the month Pachon"—which would make the date, in our reckoning, 20 May. Elsewhere the same Father of the Church says: "Some say that he was born on the 24th or 25th of the month Pharmuthi"—19 or 20 April.

It will be observed that the earliest traditions apparently were agreed upon the *day,* if not upon the *month;* but in Clement's time—he was writing early in the third century of our era—the Nativity was celebrated on 6 January: as it still is in the Armenian Church.

St. Chrysostom favoured 25 December as the date of the Nativity; St. Epiphanius preferred to believe that it had taken place on 6 January. Neither saint gives very convincing reasons why we should accept either date, but St. Chrysostom does add the interesting information that, by a very ancient tradition, the West—that is, all Europe from Thrace to Cadiz—celebrated the Nativity on 25 December; and certainly the ancient Roman Calendar, made in the year A.D. 354, gives 25 December as the date. All this uncertainty arose from the fact that, at the time of the Nativity, there were no fewer than five systems of time-reckoning in use.

All the same there has been, and probably will continue to be, much argument in attempting to fix the exact date.

There have been contenders for placing the date—apart from 25 December—on 1 January, 6 January, 21 March (the Vernal Equinox), 29 March, the time of the Jewish Passover, and 29 September, or the Feast of Tabernacles among the Jews. The modern biblical commentator, Wiesseler, gives his reasons for placing the date of the Nativity at 10 January, while another commentator, Gresswell, thinks that we must place the date of Christ's birth at 9 April, 4 B.C. Modern scholarship inclines to date the Nativity, for astronomical and other reasons, at 2 a.m., 16-17 May, 8 B.C.

It seems most probable that it was Julius I, Bishop of Rome from A.D. 337-352, who first authoritatively contended that the Nativity took place on 25 December. St. Chrysostom tells us that Julius made strict inquiries on the subject, at the request of St. Cyril of Jerusalem, and fixed upon 25 December as the most probable date. Eventually the whole of the Church came around to Pope Julius's opinion: all but the Armenian Church, which remained faithful to its opinion that the date of the Nativity should be 6 January.

At any rate, it is certain that, from the time of St. Chrysostom onwards—say from the beginning of the fifth century of our era—the feast of the Nativity of our Saviour was celebrated throughout Christendom on 25 December, except for the small section represented by those Christians observing the Armenian rite.

Well, correctly or incorrectly, the date of the Nativity has been fixed for ever. Even if scholars' research should establish, beyond a shadow of doubt, that Christ was born on some other day of the year, it is unthinkable that 25 December—a date so hallowed by centuries of worship—should be abandoned in favour of another date. We may say with confidence that 25 December will continue to be celebrated as Christmas Day until the end of time.

The date fixed, then how did the feast come by its various names? We have seen the derivations of *Yule*—the ancient Teutonic name, still used to some extent among us—and *Christmas* is not difficult to explain. The word is simply derived from "Christ" and "mas"—an old English word, meaning feast or festival.

This word is found spelt in various ways in olden times: Crystmasse, Cristmes, Cristmas, Crestenmes, Crestenmas, Cristemes, Cristynmes, Crismas, Kyrsomas, Xtemas, Cristesmesse, Cristemesse, Cristemasse, Crystenmas, Crystynmas, Chrystmas, Chrystemes, Chrystemasse, Chrystymesse, Christenmas, Christmass and Christmes are only *some* of the variant spellings to be encountered in old manuscripts and printed books.

The name, though, is thoroughly English, no matter how it is spelt, and typically German is the German name for the festival: *Weihnacht,* which, supposedly derived from the words *weihen,* "to consecrate, to inaugurate," and *nacht,* "night," has been held by some scholars to be proof that the Christian Christmas does derive directly from the Jewish Feast of the Dedication of the Temple, since Weihnacht would seem to mean *The Night of Dedication.*

But there is another word for Christmas, whose derivation is held to be far more obscure than that either of *Yule* or *Weihnacht.* It came into English usage apparently in Anglo-Saxon times, and is certainly the English form of a French word.

This is *Nowel—*

"Nowel, Nowel, the Angels did sing. . . ."

And Nowel is nothing but Englished "Noël," that we find in use in France today and used in a twelfth-century Anglo-Norman manuscript in the British Museum. This is one of the earliest carols known, and I give a stanza of it, with my own (very free) translation.

*Seignors io vus di par Noel,*
*E par li sires de cest hostel,*
*Car beuez ben:*
*E io primes beurai le men,*
*E pois apres chescon le soen,*
*Par mon conseil,*
*Si io vus di trestoz Wesseyl*
*Dehaiz eit qui ne dirra Drincgeyl!*

Sirs, I charge you by Nowel,
And by our friends that here do dwell,
To drink full well!
So let me pledge you, Sirs, the first:
Then all you others quench your thirst!
Grant me to tell
That when I pledge you all "Wassail!"
I trust you'll *all* respond "Drink-hail!"

But the derivation of "Noël" seems to me obvious. The Northern Gauls, when they came to speak the Latin of the conquering Roman legionaries, pronounced the Latin words in their own fashion, as the Hindu pronounced the English that he learnt of the conquering British. One of the peculiarities of this Gaulish Latin was a tendency to drop a "t" when that consonant came between two unstressed vowels, and to replace the "t" by a sort of abrupt pause, known to grammarians as "the glottal stop." Latin *pater*—"father"—became, on Gaulish lips, *pa'er*, and so the modern French *père*. And, in the same way, original Latin *natalis* became, first, *na'al* and then *Noël.*

For the other Romance languages—languages owing their origin to Latin—such as Spanish, Portuguese, Provençal, Italian, Romansch, Ladino, Catalan, retain the original "t" of *natalis*, which is what we may call the shorthand version of the original phrase, *Dies Christi Natalis*—The Birthday of Christ.

Christmas, in Spanish, is *El Natal*; in Portuguese, *O Natal*; in Italian, *Il Natale*; in Provençal, *Lo Nadal* or *Lo Nadaü*; and in Welsh, *Nadolig*.

It should be remarked here that there are also those who would derive the word *Noël* from the French word *nouvelles*—"news" or "tidings"; i.e., the "good news" of the Gospel. But philology is against this explanation, even if plausibility seem to favour it, and the derivation of *Noël* from (*Dies*) *Natalis* seems to be correct.

Says Chaucer, in *The Franklin's Tale*:

And Nowel cryen everich lustye man!

## CHAPTER TWO

# CHRISTIANITY IN THE ROMAN WORLD

THAT Christianity in its earliest days was persecuted may not be doubted, but the nature of this persecution has often been misunderstood and rather more frequently misrepresented.

The orthodox Jews, who had powerful commercial interests in many cities around the Mediterranean—particularly at Antioch and Alexandria—regarded the Christians, not without reason, as heretics attempting to pervert the pure essence of Judaism; and the opposition of the higher-class Romans to Christianity was based rather on snobbish than on religious grounds.

St. Paul, in his *Epistle to the Hebrews*, refers to this persecution—or, at least, to the difficulties with which the early Christians practised their faith. "They wandered in deserts, and in mountains, and in dens and caves of the earth."

So they may have done: but the evidence of the catacombs has been far too often misinterpreted. It must be borne in mind that the vast subterranean building-complex, to which we give the name "catacomb," was a place of privacy and not a place of refuge—at least, not in its primary purpose. It needs but a moment's reflection to realize that the immense constructional operation that the Roman catacombs represent could not have been undertaken in conditions of secrecy. The catacombs were burial-places as well as places of association and religious celebration, and the burial-laws of ancient Rome were exceedingly strict. Clandestine burials, on the scale exhibited in the catacombs, simply could not have taken place. The authorities would early have been made aware of mass irregularities in the observation of the burial-laws of the city, and would promptly have interfered.

The fact is that Christianity, in choosing to "go underground," was only adopting a custom already practised by other contemporary religions, and that Christians sought their privacy under rather than above ground does not imply that they were hiding anything more than the "mysteries" of their religion—from the vulgar gaze, too, and not from the police.

For instance, the rites of Mithraism were always celebrated in an underground chapel, or *cella* (whence our own word), a fine example of which may be seen in the ancient Roman city of Colchester, in the county of Essex, in England.

Now, Mithraism was the official religion of the Roman legions, and most of the political power of the Empire came to be concentrated in the hands of the military. So far no one has suggested that Mithraism, which went "underground," did so because of persecution.

We shall find, indeed, that just as the early Christians, who were exceedingly jealous of the "secrets" of their new faith, went "underground" in conformation to an established religious custom, so when Christianity became the state religion of the Empire under Constantine it adopted many of the conventions of the state religion that it had supplemented.

However, to the catacombs, where there are many evidences that Christmas was celebrated by the early Christians. Evidences, too, that the feast was celebrated in a fashion not unlike that observed by the pagan crowds above ground in their *Bacchanalia* and *Saturnalia* and *Lupercalia*. Later, bishops were to denounce this adoption, by Christians, of pagan celebrations; but in the early days of Christianity it seems that the Christians were content to celebrate the popular festivals, though in the consciousness that they were celebrating the events of Christ's life, rather than those of heathen deities.

One of the most interesting facts to be gathered from a study of the wall-frescoes—often executed with considerable artistic skill—which abound in the catacombs, is that the "master legends" of Christianity—especially those connected with Christmas—were already current in the very earliest days of the faith. Thus the traditional presence of the ox and the ass at the manger is recorded on the stuccoed walls, as is the Adoration of the Magi and the shining of the Nativity star.

All these frescoes are interspersed, let it be noticed, with those of a purely pagan character. For we find, side by side with scenes and characters from the Bible and from Christian story, Orpheus charming the beasts with his lyre, Bacchus presiding over the grape-gathering; even Mithra—the great rival of Christ for the worship of the Roman world—slaying the bull which is the emblem of darkness and death.

But there are other evidences in these frescoes which go to prove that the early Christians had celebrations of a more sober kind.

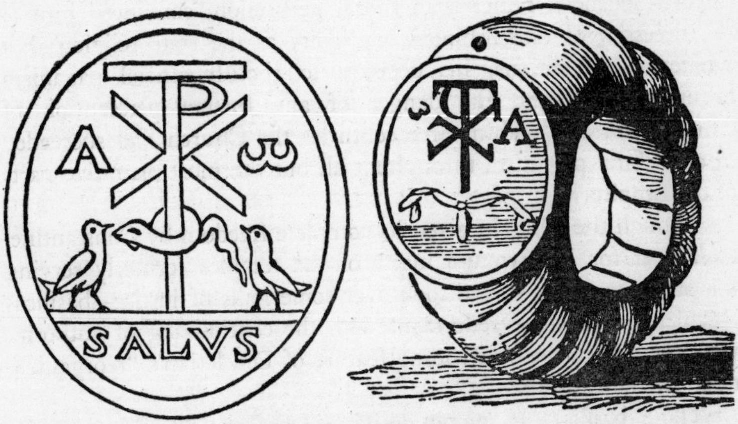


Early Christian emblems.

One very ancient fresco shows a group of five persons seated around a semicircular table, and being served by a youth who presides over the drinks set on a three-legged table. Over the heads of the seated figures two sentences are written, in the very slangiest sort of Latin: "Peace, give me some hot water!" and "Love, mix me wine with water!"—an allusion to the ancient custom of mixing wine with water, hot or cold; a custom which is still observed in the Roman Church, when the priest celebrates the Mass.

There are other evidences, too, to show that the early Christians were separated from their pagan brothers only by religious differences and not by any differences in modes of living.

This was made abundantly clear when, Christianity having been established as the state religion of the Roman Empire by that really appalling murderer, Constantine, the Christians abandoned their catacombs and took over such of the once-pagan temples that he allotted to the new Faith. He kept the largest and the most richly endowed for himself, leaving what he did not want to the Church that he established in place of the one that he had robbed: a policy which was to be copied twelve hundred years later by Bluff King Hal of England.

Britain has the doubtful honour of being able to claim Constantine as one of her sons, for Constantine—son of the sub-Emperor, Constantius, and a British princess, Helena—was born at York, A.D. 274, and was himself proclaimed Emperor in the land of his birth. Superstitiousness, rather than moral persuasion, convinced him of the necessity of establishing Christianity as the state religion; but whatever his reasons, his decision to abolish official paganism brought to an end the danger of any further persecution of Christianity, and within three centuries the Church had succeeded in abolishing paganism throughout all but the most primitive parts of the Empire.

Though the Church, given its complete freedom by Constantine, took over for its own use many of the temples formerly serving for pagan worship, it also took over some halls of justice—basilicas—which had become redundant with the centralizing of authority which had been the outstanding feature of Diocletian's "reorganization" of the Empire.

These basilicas (a name deriving from the Greek word for "king") suited the Church authorities much better than the buildings actually designed for religious worship, and it was the basilica—the hall of justice—rather than the temple, which was destined to serve as a model for the Christian church and cathedral. In Rome today you may see an ancient temple—built in 200 B.C.—converted, without structural alteration, to the service of Christian worship. This is the Pantheon. You may also see a basilica of the reign of Constantine turned over—and again without structural alteration—to Christian service.

This is the famous church of St. Mary Major; and if you would appreciate how much the modern church owes to the basilica, rather than to the temple, see how "modern" an aspect St. Mary Major has compared with the sense of remote antiquity which the Pantheon inspires.

Still, whether in converted temple or commandeered basilica, the Church now had come to the people. With the catacomb it had left its exclusiveness behind; and now that Christianity was the religion of the state, it was the pagans who, in the Church's opinion, were the outsiders, the Odd Folk.

Contact between Christians and the others was closer now than it had ever been, but the influence worked both ways: if the Empire was gradually converted to Christianity, Christianity itself was mellowed and broadened by its contact with ancient and ineradicable social customs which had their source in the very founding of the Latin people. Customs, then, which had a sanction in something more potent than religion: in a basic patriotism too primitive, too pure, ever to have been corrupted by political expediency.

In brief: if the Church christianized the Roman Empire, the Roman people humanized the Church. And certainly neither was the sufferer.

Still, the Church fought hard against the excessive humanizing powers of the people. It was all very well to see the *Saturnalia* the gentler for certain Christian characteristics: it would not have done to see the ceremonies of the Church insidiously altered by pagan sentiment.

Thus we find St. Gregory Nazianzen—he died in A.D. 389—warning his flock against "feasting to excess, dancing and crowning the doors" (a practice taken from the pagans, and still practised in modern times). He urged "the celebration of the festival after an heavenly and not after an earthly manner."

The warning was repeated—time and time again. It needed to be repeated. "Stage plays and spectacles" were forbidden on the Lord's Day, Christmas Day and other solemn Christian festivals by the African Council, held A.D. 408; and in the laws, *De Spectaculis*—"Concerning Public Shows"—Theodosius the Younger forbade, in the year 425, shows or games on the Nativity.

The practice of "dressing up"—either in the clothes of slaves or of women, of buffoons or of demons; in the skins of wild beasts or in nothing at all—evidently long survived the introduction of Christianity. (It survives today, if we regard putting on paper hats at Christmas as "dressing up.")

This custom was banned by the Council of Auxerre in A.D. 578; and another Council of the Church, in 614, repeated the prohibition. The latter prohibition was made in much stronger terms, "declaring it to be unlawful to make any indecent plays upon the Kalends of January" (i.e., 1 January—the Feast of Circumcision: a feast within

Second-century wall-fresco, showing Orpheus charming the beasts with his lyre. The eclectic nature of early Roman Christianity is well exemplified by the persistence of this and other essentially "pagan" themes in primitive Christian iconography.

the "Christmas" period, which extended from 12 December to 6 January).

The Church, as it happened, never quite succeeded in purging the traditional winter festival of "the profane practices of the pagans": what it has succeeded in doing is to purge those practices of gross elements, and to make, paradoxically enough, Christmas into a feast that even a pagan may celebrate in joyous sincerity.

Indeed, the "modern" Christmas, in which believer and unbeliever may join in feasting, is one of the triumphs of tolerance born of human understanding matured over centuries of trial and error.

Christmas is the feast, not only of man's redemption, but of man himself. It is *the* feast of humankind, because it releases—if only for a few days every year—tendencies that a savage self-interest causes mankind, in the ordinary way, to repress.

At Christmas-tide tyrants grow benevolent—even merciful; misers spend, not only freely, but willingly; the fierce flames of religious and political prejudice die for a short while to a cold cinder; selfish memories are stirred by the recollection—tardy but intense—of the neglected and the outcast.

For a few days, once a year, the atrophied souls of the grown-ups are filled again with that spirit which inspires the wisdom of fools and children.

So the history of Christmas, unlike the history of so many other human things, is consistently a pleasant one.

## CHAPTER THREE

# CHRISTIANITY COMES TO BRITAIN

THAT Christianity was introduced into Britain before the conquest of the island by the Anglo-Saxons we know; but the evidences of that religion are so very scanty among both legendary and material remains that we are forced to conclude that Christianity did not make a very strong appeal to the British Celts, at least to those who inhabited the southern parts of Britain.

We knew that there were executions—"martyrdoms"—of Christian officers in Britain: Alban, who was killed at Verulamium under Diocletian, being the best known of these victims to religio-political prejudice. But the number of such "martyrs" is small, and seeing that Christian legend has a tendency to make the most of such executions, the fact that the number is still reported to be exceedingly small surely implies that the number of Christians in Britain remained small even to the very end of Roman dominion in Britain.

Three British bishops—those of York, London and Colchester[1]—attended the Council of Arles in the year 314, and there seems reason to believe that the ancient Roman building known now as St. Martin's Church, Canterbury, was used as a place of Christian worship before the withdrawal of the legions from Britannia Prima and Britannia Secunda. There are a few—a very few—gravestones and other funerary objects surviving from the days of the Roman Empire which are marked with Christian emblems, but the evidences of Christianity among the Romano-Britons are so slight as

[1] Commonly it is accepted that Colchester marks the site of the Romano-British city of Camulodunum, but Maldon, in Essex, may really mark the site.

to lead us to believe that Christianity was never a state religion in Roman Britain as it became in Roman Italy.

There is, however, both in tradition and in custom-survival, a pointer to a different explanation of the fact of there being so few remains of "official" Christianity in Britain. The other explanation is that the British had their own form of Christianity before the Faith was introduced from Roman sources, and that the well-known conservatism—not to say prejudice—of the Celt permitted them to practise only "their own" form of Christianity.

Legend, supporting the theory that British Christianity was derived from non-Roman sources—and let us not forget that there had been trade-links between the Levant and Britain since some two thousand years (at least) before the Roman invasion of Kent—says that it was a British king, Bran, captured by the Romans and imprisoned in the same cell at Rome as St. Peter, who—on his release from captivity—brought the Faith to Britain; and the seventeenth-century English historian, Selden, quoting the Venerable Bede, uses another version of the legend when he tells us that a British king, Lucius Verus, at the time when Eleutherius was Bishop of Rome, asked to be instructed in the Faith. "This great and illustrious Prince, King Lucy" as Selden quaintly calls him—lived in the latter part of the second century of our era; later, by a hundred years or more, than the legendary Bran. But the legend is strong in contention of the fact that Christianity did enter Britain through other than a purely Roman source.

And that this non-Roman British Christian Church—whatever its origins—did develop on independent lines we know from our history books. Retiring to the northern parts of Britain and to Ireland, so as to escape the persecution of the Anglo-Saxons, the British Christian priests established a focus of culture which was later to play an important part in re-educating the West after the appalling anarchy of the Dark Ages.

It must have been a Church, this early British Church, singularly jealous of its national character, and that it did not share the Roman official prejudice against the Druids—or perhaps it was that the Druid priesthood merged itself into the newer faith—is shown by traditions and customs surviving today which derive from pre-Christian sources. I shall mention these specifically later in the book, and it will suffice here to point out that the Christmas mistletoe is a proof that objects held to be sacred in Druidical times were not deprived of their "magic" through the change from Druidism to Christianity.

Indeed, when Pope Gregory sent a mission under Augustine to England at the very end of the sixth century, the Roman missionaries appeared to differentiate little if anything between the pagan Anglo-Saxons and the British Christians, whose spiritual headquarters was situated on the rocky island of Iona, in the Hebrides. Fierce and bloody encounters, indeed, took place between the aggressive Roman missionaries and the cultured priesthood of the British Church. There was a fearful massacre of British monks at Bangor, but peace was established between the two branches of Christianity by the Synod of Whitby, in A.D. 664, by which the British Church agreed to accept the Roman usage and surrendered its independence as a Christian Church.

We shall see later, however, that this fusion of British and Roman elements in our ancient national religion preserved customs which were older than Christianity, either Roman or British.

In the meanwhile, the Roman missionaries were making much headway in converting the pagan Saxons: mostly because the missionaries used far more tolerance in dealing with these hardy, simple Teutons than with the almost over-civilized fellow-Christians of the North.

In a famous letter to Augustine, Pope Gregory directs the great missionary to "accommodate the ceremonies of the Christian worship as much as possible to those of the heathen, that the people might not be much startled at the change; and in particular the Pope advised Augustine to allow converts to kill and eat at the Christmas festival a great number of oxen to the glory of God, as they had formerly done to the devil." It is this oft-quoted letter which gives us our clue to the reason why so many of the ancient Teutonic Yule customs have survived into our modern Christmas, which received a further Teutonization from even more ancient sources—with the Germanizing of the British Royal Family in the eighteenth century: a Teutonization which will be duly considered and described in a later chapter.

This calculated tolerance on the part of Rome served its purpose well. King Aethelberht of Kent—who was married to a Christian princess—Bercta, daughter of the Frankish king, Charibert of

Paris—assigned the missionaries headquarters at Canterbury (in which city there was possibly a Christian community which had survived the passing of Roman rule in Britain), and on Christmas Day, 597, no fewer than ten thousand persons were baptized, "at the wish" of their newly converted king.

The reverence in which the Teutonic peoples had always held Yule they now transferred willingly to the feast of Christmas: the period about which date they called *Haelig-monath* (the Holy Month). But the truth is that Christmas was so easily established in England as a national festival because it coincided with a feast already traditionally celebrated.

There is a legend that King Arthur, who was not the purely mythical character that he was considered during the eighteenth and nineteenth centuries, celebrated his great victory over the Saxons at York by resting his army and holding a great feast in the ancient city that he had retaken from the invaders. He was, says Geoffrey of Monmouth, "a prince of unparalleled magnificence," and he tells us that Arthur's Christmas at York was kept with the greatest joy and festivity. "Then was the Round Table filled with jocund guests; and the minstrels, gleemen, harpers, pipe-players, jugglers and dancers were as happy about their log fires as if they had shone in the blaze of a thousand gas-lights," says a nineteenth-century historian.

Sir Thomas Malory—a little nearer, in the fifteenth century, to Arthur's time—gives *his* version of King Arthur's manner of celebrating Christmas.

"So," says Sir Thomas, "passed forth all the winter with all manner of hunting and hawking, and jousts and tourneys were many between many great lords. And ever, in all manner of places, Sir Lavaine got great worship, that he was nobly renowned among many of the knights of the Round Table. Thus it passed on until Christmas, and every day there were jousts made for a diamond, that whosoever joust best should have a diamond. But Sir Lancelot would not joust, but if it were a great joust cried; but Sir Lavaine jousted there all the Christmas passing well, and most was praised."

Gildas, writing in the sixth century, makes a significant reference to the then existing division of Britain among those who spoke Saxon, British (i.e., Celtic) and Latin. This is a reference which so far seems to have escaped the attention of the historians, but its implication is that a sort of "pocket of resistance," where the people still preserved the shadowy allegiance to Roman civilization, survived, by many years, the all-but-complete conquest of Britain by the Anglo-Saxons. It is almost certain that, if Arthur did not exist as a person, he did exist as a composite of the princes who ruled this "free British" territory almost to Norman times.

The two civilizations—perhaps cultures is the better word—existing side by side in a small country like ours have certainly combined to fuse Teutonic and Celtic customs into a synthesis of habit which has given that essentially "British" cast even to customs imported from abroad.

The Saxons themselves—though they, too, spent their winters in the active sports (mostly involving fighting) which are customary among primitive peoples—liked peaceful amusements as well. They were extremely fond of chess and backgammon, and in their passionate addiction to gambling of all sorts—especially dicing—the thoughtful may see the reason why football pools flourish in modern Britain despite the protests of the "unco guid."

Gambling, indeed, has an old history among the Teutonic peoples: the ancient Germans—Tacitus, the Roman historian, tells—would stake, not only their entire wealth, but even their personal liberty, on the roll of the dice. "He who loses," says Tacitus, "submits to servitude, though younger and stronger than his antagonist, and patiently permits himself to be bound and sold in the market; and this madness they dignify by the name of honour."

The social historian may see the origins of another modern custom in the remark of an ancient chronicler, in talking of the Anglo-Saxons: "When all were satisfied with dinner," he says, "they continued drinking all the evening"—but the duties on wine were not so heavy as they are now!

The boar was, in those days, to be found wild in many parts of Britain, which was much more thickly wooded then than it is now; and this plenitude of boar-meat (relished by both the Celts and the Saxons) developed a liking for the flesh which became gradually an unalterable custom, so that the boar's head was inseparably connected with Yule rejoicings.

The "brawn of the tusked swine"—as Chaucer calls it—was the first dish at Christmas, and even today the boar's head is carried with great solemnity into Hall at Queen's College, Oxford, to the chanting of a Latin carol—or, rather, Latin and English (a poem which is called a *macarontic*):

> *Caput apri defero,*
> *Reddens laudes Domino.*
> The boar's head in hand bring I,
> With garlands gay and rosemary.
> I pray you all sing merrily:
> *Qui estis in convivio.*

Studying the Christmas activities of the Anglo-Saxons, in the period when—clumsily, savagely even, but still certainly, and with indomitable purpose—they were making the scattered and divided principalities of Britain into one nation—one is aware of the fact that modern Christmas, itself a fusion of originally different national customs, was then being cast into an unalterable pattern. Indeed, we may say that though the pantomime, the Christmas-tree, the plum-pudding and other attributes of Yule were to come in the near or the distant future, the modern British Christmas was being patterned in the centuries immediately following the Saxon conquest.

It was in this period that a very famous Christmas Day impressed itself upon the mind of the West: the day on which Charles the Great—Charlemagne—was crowned, by Pope Leo, "Charles Augustus, Emperor of the Romans."

This day marked a turning-point in history, for though we may agree with some critics that there was something distinctly spurious in Charlemagne's attempt to set himself up as the heir of the Caesars, we cannot deny that the "re-creation of the Roman Empire" put a limit to the drift towards anarchy which had set in with the collapse of the old Empire. The political and cultural and administrative powers of Rome, though horribly enfeebled by attacks from without and by the despairing consciousness of defeat from within, had been preserved, through the almost total collapse of the central authority, by the Church.

When the true power seemed to have passed into the hands of illiterate brigand princes, "she did preserve, no matter in what vestigial and corrupt degree, the rule of law." She kept the flame of learning and art—however dim—still alight; and she offered to men, in an age when only force seemed to justify men's respect, the promise of authority deriving from rule rather than from repression; from code rather than from caprice; from a recognition of human dignity and human rights rather than from an appreciation of how completely men may be enslaved by the unscrupulous use of physical violence.

It is possible to make out a case for the contention that mankind can do today without churches; it is certainly not possible to make out the ghost of a case for the contention that mankind, between the fourth and the ninth centuries of our era, did not need the Church.

To Charlemagne, who represented the rebirth of a civil authority—who represented the restoration of that *Pax Romana* under whose sometimes severe but mostly just guidance the world had known peace for nearly half a millennium—the Church handed over its own authority, the debilitated but carefully tended legacy that she had received as the heir of the Caesars.

As the empire of Charlemagne, the new Roman Empire did not last long; he could not beget sons of a stature equal to his own, and they soon broke up the empire that their father had erected. But, though the actual empire of Charlemagne was transformed, there was no real retrograde step towards the earlier anarchy.

The concept of centralized authority had been reintroduced to the consciousness of intelligent men, and it was an ideal which was never again to be entirely abandoned. Like all other ideals, it was to be employed by rogues to make a trap for fools; but because it is, in its essence, a *good* ideal, it can never be entirely or for long perverted to base ends; for on it the happiness of mankind in general depends.

Christmas Day, 800, then, may be held to mean as much to man, in the material sense, as Christmas Day itself—the first Christmas Day of all—means to man in the spiritual sense.

If, with the crowning of Emperor Charlemagne, the seeds of civil peace were sown in anarchic Europe, the ninth century also brought political unity and consequent civil authority to England.

That century saw the uniting of the seven petty kingdoms of the Heptarchy into the Kingdom of England—as it saw that kingdom take its place among the comity of nations under the rule of the first truly able king to sit on the English throne: Alfred the Great—the first Englishman to have authority over the nation, who was

*Right:* A Bacchante making "rough music" in an ancient Roman *Saturnalia*. From a cornelian intaglio of the first century A.D.

*Below:* "Mummers," from an English MS. of the twelfth century. A thousand years of banning by the Church failed to kill the ancient custom of "disguising."

The murder of St. Thomas à Becket, Archbishop of Canterbury, at Christmastide, 1170/1. The illustration, from an illuminated MS. of the early thirteenth century, shows Sir Hugh de Morville, Sir Reginald Fitz Urse, Sir William de Tracy and Sir Richard Brito killing the Saint at the altar of Canterbury Cathedral.

also, in the best sense of the word, a "European."

In his reign England both gave and received culture; the country shared in the revival of learning which marked the end of the Dark Ages, and made its own contribution to the general enlightenment.

Yet Alfred made his mistakes, and some historians hold that, but for the king's strict observance of the law (that he himself had passed) by which the twelve days of Christmas-tide were set apart for celebration, he would not have been defeated by the Danes in 878.

It was on Twelfth Night that the invaders suddenly appeared at Chippenham.

"They rode through the West Saxons' land, and there sat down; and mickle of the folk over sea they drave, and of others the most deal they rode over. All but King Alfred. He, with a little band, hardly fared after the woods and on the moor-fastnesses."

There is an ancient legend which tells us how the King, wishing to spy out the Danish defences, passed through the enemy lines in the disguise of a Christmas minstrel, and spent several days among the Danish invaders, charming them with his singing, and staying and leaving with his true identity still hidden.

There were Danish kings in England after Alfred, and these invaders suffered the same fate as all the other invaders who have landed on this small island: they came as conquerors, and they stayed to become just one more racial element in that astonishing blend of bloods that we call "the British race."

They have left their traces, of course—all invaders do that. Names ending in "by"—such as Whitby, Maltby, Appleby—showed where the Danes had their original settlements; and that we say "the," "that," "then," "those," rather than "se," "sat," "sen," "sose," we owe to the influence of the Danish speech. The Church of St. Clement Danes, in the Strand, London, preserves, in its name, the memory of a Danish *enclave* of the ninth century, which stood just outside the city wall, at the gate later to be called Temple Bar. Whenever English-speaking children, all over the world, sing the nursery rhyme which begins:

Oranges and lemons,
The bells of St. Clemens[1]

[1] It is interesting to see how the nursery rhyme preserves the correct pronunciation. *Clemens* is Latin for "Loving."

they recall the Danes who settled in London a thousand years ago.

The greatest of the Danish kings of England was Cnut (Canute), whose symbolical act by the sea has so often, misrepresented, been held against the man for childish arrogance.

"Cnut's first acts of government in England," says Dawson, "were a series of murders; but he afterwards became a wise and temperate king. . . . He joined heartily in the festivities of Christmas-tide, and atoned for his father's ravages by costly gifts to the religious houses. His love for monks broke out in the song which he composed as he listened to their chant at Ely—'Merrily sang the monks in Ely when King Cnut rowed by'—across the vast fen-waters that surrounded their abbey. 'Row, boatmen, near the land, and hear we these monks sing!' "

Still, despite the "wisdom and temperance" that Canute developed "later," he reverted to his old form pretty thoroughly one Christmas. The Saxon, Edric, was boasting of the treacherous services that he had rendered to Canute, when the King, disgusted by the traitor's glorying in his infamy (for all that the King had not hesitated to take advantage of the treachery), shouted to another Edric who stood by—Edric, Earl of Northumberland: "Then let him receive his deserts, that he may not betray *us* as he betrayed Ethelred and Edmund!"

Upon which, as we are told, "the ready Norwegian disposed of all fear on that score by cutting down the boaster with his axe, and throwing his body into the Thames."

There were only two more Danish kings after Canute: his incompetent sons, Harold and Hardicanute. On the death of the survivor the crown reverted to the English line in Edward, surnamed the Confessor. Edward, the son of Ethelred and Emma (who after her husband's death married King Canute), had been brought up in Normandy, and was much more a Norman than an Englishman, a fact which was later to facilitate the Norman Conquest. This fact is often held against Edward, but it was a fact which had a beneficial effect upon English customs, since Edward's coming to the English throne established a cultural union of England with the Continent, to the vast improvement of the national taste, especially in matters of art. It is from Edward's reign that the great "Norman" abbeys date, and if one would wish to realize just how much English art owes to the coming of Edward one has only to compare, say, the

Romanesque of the Chapel of St. John in the Tower of London with the primitive long-and-short work of any surviving Saxon church.

But with the great development in *taste* that Norman influences caused came also the love of magnificence which now appears for the first time in English social life—for the only social life of any importance in those early days was the life which had its centre in the royal household and in the palaces of the higher clergy.

Earlier kings had lived well, but never magnificently: whether or not the story of Alfred, letting the cakes burn in the country wife's cottage, be true, it must always be read as a significant allegory, of which the purpose is to show how close was the union, in the days of the Anglo-Saxon monarchy, of aristocracy with people.

Or, in other words, how slightly differentiated were the classes in Anglo-Saxon days save by the possession of actual power. For in their home-life—save that they had more—the jarls and the thegns and the ealdormen shared the same tastes with the humblest.

The accession of Edward the Confessor changed all this: and changed it quickly. For the Normans, though they were descended from the same stock as had produced the rulers of England, had adopted the feudal system—which had had its origin in the collapse of the Roman Empire. This system depended for its success on a rigid caste-system, the unalterable division of society into classes, rising in a carefully devised gradation from the serf to the source of all authority (in theory): the king.

Thus, with Edward, a luxury-loving aristocracy was introduced into the fabric of English society. And, since the luxurious habits of the new Continental aristocracy were indulged quite as much as one of the duties of their feudal class as by any love of fine living, the celebration of public holidays and state occasions immediately took on a splendour never before seen in these islands.

Edward's reign was troubled enough, and one of his rebellious subjects, Earl Tostig, brother of that Harold who was afterwards to be king for a short while, celebrated the Christmas of 1064 by murdering Gospatric, one of the chief thegns.

His last Christmas of all was an important one for Edward. It saw the dedication of the new abbey-church of St. Peter at Westminster, whose completion was one of the fondest dreams of the King's life; it saw the frustration of that ambition in the King's death; and it saw the coronation of Harold as the last of our Saxon kings.

If the majority of the British people know nothing more of their history, they remember what happened to Harold at Hastings in 1066!

On the following Christmas Day, William, Duke of Normandy —William the Conqueror—was anointed King of England. He was a foreigner and a man whose intention to establish order—*his* conception of order—was to be set aside by no mawkish considerations for the customs—or even the lives—of his subjects. He appeared to very many of them to be a tyrant.

And so he was. But no opposition could shake his hold upon the kingdom, and one of his descendants still sits today upon the throne that William conquered.

## CHAPTER FOUR

# CHRISTMAS PRESENTS

THE custom of giving presents at Christmas is, one would imagine, of ancient usage—for did not the Three Kings, Gaspar, Melchior and Balthasar, who followed the Star, bring royal offerings to the Babe in His manger?

And, given that intense faith of the earlier Christians—which was not less intense, even though we choose to dismiss it contemptuously as "superstition"—one would have expected to find that the custom of giving Christmas presents was one which would early have recommended itself as desirable to the Christian world.

That it did not—at least until many centuries had passed since the first Christmas—we can only attribute to the fact that the giving of presents was one of the most notable customs of the pagan winter festival, and so would be a custom that Christians would have a tendency to neglect.

But with the revival of culture in Europe, and that more settled social life which made it possible for artists to find patrons, and so art to flourish, there came a new magnificence, which sought expression mostly in the giving of costly presents: sometimes to worthy corporations, such as abbeys and monasteries and schools, sometimes to persons of importance.

The great feasts of the Church were made the occasion for the exchanging of presents, but Christmas, being the supreme festival of the calendar, it was around this date that the costliest presents were given—as it is today.

Christmas, then, certainly seemed the most suitable time that William the Conqueror could have chosen for making the Pope a present of rare magnificence. On Christmas Day, 1067, William dispatched to Rome the major part of the plunder captured by the Conqueror at Hastings and afterwards. Among the booty sent to the Pope was the banner of the defeated Saxon king.

Eight months William had spent in distributing the wealth that he had gained by his victory over Harold. He had replaced the ancient English aristocracy by one made up of his own Norman supporters, and had "capitalized" them with lavish gifts made out of the plundered treasure of England. At least, his new noblemen would not complain that they had insufficient funds wherewith to support their new dignities!

But the money had been given for a specific purpose: William, in giving it, had no wish to see it salted away. It had been given to enable the nobles to reflect the glory of their king. He expected them to spend it. To make a show with it.

And William was a man whose wishes were not lightly to be disregarded—as those Saxons who rose against him throughout the north of England found to their bitter cost.

"And now," says Freeman, "William did one of the most frightful deeds of his life. He caused all northern England, beginning with Yorkshire, to be utterly laid waste, that its people might not be able to fight against him any more. The havoc was fearful; men were starved or sold themselves as slaves, and the land did not recover for many years. Then King William wore his crown and kept his Christmas at York."

The people of the ravaged territories were long to remember that Christmas of 1069. Indeed, it has never been quite forgotten, and a curious custom in Norfolk owes its origin to the dark events of the autumn of 1069, when King William set out to make a "Lidice" of a third of his kingdom. At harvest-time in Norfolk the children are permitted by ancient custom to ask a penny "for luck" of the harvesters. And it is held very unlucky to refuse the children, for they use a magic word in asking. They use the word "largesse" —the very word that the starving, utterly forlorn people of England, a thousand years ago, learnt, so as to beg of their French-speaking persecutors!

Christmas, 1085, has more peaceable memories for us, since it was at the gathering of William's advisers of that time—his Great Council—that it was decided to make the survey of England known to history as the Domesday Book. It was at Gloucester—the ancient Roman military city of Glevum: which must then still have possessed many remains of Imperial Roman architecture—that William held his Council in that year. The Domesday Book, says Freeman, "is a most wonderful record, and tells us more of the state of England just at that moment than we know of it for a long time before or after." It is true to say that nothing comparable to this survey, in boldness of planning or efficiency of execution, was undertaken until our own times.

William's son, William Rufus, was a sad degenerate whose Christmasses combined, as one might expect to read, the magnificence introduced by his father with coarser elements of conviviality that the man's character would find irresistible.

There was a memorable Christmas in the reign of William Rufus's brother, Henry, who succeeded him on the throne. Henry's daughter, Matilda, had married the Emperor, Henry V of Germany, and on the death of the Emperor the English king resolved to secure, for his widowed daughter, the succession to the throne of England and the lordship of Normandy.

With this object in view Henry summoned the chief men of his kingdom to gather at Windsor at Christmas, 1126, and there to take oath to serve Matilda as their queen on the death of her father.

That there was a symbolical significance to be observed in this summoning the Great Council of the Realm to meet at Christmas is clear enough when we remember that it was at a previous Christmas, six years earlier, that Henry lost his only son—his only legitimate son, rather—William, who perished in the wreck of the *White Ship*.

Learning Mrs. Hemans's stanzas, inspired by a complete misunderstanding of the young Prince William's character, is one of the least pleasant memories of my own childhood. Contemporary Christendom, indeed, was so far from sharing the nineteenth-century poetess's sentimental conception of the character of Henry and his heir that most people not in the King's "set" openly declared that the loss of the *White Ship,* with about a hundred and fifty of the noble youth of England and Normandy, was God's judgment on the corruption of the Court!

A strange legend of Christmas belongs to this reign. It is related by William of Malmesbury, in the words of one of the chief characters of the story, which relates, be it noted, to a time when one of the periodic "dancing manias" was affecting Europe.

It appears that some young men and women, dancing, disturbed a priest who was saying Mass on Christmas Eve. Othbert was one of the disrespectful band, and it is he who tells what happened to the dancers.

"I, Othbert, a sinner, have lived to tell the tale. The priest, Rathbertus, had just begun the Mass, and I, with my comrades, fifteen young women and seventeen young men, were dancing outside the church. And we were singing so loud that our songs were distinctly heard inside the building, and interrupted the service of the Mass. And the priest came out and told us to desist. And when we did not, he prayed God and St. Magnus that as our punishment we might dance for a year to come. A youth whose sister was dancing with us seized her by the arm to drag her away; but it came off in his hand, and she danced on.

"For a whole year we continued. No rain fell on us; cold, nor heat, nor hunger, nor thirst, nor fatigue affected us; neither our shoes nor our clothes wore out; but still we went on dancing. We trod the earth down to our knees, next to our middles, and at last we were dancing in a pit. At the end of the year release came."

Boxing Day—26 December, 1135—ushered in a period of extraordinary civil disorder, for it was on this day that Stephen of Blois was crowned king in Westminster Abbey.

Matilda, widow of the Emperor, Henry V, and daughter of the English king, Henry I, disputed Stephen's right to the crown, and war ensued between Stephen and Matilda, who claimed the crown on behalf of her son, Henry.

At Christmas, 1142, Matilda had been besieged in Wallingford for three months. Supplies were almost exhausted; hope completely so. Matilda resolved on flight, and the story goes that, as the bells were sounding across the sedgy flats of the Thames, Matilda—one bitter Christmas night, when the snow lay thick as on a Christmas-card—escaped from the beleaguered town with four trusty knights, and that to escape observation by Stephen's patrols the five fugitives "camouflaged" themselves with white cloaks.

By the Treaty of Wallingford, 1153, the civil war came to an end, and Henry was recognized as Stephen's heir.

A year after the signing of the treaty Stephen died, and Henry was crowned King of England at Christmas, 1154.

Under Henry II something of order crept back into English

social life, and to encourage the nationalism which had been so grievously undermined in the period of civil war, Henry solemnly promised, during his first Christmas festivities—held with great pomp at Bermondsey—to expel all foreigners from the kingdom. This seems to be an uncharitable act, little in accord with the traditional spirit of Christmas; but it must be remembered that the English people had suffered much from the activities of foreigners, and the nation breathed the more easily when William of Ypres and his fellow Flemings, without waiting for further notice to go, hurriedly left the country.

Henry, indeed, was a good king—judged by the standards of the time. It is true that the King marked one of his Christmasses in a regrettable fashion by causing Thomas à Becket, Archbishop of Canterbury, to be assassinated in his own cathedral within the octave of the Nativity (29 December, 1170), but the King made expiation, and, if he brought death to Becket, Henry brought peace and some measure of social security within the law to the people of England.

Indeed, the manners of this reign set a new standard in magnificence of living, and it is related that the Irish kings and princes, invited to the great Christmas feast of 1171, were as much overawed as astonished at the sumptuousness of the banquet provided. Only with difficulty could they be prevailed upon to eat roasted crane—a dish to which they were quite unaccustomed.

The descriptions of the repasts of those times make astounding reading, and then, as now, the Court set the example for the national behaviour. Small wonder, then, that we find the taste for costly overeating diffusing itself among all classes; but naturally the taste taking a firmer hold upon those who had the means to gratify their gluttony.

Some abbots, alarmed by the greed of their monks, framed rules designed to curb the gluttonous propensities of the friars. The friars resented this—one may easily understand why!—and strongly deprecated the attempts of their lord abbots to curtail their "liberty." The monks of St. Swithun's monastery, at Winchester, resented it so much that they appealed directly to the King, making a formal complaint against their abbot that he had taken away three of the thirteen dishes that they were accustomed to have for dinner! There is no record that the monks of Canterbury suffered any pruning of their customary seventeen dinner-dishes!

King Richard Lion-heart did nothing by his romantic excursions—and expensive excursions they were as well, to the people who had to ransom him!—to diminish the prevailing taste for exotic luxuries. His taking so many knights and their humbler followers with him from London to Jerusalem was but a certain way of strengthening the love of foreign indulgences. It is curious to recall that fox-hunting—that most English of all sports, surely?—was an importation from Syria by the knights who had hunted the fox there, in the intervals between fighting the Paynim. Yet the sport preserves to this day even the phrase that the original Crusading fox-hunters learned from their Syrian whippers-in: *Tally-ho!*—which is only very slightly altered, *Tala ha!*—Arabic for "Go there!" or "Straight ahead!"

Most of Richard's Christmasses were spent abroad; but none apparently—if we are to believe the records of the time—in any "austerity" fashion, for all that Richard was engaged in a war. The old ballad of *Richard Coeur de Lion* tells us that:

> Christmas is a time full honest;
> Kyng Richard it honoured with gret feste.
> All his clerkes and barouns,
> Were set in their pavylouns,
> And served with grete plente
> Of mete and drink and each dainte.

In 1190 the two kings of England and France "held their Christmasse this yeare at Messina, and still the King of England used great liberalitie in bestowing his treasure freelie among knights and other men of warre, so that it was thought he spent more in a moneth than anie of his predecessours ever spent in a whole yeare."

John was meaner than his brother, but his meanness never took the form of miserliness. John was as extravagantly self-indulgent as the Lion-heart, and the Christmas that John spent at his palace of Guildford was distinguished by the same costliness which had marked the hospitality of his brother.

John, at Guildford, "gave to his servants manie faire liveries and suits of apparell. The archbishop of Canturburie did also the like at Canturburie, seeming in deed to strive with the king, which of them should pass the other in such sumptuous appareling of their men:

whereat the king [and not without good cause] was greatlie mooved to indignation against him, although, for a time, he coloured the same."

All the same, John had his revenge: an odd one, as it happened. "From thence he returned and came to Canturburie, where he held his Easter, which fell that yeare on the day of the Annunciation of our Ladie, at which feast he sat crowned, together with his wife, queen Isabell, *the archbishop of Canturburie bearing the charges of them and their trains while they remained there.*"

John's name, of course, will always be associated in the memories of the British with that greatly misunderstood and highly overrated document, Magna Charta, which was less the granting of liberty to the English people than an admission by one brigand that a combination of rival brigands was too strong for him.

It was at Christmas, 1214, that the barons, in concert (and fully armed), demanded from John that he sign a charter to restore to them the privileges that they had enjoyed under previous kings.

In the end, though, John accepted what he saw to be the inevitable and summoned the barons to meet him on the small island of Runnymede, in the River Thames, where he signed Magna Charta.

There was no Christmas for the wretched John in 1216: two months before that feast he died miserably in his castle of Newark on Trent; his bodily strength debilitated by the disappointments and frustrations that he had suffered at the hands of his subjects. His baggage, as every schoolboy knows—which means, in the language of the old chroniclers, his treasure—was lost in the Wash; and John himself was poisoned by some lampreys that he had eaten. He died, the old chronicles say, in "an extremity of agony and remorse"; what one might expect, indeed, from acute indigestion. An unpleasant death for a man no more selfish than his enemies.

## CHAPTER FIVE

# FEASTING, JOUSTING AND PLOTTING

HENRY III—sometimes called "Henry of Winchester"—was under ten years of age when he came to the throne; and his training was such that he became a compliant—not to say subservient—son of the Church. Indeed, his attachment to the Holy See was interpreted, particularly by Simon de Montfort, as a betrayal of his duty towards his kingdom, and this interpretation of the king's pious obedience to his spiritual overlords was to lead, first to civil war, and then—as a result of that internal dissension—to the establishment of Parliament: the first in the world and the model of all its successors from Russian to Indian.

Ecclesiastical influence, however, was nothing whereby Henry was forced to give up the luxurious habits of former kings, since the courts of the archbishops and other Church dignitaries used often to rival that of the king in the splendour of their appointments and in the lavishness of their entertainment.

At Christmas, 1252, Henry married his daughter, Margaret, to Alexander, King of Scots, and the accompanying festivities were held in the ancient city of York. The marriage ceremony itself was solemnized on Christmas Day, and there were a thousand English knights in the King's train—Alexander having brought a mere sixty sumptuously attired Scottish knights with him.

The eating was on a literally gargantuan scale: no fewer than six hundred fat oxen being slaughtered to feed the guests. The refreshments were paid for by the Archbishop of York—who, in fact if not within the strict letter of the law, was the kingly *owner* of his cathedral city. In addition to his paying for the six hundred oxen, the Archbishop made a contribution of the truly enormous sum of four thousand marks to the cost of the wedding-feast—£2,700 in nominal value, but impossible to give in modern value, comparing our age with theirs, in which a sheep cost a penny and a bullock fourpence. Gold, of course, owing to the primitive methods then employed of mining and crushing the ore, was incredibly dear—which is why the sheep, and so forth, appear so incredibly cheap. But though we cannot—we simply cannot—express the Archbishop's £2,700 in terms of modern currency, we may still say that this sum represented a princely gift from a treasure of almost fabulous worth.

There is an order of Henry's, addressed to his "boteler," directing him to deliver two tuns of white wine and one of red, to make "garhiofilac,"[1] and claret—*as usual*—for the Christmas drinks.

Dawson, in his *Christmas and its Association*, when describing the lavish tables kept by kings and aristocrats of the Middle Ages, rightly points out that this lavishness was necessary, in so much as the poor as well as the rich had to be fed from the king's table. It is on record that Richard II daily fed ten thousand persons. In the metrical chronicle of John Hardyng, he tells us that:

> Truly I herd Robert Ireleffe saye,
> (Clerke of the grene cloth) that to the household,
> Came euery daye for moost partie alwaye,
> Ten thousand folke by his messis tould,
> That folowed the hous aye as thei would,
> And in the ketchin three hundred seruitors,
> And in eche office many occupiours;
> And ladies faire with their gentilwomen,
> Chamberers also and launderers,
> Three hundred of them were occupied then.

Hardyng, in fact, minimizes the numbers of the king's staff; for Stow credits Richard with the possession—or employment—of no fewer than two thousand cooks!

But Richard lived a century and a half after Henry III, so that "progress" alone would be enough to account for the increase in expenditure—royal expenditure at least!

All the same, Henry was no niggard. At the Christmas of 1248, while Henry was feasting at Winchester, Westminster Hall was, by the King's command, filled with poor persons for a whole week—and fed royally.

Dawson relates how, twenty years after this, Henry kept his

[1] A spiced wine, with honey.

Christmas in London, and ordered the shops to be closed for the fifteen days of the festival that he held. The ban on trading offended the shopkeepers of the capital, but Henry would not let them reopen their shops until they had consented to make him a "present" of two thousand pounds!

While Henry's relations with his pensioners must have been cordial enough, his relations with the great barons went from bad to worse, since they charged him with wilful betrayal of Magna Charta. The quarrel deepened until it had culminated in civil war. Leading the forces against the King was the ambitious and unscrupulous Simon de Montfort, Earl of Leicester, who, holding the King prisoner, summoned representatives of the cities and boroughs, as well as barons, bishops, and knights of the shires, to meet at Westminster, in a national assembly. It was the first time such an assembly had been called since the days of the Saxon kings, and that meeting—Christmas, 1265—saw the birth of the English parliament. It will be noted that it was established neither by the initiative nor with the consent of the reigning sovereign.

It was in Henry's reign—a troubled period, but a constructive one—that the great Robin Hood died. The date of his death is given as Christmas Eve, 1247, and though poor Robin has become, by the unimaginative efforts of the folk-lorists, a Nature-myth, neither the historian, Stow, writing of Robin Hood in 1590, nor the makers of several Hollywood films, have doubted his reality. To them he was very much a genuinely historical character, and Stow says of him that "he suffered no woman to be oppressed. Poor men's goods he spared, abundantly relieving them with that which by theft he got from the abbeys and the houses of rich old earls."

Edward I we may care to recall as the first truly English king since the Conquest, and the first, too, who sought to invest the glory of his own days with the added prestige derived from recalling ancient glories. So that, at Kenilworth, the King held a great Christmas feast, with a "Round Table" in honoured memory of King Arthur's, around which a hundred lords and ladies "clad all in silk" sat.

The Christmas of 1281-2[1] was spent less pleasantly, for at

[1] In those days—and until 1752—the New Year began officially on 25 March, though the people began their New Year on 1 January. Thus we write 1281-2 to indicate that fact.

Worcester, where Edward that year held his court, "there was such a frost and snow as no man living could remember the like." It was no warmer in London, and five of the arches of London Bridge were carried away when the ice broke up.

Christmas, 1286, passed by the King at Oxford, was marked by the hanging of the Mayor of Oxford, and that of 1301, spent at Linlithgow, during Edward's Scottish campaign, by the building of a castle in which to celebrate the festival.

They remember the Christmas of 1332 in Scotland, for it was at that time that Edward Balliol, the "Phantom King" of the Scots, was defeated by the Earl of Moray and Sir Simon Fraser, after having reigned only a few months. Balliol escaped upon an unsaddled horse, leaving his brother Henry dead in the ambush; and coming to England, the "Phantom King" was well received by Edward III, who even organized expeditions against the Scots with the object of restoring Balliol to his throne. The English king was completely unsuccessful: on his entry into Scotland the "rebels" retired into the mountains, to come forth again as soon as Edward—flattering himself that he had subdued the North—left for his own country.

It was during the Christmas festivities of 1346 that King Edward III instituted the senior English order of chivalry: that of the Garter. The King had invaded France, and during his absence the Scottish king, David II, had invaded England.

The Scots were met by Queen Philippa, who soundly defeated them and took their king prisoner. The Queen then joined her lord at Calais, and spent her Christmas there.

It seems that the popular explanation of the institution of the Most Noble Order of the Garter is the true one, for all that some scholars have dismissed it as vulgar fable. But modern research tends to accept the tale that, at a feast given by the King, the Countess of Huntingdon *did* lose her garter, and a knight, with a snigger, picked it up and held it aloft for all to see. And that the King did take it away from the knight and put it around his royal knee, with the rebuke to the knight: *"Honi soit qui mal y pense!"*—the the motto of the Order, "To the Evil, all things are evil!"[1]

The description of the entertainments at the Christmas of 1348, which was held by Edward III at Guildford, reveals that the ancient

[1] *Literally:* Evil to him who thinks evil of it!

pagan habit of "dressing up" at the winter festival had survived the change-over to Christianity and the thundering denunciations of the Church.

Orders were given to manufacture for the Christmas sports eighty tunics of buckram of different colours, and a large number of masks —some with faces of women, some with beards, some like angel-heads of silver. There were to be mantles embroidered with heads of dragons, tunics wrought with heads and wings of peacocks, and embroidered in other fantastic ways!

The weather recorded by our ancestors seems to have been less temperate than that now enjoyed: even the weather of my own childhood seems—at least in memory—to have been characterized by endless days of unbroken sunshine for summer, and equally interminable spells of nightmare cold for winter. Was it truly so? Or does the human memory tend to record only extremes, forgetting intermediate states?

At any rate, one of those classical tempests which seem to have passed with the coming of modern times made one of Edward III's Christmasses most memorable. It occurred at Christmas, 1362-3, when the King was staying at Windsor. Stow thus refers to the event: "a sore and vehement south-west winde brake forth, so hideous that it overthrew high houses, towers, steeples and trees, and so bowed them, that the residue which fell not, but remained standing, were weaker."

It was at that same Christmas of 1362-3 that three kings sat down together at Windsor, when the King of Scots and the King of Cyprus were Edward's guests. Such a thing had happened at an earlier Christmas, that of 1358, when the Scots and French kings had been entertained at Westminster—but on that occasion the French king was hardly a willing guest, being held a captive for ransom; and the King of Scots was "free" only by a polite fiction.

Richard II—whom the genius of Shakespeare has made one of the best known of English kings by name—was the son of the Black Prince, but he bore little resemblance to his father, either in appearance or in character. The Black Prince loved the rough pleasures of the battlefield; Richard preferred joys softer and more calculated to appeal to that feminine aspect which was so well developed in him.

But Richard of Bordeaux was truly the first civilized king to sit on the throne of England. He was, too, the first "modern" king, in so much as he belongs, spiritually, rather to the post-Renascence than to the pre-Renascence world.

He was born too soon. He lived in a world which was still medieval, and his modernity shocked and frightened men who felt that their only hope of survival was to remain what they were: the children of the Dark Ages.

His Christmasses, as I have already mentioned, were sumptuous on a scale to shame the feasts of earlier days—splendid though these may have been.

Recalling for a moment Hardyng's statement that the King fed ten thousand persons at a sitting, it is understandable that he should have been credited with the employment of two thousand cooks (though one cook to five people seems excessive, even for the days of non-labour-saving kitchens!), and it seems just that the earliest English cookery-book which has come down to us should have been compiled in the reign of this luxury-loving prince.

This fourteenth-century Mrs. Beeton is called *The Forme of Cury*, and was compiled "of the chef Mairt Cok of King Richard the Secunde, Kyng of Englond aftir the Conquest."

The book, doubtless, represented the supplying of a felt need, since twenty-eight oxen, three hundred sheep and countless fowls were killed every morning for the use of Richard's personal table.

The Royal Palace of Eltham—nine miles from London—was the most favoured by Richard, who had greatly modernized and enlarged the original palace built by King John two hundred years earlier. This royal residence still exists; after having fallen into disrepair, it was bought and restored at considerable cost by a member of the Courtauld family, the millionaire manufacturers of artificial silk.

In 1386, disregarding the prevalent scarcity of money in the country, Richard here entertained most nobly the Armenian king, Leon, treating his guest to one of those costly spectacles in which Richard's love of extravagance and theatrical sense took an equal delight.

Pageants and plays were the favourite form of entertainment at this time, and all classes joined to present them, even the parish clerks of Smithfield putting on a play at Skinner's Wells, lasting three days, at which the King, Queen and many of the great nobles were present.

Every baron's castle saw these performances, which were usually performed by wandering minstrels, jugglers, tumblers, dancers and bourdours (or jesters), though fairly often we find the shows put on by the noblemen's servants.

The plays and pageants done by these wandering players always had a religious theme, though the presentation of, for instance, the story of Noah's Ark, or of Abraham and his son, was not always either dignified or even proper.

The Church used to put on rival plays, and that the secular showmen appeared to enjoy a greater popularity was the cause of bitter enmity on the part of the Church-players. According to the Church-players, the secular plays were full of indecency, and there is on record a petition, presented by the scholars of St. Paul's School to Richard II, "wherein complaint is made against the secular actors, because they took upon themselves to act plays composed from Scripture history, to the great prejudice of the clergy, who had been at much expense to prepare such performances for public exhibition at the festival of Christmas."

A famous play has come down to us from this time in which the Shepherds and Mak, a character of doubtful repute—the first "comic" character in English literature—find themselves in the honoured position of being the witness to the Nativity.

We shall later see how such a comic character as "Mak" developed into the Pantaloon of the pantomime; but in this early play his "type" is already, as we see, fixed. In other words, he must have a considerable history of development behind him before he appears as the finished type in this rich old play. The three shepherds, grumbling very heartily against the crippling taxes and the general tyranny of "men that are gretter" in a free manner which astonishes the reader who has believed that the serfs of the Middle Ages were too browbeaten to indulge some "socialistic" grumbling, sing a catch, and are then joined by Mak, who has a reputation for thievery. They all go to sleep, but make Mak lie down between them, so as to prevent his stealing their sheep. Mak, however, who has come out to do just what the shepherds fear that he will, keeps awake, and gets up as soon as the others have dozed off. He says:

Now were tyme for a man, that lakkys what he wold,
To stalk prevely than unto a fold,
And neemly to wyrk than, and be not to bold,
That he myght aby the bargan, if it were told
At the endyng.
Now were tyme for to reylle;
Bot he nedes good counselle
That fayn wold fare weylle,
And has bot lytylle spendyng.

A fat shepe I dar say,
A good flese dar I lay,
Eft-whyte when I may,
Bot this wille I borow.

So he steals the sheep and takes it home to his wife.

How, Gylle, art thou in? Gett us som lyght!

His wife then asks:

Who makys sich dyn this tyme of the nyght?
I am sett for to spyn: I hope not I myght
Ryse a penny to wyn: I shrew them on hight.
So farys
A huswyff that has bene
To be rasyd thus betwene:
There may no note be sene
For sich smalle charys.

Mak, having given the sheep to his wife, goes back to the fields and lies down between the still-sleeping shepherds. When they wake, and miss a sheep, they suspect Mak, and he is forced to take them home. They search the house and find nothing until it occurs to one of the shepherds that they have given nothing to Mak's child. Mak tries to pretend that the sheep, who has been put in the cot, is his own child, changed by the fairies; but for all that the Middle Ages are supposed to be the age of black superstition, the shepherds do not swallow this explanation, and toss Mak in a canvas, until Mak screams out:

Lord, what I am sore, in point for to bryst!
In fayth I may no more, therfor wylle I ryst.

Back go the shepherds to their field.

> Now, I pray you,
> Lyg downe on this grene.

And, right following this slapstick, this ultra-broad farce, comes the Angel, singing "*Gloria in excelsis Deo.*"

The Angel, in language as simple as the shepherds', bids them go to "Bedlem" to see the Child "in a cryb poorely, betwyx two bestys."

So, still in the same language of everyday use—the talk of the simple people—the play takes the shepherds into the presence of the Mother and her Child.

It is easy to understand that this "treatment" might well have seemed, to the Church dignitaries—even more to the professional impresarios acting under the patronage of the Church—somewhat lacking in dignity, if not in actual reverence. Yet we see that this very simplicity of language and conception is the mark of, and is derived from, a true reverence, in that the writers of such plays accepted the marvellous works of God as the most natural things in the world. They really had the only possible point of view open to those who would be at peace with God: to accept Him as an integral and perfectly to-be-taken-for-granted part of their everyday.

Though the play of Mak and the shepherds is of a little later date, Richard II must have seen many similar plays; and we shall notice in a further chapter how greatly the modern play is indebted to the material, if not always to the spiritual, elements in the composition in these early dramas.

Richard, like many other kings both before and after his day, took great pleasure in the tournament, which is—when all is said and done—only another aspect of the drama, even when it is "in earnest" (but a dramatist would rather add, *especially* when it is "in earnest"). One may reflect, at this point, that the elaborately ritualized killing of the bull in the Spanish *corrida*, or bull-fight, was derived from an original pre-Christian ritual dance in honour of the sun; and that the addition of the "serious business" of the bull-fighting has not diminished the essential dramatic content of the *corrida*.

Just so, the tournament, highly ritualized, depended as much for its effect on the spectators on its ritual as on its physical combat.

Richard spent vast sums of money on these tournaments, and one of the most splendid was held in London at Christmas, 1389, in imitation of one which had been held in Paris to celebrate the entry into the French capital of the Queen of France.

In Richard's tournament sixty knights, conducted by sixty ladies, challenged all foreign knights. Heralds were sent as far afield as Italy, to carry the challenge to "all valorous knights and squires" who might wish to accept the Englishmen's invitation to meet in the tourney.

The lists were set up at Smithfield, and since the challenge had attracted many foreign knights—who came as much from a desire to see England as from a desire to break their necks—the procession to the lists was vastly impressive in its numbers.

Each of the challenging knights, mounted and armed save for helm, buckler and lance, was "led" by a young lady, herself mounted on a palfrey, by a silver chain, attached to the knight's neck. Arrived at the lists, the ladies let go their chains, and the fair conductresses were then lifted down from their mounts and taken to the rooms provided for them. The knights entered the lists, and "charged before the eyes of ladies and of kings."

As darkness came, and put an end to the day's jousting, the combatants and other guests were led to the palace of the Bishop of London, and there they sat down to a supper spread in the lavish manner that Richard's taste always commanded.

The prize for the best joust done by a foreign knight—a golden crown—went to the "Earl of St. Paul" ("de St. Pol" or "da Sao Paolo"?), and that for the best performance by an Englishman to the Earl of Huntingdon. His lordship won a rich girdle, adorned with gold and precious stones.

The tournament, which had begun on a Sunday, lasted the whole of the ensuing week, and on the following Saturday the King, with all his guests, moved to Windsor, where the celebrations were continued—for had not the good King Alfred, himself following the wise opinion of the Fathers, set aside twelve whole days for the proper observation of Christ's Nativity?

As Christmas-tide ended, the visitors from foreign lands returned home laden with rich presents, which testified both to the generosity and the improvidence of the English King.

The same Earl of Huntingdon it was who was a conspirator in a plot, hatched at Christmas, 1399-1400, to assassinate Henry Bolingbroke, that cousin of Richard's who had usurped his throne and finally murdered him. This Henry has got much undeserved credit, because Shakespeare—who was by no means infallible in his judgments—admired the man. In fact, Henry was a detestable bigot, besides being more than something of a bloodthirsty savage. But when we add that he was a very sick man—sick in mind and in body—we may find some excuse for his primitive cruelties and primitive fears.

The plotters, though, needed no excuse for their attempt on Henry's life. No one would have missed him, and he would only have received for himself what he so cheerfully had served up for another.

Indeed, it would have been better for the plotters had they succeeded, for their failure convinced Henry that he had received Divine protection, which must be acknowledged by sacrificing both the innocent and the guilty to his blood-lust.

The conspirators gathered during the Christmas holidays of 1399-1400 at the home of the Abbot of Westminster, and the plan upon which they eventually came to resolve was this:

A great tournament was to be given by Lord Huntingdon, Lord Rutland, and others, on 3 January, 1400, at Oxford. Henry was to be asked to preside—for his love of jousting was as great as that of the king whose throne Henry had usurped—and while watching the games Henry and his sons were to be assassinated by bullies hired for that purpose. The Earl of Huntingdon delivered the invitation to the King at Windsor, where Henry was spending his first Christmas as king. It was accepted, and the scheme would doubtless have been successful had not the Earl of Rutland, from motives of unadulterated self-interest, warned Henry on the eve of the tournament, so that the conspirators assembled at Oxford to wait in vain for their pre-condemned guest.

Open rebellion now offered the only hope to the plotters, and in that means of ridding themselves of their enemy they failed, too. The vengeance that Henry took upon the losers was as sanguinary as deliberate.

Henry, as though driven by some urge to prove to the world that *he* at least did not regard his taking the crown from Richard as usurpation, took great care to adopt the murdered man's habits, and to give patronage to Richard's favourite customs.

Thus Eltham, which had been Richard's best-loved palace, was that most favoured by Henry. Here it was that the second Christmas of Henry's reign—that of 1400-1—was held with imperial splendour.

The adjective is literally correct, for the guest of honour that year was Manuel II Palaeologus, Emperor of Byzantium, Lord of Eastern Rome, the structure of whose state, like wormy wood under gilding, was destined to crumble into nothingness only fifty years from that day.

But Golden Byzantium, for all the corruption which had sapped its vigour, drained it of its vitality, and left it only the phosphorescent radiance of rotten timber, Golden Byzantium was golden still—the one remaining city of classical art in a West which was only just beginning to be touched with the stirring breath of the Renascence.

Benjamin of Tudela, a Spanish Jew who visited the imperial city in the middle of the twelfth century, has left us a description of its wonders; wonders magic enough, in all conscience, to make the Jew cry out, in honest, involuntary delight: "There is no such sight to be seen in all the world!"

Benjamin tells us how, every year "on the day of the birth of Jesus the Nazarene," the King gave a grand entertainment, "in a place called the hippodrome, near to the wall of the palace."

Writing a hundred and fifty years before Henry IV's day, the Jewish traveller describes a Byzantine pageant in terms which may well make us wonder what Manuel Palaeologus thought privately of the Christmas show that Henry had put on for his distinguished guest.

That year it was the Aldermen of the City of London who had produced and presented the entertainment—a costly business, since the Middle Ages were universally agreed that any deficiency in wit could always be amply compensated for by a pageant's lavishness of costume—a foolish belief which is still with us to ruin many a Hollywood "musical" or London "revue."

Art had become as stereotyped in Byzantium as its ancient culture. Behind the towering, "impregnable" walls, which were to fall only when gunpowder had been introduced into the West, the Byzantines, writing in a script and a phraseology unchanged since the days of Plato, had permitted a love of tradition to narrow their minds and ossify or petrify their imaginations. Nothing became for them so important—so vitally important—as to do today exactly what was done yesterday. They developed, by this principle, a caste-system compared with which the caste-system of the Hindoo is a chaotic condition of social flux. Form took the place of spirit, and formalism usurped the place of progress. Life in Byzantium became as unchanging, from one day to another, as the lifeless faces of their saints in the mosaic frescoes.

But in the days of Manuel Palaeologus the relics of a classical antiquity were everywhere to be seen in Byzantium in splendid profusion and in a state of marvellous preservation. The great hippodrome, where Benjamin of Tudela saw the Christmas pageant, was still as perfect as it had been in the days of Justinian, and the noble cathedral of the Holy Wisdom—already nine hundred years old—had not yet had its Moslem minarets added to mar its strangely utilitarian beauty.

Effete though they were, the last emperors of Byzantium were possibly the only completely cultured persons to be found in the Europe of their day. It was not until the days of Pico della Mirandola and Gian Visconti that culture may be said to have come to Europe, and not even the Italians of the Renascence may be held to have been really civilized. Polished, yes; but there was too much of the lusty savage about them that they may be held to compare with a Palaeologus for that perfect polish which is the last gift of old, tired empires. Even the Medicis themselves acquired it only when Tuscany was as dying as dying Byzantium had once been.

For the delectation of the Emperor the Aldermen of the City of London provided a "gret mummyng to him of XII Aldermen and their sones, for which they had gret thank."

One can imagine the cynical smile on the lips of the Palaeologus Emperor as he gave the City Fathers "gret thank.". . . .

Henry V was a typical man of his time—which must be the best (for it will be the only) excuse for his behaviour. If he inherited physical courage from his father, he inherited, too, the father's savage bigotry, which implied, of course, a criminal indifference to human suffering.

Henry IV had been too short a time on the throne that he had seized for the son to feel altogether secure upon it. His son—Henry V, Shakespeare's "Star of England"—needed—or was persuaded that he needed—the help of the Church to keep his throne safe, and he proceeded against the Church's enemies with an ardour which satisfied the ecclesiastical authorities that they need have no fear of Henry's orthodox views.

Both in the technique of his attack upon those enemies and in the ruthlessness of that attack Henry's campaign against the Lollards—they were conveniently dubbed "heretics," so as to judge and condemn them beyond the possibility of any appeal to justice—reminds us too uncomfortably of similar campaigns—"purges"—against "Trotskyites" and "Fascists" in Russia. Condemned by a phrase, hunted with all the resources of the State, "tried" by venal judges and handed over to a compliant executioner for the cruellest of all deaths: one reads of their fate and sighs, indeed, to think that no one country has the monopoly of calculated savagery.

For his "discovery" of a "plot" against the security of his filched throne Henry V chose Christmas-time of 1414 as the most suitable period. With plenty of "evidence" collected by his agents, the King proceeded to round up the Lollards on the grounds that they were plotting to overthrow the monarchy, dispossess the Church, and to set up—what? Anyhow, to set up a rival kingdom, in which neither the House of Lancaster nor the Church of Rome would play a part.

That there was no evidence worth a jot to prove this charge did not trouble the King or his churchly accomplices. Nor need it trouble us. The fact is that the Church had declared total and unrelenting war against the Lollards—who had been guilty of the unspeakable crime of suggesting that the Church devote more of its time to educating men in Christian principles and less in accumulating vast fortunes for its dignitaries—and Henry, in exchange for the Church's supporting his claim to the throne of England, showed himself willing to do the Church's dirty work.

It must be conceded that he did it extremely well.

Christmas was a favourite time for important actions in Henry's life (historians have called attention to this fact as a mark of his "piety"!), and just as he had announced the "plot" to murder him at Christmas, so now he chose Christmas Day, 1418, as that most suitable for the death by torture of Sir John Oldcastle, Lord Cobham, the leader of the Lollards, who had voluntarily surrendered himself in order to avoid further persecution of his followers.

On Christmas Day, 1418—as Lord Cobham, in distant St. Giles's Fields, was dying his cruel, undignified and protracted death—Henry, "the Star of England," was besieging Rouen, whose garrison was starving behind the city walls.

But no man is altogether vile, and Henry V's natural qualities had been corrupted by that great quietener of consciences: the concept that morality may justly be set aside for what is called political expediency, or (as some say) "the good of the community."

Holinshed, the Elizabethan chronicler, thus describes the one recorded instance of mercy in the soldier-king's brief and "glorious" career.

"If I should rehearse," says old Holinshed—who was the main source of Shakespeare's historical knowledge—(according to the reports of diverse writers), "how deerlie dogs, rats, mise, and cats were sold within the towne, and how greedilie they were by the poore people eaten and devoured, and how the people dailie died for fault of food, and young infants laie sucking in the streets on their mother's breasts, lieing dead, starved for hunger; the reader might lament their extreme miseries. A great number of poore sillie creatures were put out at the gates, which were—by the Englishmen that kept the trenches—beaten and driven back againe to the same gates, which they found closed and shut against them. And so they laie betweene the wals of the citie and the trenches of the enimies, still crieing for help and releefe, for lacke whereof great numbers of them dailie died.

"Howbeit, King Henrie, moved with pitie, upon Christmasse daie, in the honor of Christes Nativitie, refreshed all the poore people with vittels, to their great comfort and his high praise."

A similar instance of the benevolent effect of the Christmas spirit on a society brutalized by false moral values is to be found in the records of the succeeding reign, when the English forces besieging Orleans under Talbot offered an armistice to the French commander, Dunois, to cover the period of Christmas.

". . . the Nativity of the Saviour was commemorated to the sound of martial music. Talbot, Suffolk and other ornaments of English chivalry made presents of fruit to the accomplished Dunois, who vied with their courtesy by presenting to Suffolk some black plush he wished for as a lining to his dress in the then winter season."

Challenges were sent, in a friendly fashion, between the knights of the contending armies. "These jousts were not held in honour of the ladies, but the challenge always declared that if there were in the other host a knight so generous and loving of his country as to be willing to combat in her defence, he was invited to present himself."

All through the French war of Henry VI's reign, and throughout the civil war—the so-called Wars of the Roses—which followed the French victory initiated, if not actually achieved, by Joan of Arc, the great occasions of the year, especially the festival of Christmas, were celebrated with no abatement of their former splendour.

Nor was this lavish entertainment confined to private persons: corporations of all sorts felt themselves free to play the open-handed and wealthy host. On Christmas Day, 1445, the mayor and borough council of King's Lynn presented a series of religious tableaux before Lord Scales at Middleton Castle, which were performed in the castle-yard, the cost of the entertainment being borne by the town.

Indeed, what interruptions Christmas festivities suffered during the Wars of the Roses were always of a purely military—and never by any chance of an economic—nature. The bloodiest battle of this civil war—that of Wakefield—was fought at Christmas.

But it took at least a battle to interrupt the celebrations: finding himself short of money as Christmas approached, Henry VI went to the moneylenders.

Henry VI had been a pious, sickly man, whose superstitious desire to "expiate his sins" caused him to spend his money rather on religious than on secular works. When, at Christmas, 1454, he showed evidences of what seemed to be an almost complete recovery from his long illness—a species of quiet madness, such as centuries later was to attack another pious English king, George III—his first act was to give thanks to God for his restored sanity. And his thanksgiving took the form of a costly gift to the shrines of St. Edward the Confessor and St. Thomas of Canterbury.

*The Paston Letters* tell us that the secretary was sent off with the offerings on St. John's Day, 1454, that is, 27 December.

We have given up the old custom of naming the days of Christtide, as we have those of Holy Week. It is true that we still refer to Boxing Day, and (in Holy Week) Good Friday; but the names of the other days have dropped out of popular usage.

In Henry VI's day, however, the days following Christmas Day, right up to Candlemas Day (2 February), were each named after a saint. A carol[1] ascribed to this period refers quaintly to this fact:

Make we myrth
For Crystes byrth,
And syng we yole tyl Candlemes.

The fyrst day of yole have we in mynd,
How God was man born of oure kynd:
For he the bondes wold onbynd
Of all oure synnes and wykednes.

The secund day we syng of Stevene,
That stoned and steyyed up even
To God that he saw stond in hevyn,
And crounned was for hys prouesse.

The iij longeth to sent Johan,
That was Crystes darlyng, derer non,
Whom he betok, whan he shuld gon,
Hys moder der for hyr clennesse.

And so on, until Twelfth Day:

The xij day offerd to hym kynges iij,
Gold, myr, and cence, thes gyftes free,
For God, and man, and kyng was he,
Thus worschyppyd thei hys worthynes.

And last day of all:

On the xl day cam Mary myld,
Unto the temple with hyr chyld,
To shew hyr clen that never was fylyd,
And therwith endyth Chrystmes.

Edward, the son of that Duke of York who should have succeeded peacefully to the throne on the death of Henry VI but who was killed on the bloody night of Wakefield, was neither a sickly nor a particularly pious man.

Brought up in the unsettled conditions which follow a civil

[1] British Museum Sloane MS. 2593.

war, he wished for internal peace more than anything else; and he sought, in a high-handed, dictatorial fashion, to curb the power of the great nobles, whose jealousies had plunged England into factional strife.

He sought this end, first by by-passing the nobles in his approach to the nation: at his first parliament he adopted the almost unprecedented measure of making the "speech from the Throne" himself; and second, by forbidding the nobles to dress their servants in livery (i.e., uniform) and to give sanctuary to hunted criminals; and third, by prohibiting the nobles—and lesser men—from permitting the playing of card-games or rolling of dice in their houses, save only during the twelve days of Christmas.

Edward used the method which was to be copied by Louis XIV in breaking the power of the territorial nobles: by establishing a splendid court, to which noblemen desirous of preferment would be bound to come, and so—as a consequence—to neglect their own estates.

The Croyland Chronicler, describing Edward's first Christmas as king, tells us that he "appeared in a variety of most costly dresses, of a form never seen before, which, he thought, displayed his person to considerable advantage," and in his reception of important foreign guests the Yorkist king set new standards of lavishness. He was helped in his search for higher standards of luxury by the fact that Constantinople, falling at last to the assault of the Sultan's troops, had released a cultural force upon Europe which was to bring it to the supreme artistic culmination of the Renascence.

It was Edward who encouraged William Caxton to introduce the art of printing into England. The King set aside, for Caxton's use, the Almonry of St. Stephen's Chapel at Westminster, on the site of which the present British Houses of Parliament stand, and of which the crypt, "the Jerusalem Chamber," still remains intact.

We shall see later how Christmas has owed much to the art of printing, and so, in the history of Christmas, Edward IV—as the earnest patron of Britain's first printer, Caxton—has an important, though too frequently unrecognized, place.

It is because the first English printing-press was set up in the Royal Chapel of St. Stephen's that, ever since, wherever the English language has been used, the printing-staff has been known as "the chapel."

The first book ever to be printed in England was dedicated to King Edward IV. It is called *The Game and Play of Chess*, and its date is 1474.

It is in the middle of the fifteenth century that we first hear of playing-cards as a popular adjunct to the Christmas festivities. It is known now that playing-cards were printed from wooden blocks (though coloured by hand) a considerable time before the introduction of the printed book, and that their import from the Continent (where, be it noticed, printing was later introduced) had already attained the proportions of a threat to the home-product is shown by the passing of an Act in 1463 prohibiting their import into England.

This Act, it seems, was passed at the request of the English manufacturers, so that the playing-card industry must already have attained considerable proportions in England for foreign competition to have been recognized as a grave threat to one aspect of her commercial prosperity.

I mentioned earlier, too, that the confining of card play to houses was restricted to the twelve days of Christmas by one of the very first Acts of Edward IV's reign.

By the middle of the last quarter of the fifteen century the references to card-playing are so numerous that we realize that the pastime had become one of the chief pleasures of Christmas.

That mine of social information, *The Paston Letters*—letters which were written among various members of the Paston family, influential Norfolk landowners, over the latter half of the fifteenth century—contains many references to the developing taste for card-playing.

Thus on Christmas Eve, 1483, Margery Paston wrote to her husband, John, to tell him that she had sent their son, John, to Lady Morley, to ask her ladyship which "sports" had been permitted in her house at Christmas, following the death of her husband.

Lady Morley apparently told young John Paston that she had forbidden harping, luting, singing and (other) loud disports, and had permitted only "playing at the tables" (probably she meant backgammon—a favourite game of the time), "and the chess, and cards."

Lady Stapleton, asked a similar question by a younger Paston son, agreed with Lady Morley's ruling. "Such disports she gave her folks leave to play, and none other."

Really stupid laws, such as are made by the bigoted for the "good" of the simple, are hard to keep enforced; and so it is not astonishing to read that it was necessary for a further attempt to be made in the reign of Henry VIII to enforce the law restricting card-playing to the Christmas holidays. That second attempt failed, too, as did its many successors.

Christmas dinner, in the fifteenth century, was served at noon, for the days of our ancestors were shortened in winter by the practical problem of lighting their houses. None but the very rich could afford candles of pure beeswax; for lesser folk there was only the illumination of the "dip"—a dried rush dipped in melted mutton-fat. The rush burnt with a dull and smoky flame, and gave off just enough light to break the darkness. Or, mostly, the family sat by the log-fire on winter's afternoons and the year's evenings,

> "Where glowing Embers through the room
> Teach light to counterfeit a gloom. . . ."

The hours of daylight, then, were the hours that simple folk kept: darkness, for them—as for the beasts that they owned—was a time for rest.

They were simple folk and they lived simple lives. Their pleasures, too, were simple . . . and home-made. They relied upon themselves for their own amusements—they had to—and we shall see later what a wealth of simple songs, simple plays and simple games came out of those quiet days and nights that they spent in their simple houses. For the traditional tale and song of Old England comes from the cottage and not from the castle.

## CHAPTER SIX

# THE LORD OF MISRULE

THE two brief reigns of Edward V and Richard III—"Richard Crookback"—add little to our history of Christmas.

Richard was slain on Bosworth Field by Henry of Richmond, who, before setting out to invade England, had promised a gathering of his supporters—on Christmas Day, 1483—that, if he conquered Richard, he would put an end for ever to the rivalry of York and Lancaster by marrying Elizabeth of York, the eldest daughter of Edward IV.

Parsimonious as he was, Henry Tudor did not begrudge money spent on show, for all that—unlike previous kings—he had the courage to tax the nobility as well as the people.

We have a description of one of Henry's riding-habits: "a doublet of green or white cloth of gold satin, with a long gown of purple velvet, furred with ermine, powdered, open at the sides, and purpled (purfled?[1]) with ermine, with a rich sarpe (scarf) and garter."

Indeed, there was no diminution in the prevailing standards of costly apparelling; but Henry's reign is of peculiar interest for us in that it saw the introduction of a new Christmas diversion, which was—as we shall see—nothing but the revival of a very ancient (indeed, pre-Christian) custom.

We remember how, in the Roman *Saturnalia*—that period of national rejoicing which centred about the primeval festival of the winter solstice—it was the custom both to "dress up" and to turn social relations topsy-turvy. Men wore the skins of animals, the dresses of women; servants were waited on at table by their masters.

I seem to see a connexion between the revival of these customs at the end of the fifteenth century and the fall of Constantinople a few decades earlier, since, as I pointed out, ancient manners and customs had become traditionally fixed in Constantinople, and for Europe

[1] ***Purfled:*** **with the outer garment cut to show an under-garment or lining through.**

The Lord of Misrule, or Master of the Revels—variously styled Emperor, Prince, Bishop, etc. During the period of Christmas the authority of this temporary dictator was absolute, even kings submitting with cheerfulness to his most impudent orders. He survived (at Downside School) until as late as 1878.

Henry VII, King of England, Prince of Wales, and Lord of Ireland, sitting in council. A strengthener of government bureaucracy, he sought to centralize authority in the Crown and to buttress its power by impoverishing the independent nobility. His reputation for parsimoniousness has survived, but in his private life he established new standards of royal splendour, and his Christmas expenditure was on a progressively extravagant scale. It was he who confirmed the prestige and power of that strange functionary, the Lord of Misrule.

to fall under the influence of Constantinople (or Byzantium, to use an older name) in the fifteenth century was, in reality, for it to fall under the influence of the manners of ancient Rome, preserved, by a curious accident, unchanged over a thousand years. For while the original culture that Europe had inherited from Rome had been modified and changed during the centuries, that culture had known hardly any change in Byzantium.

I feel, then, that we may attribute the revival of the *Saturnalia* at the end of the fifteenth century to this spreading of Byzantine influence over Europe.

At any rate, whatever the cause, certain it is that the *Saturnalia was* revived—and it flourished, unchecked or unrebuked by the Church, simply because the Church did not see in the apparently new custom merely a revival of an old custom that it had once—ages ago—strongly denounced.

We have the first hints of the revival in "The Kyng's boke of paymentis," where the Lord of Misrule—sometimes called the Abbot of Misrule—is credited "in rewarde for his besynes in Crestenmes holydays, £6 13s. 4d." (ten marks).

Leland, the historian, makes reference, in 1489, to the new custom: "This Cristmas I saw no disgysyngs, and but right few plays. But ther was an Abbot of Misrule, that made much sport and did right well in his office."

The reflective reader may be struck by the curious and apparently contradictory fact that this "guying" of authority—paid for, out of official funds, by authority itself—became a craze at the very time that the rulers of Europe were adopting the modern policy of centralized authority; were striving to impose the power of the State on nations—as they were seemingly paying so that authority might be held up to ridicule.

But so it was; and the Lord of Misrule became one of the most important figures in British social life, while his influence abroad was possibly even more strong. Traces of him are still to be found—as when on Christmas Day, in the British Army, the officers wait upon the rankers—but in his heyday he was exceedingly powerful. And extraordinarily costly, as we shall see.

Briefly, his powers were absolute, and fixed by a convention which had all the force of law—and something over. His duties were to invert ordinary usage for the period of Christmas—the whole twelve days from Christmas Day to Twelfth Night—in any manner most appealing to his impudent ingenuity, so long as it amused the spectators.

The sailor is possibly the most traditional man in our modern world, and customs live longer among sailors than among landsmen. So that it is not astonishing to find that the Lord of Misrule is still to be found at sea, even if he has died more of neglect than of old age on land.

At sea he is called "Father Neptune," and those who, in "crossing the Line" (the present King of Great Britain among them) have had to suffer, with real or assumed cheerfulness, the "lathering" and other indignities that Father Neptune puts upon his hapless victims, may find what consolation they may in reflecting that they were the victims of a custom of most respectable antiquity——a picturesque survival, into our modern times, from a ruder, more boisterous past.

Connected with the Lord of Misrule, by the sentiment of "topsy-turvydom" which inspired both, was the "subtlety" or "soteltie," as it was spelled in the fifteenth century.

This was a dish disguised to look like anything but food; and a description of one or two actually served may explain to the reader exactly in what a "subtlety" consisted.

We find them a feature of the state banquets at the beginning of the century, but they become increasingly popular—and increasingly expensive—as the century progressed, until they reached the summit of ingenuity and costliness in the reign of Henry VIII—the "Bluff King Hal" of matrimonial fame.

Here are three "subtleties" which were served at the grand banquet in Westminster Hall given to celebrate the marriage of Henry V to the Princess Katherine of France.

"Then came a subtlety representing a pelican sitting on her nest with her young, and an image of St. Katherine bearing a book and disputing with the doctors, bearing a reason (i.e., motto) in her right hand, saying, *Madame le Royne,* and the pelican, as an answer:

> "*Ce est la signe*
> *Et lu Roy*
> *Pur tenir ioy*
> *Et a tout sa gent,*
> *Elle met sa entent.*

"Then a subtlety representing a panther with an image of St. Katherine, having a wheel[1] in one hand and a roll with a reason in the other, saying:

*" La royne ma file,*
*In ceste ile,*
*Par bon reson*
*Alues renoun.*

"A leche called the white leche, flourished with hawthorn leaves and red haws, and a march-pane, garnished with figures of angels, having among them an image of St. Katherine, holding this reason:

*" Il est ecrit,*
*Pour voir et dit*
*Per mariage pur*
*C'est guerre ne dure.*

"And lastly a subtlety representing a tiger looking into a mirror, and a man sitting on horseback, fully armed, holding in his arms a tiger's whelp, with this reason *Par force sanz reson il ay prise ceste beste,* and with his one hand making a countenance of throwing mirrors at the great tiger, the which held this reason:

*" Gile de mirror,*
*Ma fete distour."*

This last "reason" referring to the old superstition—to be found repeated in all the medieval bestiaries—that the lion and the tiger are so vain that the eastern hunters may trap them by leaving mirrors lying about in the places that the beasts frequent. The lions and tigers, seeing the mirrors, are unable—by their vain nature—to resist the opportunity to admire themselves, and thus present a sitting target to the hunters. The Harleian MS.4751, in the British Museum—dated at about the end of the twelfth century—is a mine of misinformation, with illustrations, concerning "bestes"—especially those of foreign lands. But the strange tales continue to be told, and to be believed, and Sir John Mandeville's "travelogue" of the beginning of the fifteenth century—written just in time to

[1] The legend is that St. Catherine was martyred by being torn upon a spiked wheel.

be printed—became a best-seller of the day. When Shakespeare, in *Othello,* refers to:

> the anthropophagi,
> And men whose heads do grow beneath their shoulders,

he is referring to tales re-told in Mandeville's book.

The subtlety, then, as its name conveys, expressed a resurgence of the ancient custom of topsy-turvydom observed around the time of the winter solstice. The Lord of Misrule, under his various names, being only another aspect of that old custom.

The end of the fifteenth century saw the old customs revived because authority no longer frowned upon them. That this was a decidedly new attitude is shown by the fact that by a statute of 6 Edward III mummers and masqueraders were ordered to be whipped out of London, and that, even as late as 6 Henry V—1418—Letter Book I of the Corporation of the City of London contains the following:

"The Mair and Aldermen chargen on the kynges byhalf, and this Cite, that no manere persone, of what astate, degre, or condicoun that euere he be, duryng this holy tyme of Christemes be so hardy in eny wyse to walk by nyght in eny manere mommyng, pleyes, enterludes, or eny other disgisynges with eny feynyd berdis,[1] peyntid visers, diffourmyd or colourid visages in eny wyse, up peyne of enprisonement of her bodyes and makyng fyne after the discrecoun of the Mair and Aldermen; ontake that hit be leful to eche persone for to be honestly mery as he can, within his owne hous dwellyng. And more ouere thei charge on the Kynges byhalf, and the Cite, that eche honest persone, dwellyng in eny hye strete or lane of this Citee, hang out of her house eche night, duryng this solempne Feste, a lanterne with a candell ther in, to brenne as long as hit may endure, up peyne to pay ivd, to the chaumbre at eche tyme that hit faillith."

In the following chapter I shall deal at some length with that revival of the old Roman *Rex ludorum*—a part that Nero played one year—in the person of the Lord (or Abbot) of Misrule; for though "mumming" and "disguising" became fashionable in the very earliest stages of our history, and have survived until the present day, the revival of the Lord of Misrule lasted only over a couple

[1] False beards.

of centuries—with some exceptions that I shall treat of in their proper place—and enjoyed his heyday in the sixteenth and seventeenth centuries; in England as in some continental countries.

I should mention here that it was in Henry VII's reign that Columbus sold to the King and Queen of Spain the secret that he had learnt at Genoa: the route to America.

He had not got the route exactly, which accounts for his uncertainty, first as to the direction in which he should go, and second, what exactly he could expect to find at the other side of the Atlantic. But, more by luck than by judgment, he did strike land in the west, and after having first seen it in the shape of Watling Island he pushed on to land on the coast of Cuba, at a bay that he christened *Navidad,* because it was on Christmas Day, 1492, that he arrived there.

The world was expanding: by betraying the secret of Cuba, which had been jealously guarded by a small band of Genoese and Venetian merchants for centuries, Columbus threw the New World open to the adventurous of all Europe. An inexhaustible mine of wealth—even if Columbus was destined never to get the share that he had bargained for so pertinaciously and so long—was suddenly available to a European civilization which had outgrown its currency: which had not enough gold to finance its growing ideals of material culture.

We shall see how the wealth which came pouring into Europe after the dawning of the sixteenth century was to set yet higher standards of luxury and refinement in living—standards which were to affect all classes of the population.

To appoint a "king" or "queen" of the revels is a custom whose origins must be found in the grey, formless shadows of remotest antiquity; for though man is a gregarious creature, he does not—in spite of the theories of some philosophers—value his independence sufficiently not to wish to have a leader, a representative of the group, to act for him: to personify, in a single mind and a single body, the minds and bodies of the clan.

"Railway Queens" and "Holiday Week Queens" and even "Radio Exhibition Queens" have a pedigree compared with which the oldest aristocracies in the world are the upstarts of yesterday.

The "Railway Queen" of the twentieth century is a lineal

descendant of the "Corn Maiden" of the days when our ancestors came, after having left the European forests, into the fertile plains of South Russia. Both represent an ancient desire to embody the mass-wish in the person of some chosen representative of the tribe.

Journeying in medieval times, with a "Christmas Fool" in front.

Every one of the numerous festivals which are common in the life of primitive peoples had its "king" or "queen"—often both; but it appears that a "king" was chosen when the event celebrated—such as the ripening of the corn—was felt to be controlled by a male deity—or Nature-force—while a "queen" was chosen to celebrate an event dominated by female forces—such as lambing or calving.

Despite the fact that the word for "sun" in Anglo-Saxon—*sonne*, or *sune*—is of the feminine gender, and that for "moon" is of the masculine gender—*mone*—those ancient festivals which were concerned with the apparent movements of the heavenly bodies were held to be regulated by powers which were conceived of as essentially masculine.

Let us put it in this way: the planetary aspects of Nature—the remote, or *first*, causes—were held to be masculine; the aspects of Nature nearer home—springing, budding, fruiting, autumnal withering—were held to be feminine. The ancient Aryan name for the spirit of Nature—we can hardly call it "God," for that represents a much later stage in human mental development—means

"Sky-father," while the earth, and all that it brings forth, are regarded primitively as feminine. The great earth-goddess of the Greeks has a name which means "pig-mother."

The winter solstice, then, since it was the most impressive—awe-inspiring, fearful—of the heavenly events by which early man adjusted his habits and his beliefs, was believed to be under a masculine influence, and so the chosen representative of the tribe to speak for the people at this festival was a male—a "king."

I have mentioned that the Romans celebrated the winter festival with extravagant carnival, involving a temporary upsetting of normal behaviour, and the "king" chosen to preside over this feast was called *Rex ludorum* or *Rex bibendi*—"King of the games" or "King of the wine-pots."

Nero, as I have mentioned, too, was *Rex bibendi* more than once, being drawn for the position by lot—though possibly not altogether by sheer chance!

Typically Neronian was the manner in which he marked one of the "Christmas" Festivals over which he presided as Master of the Revels: while he circulated the cup and led the choruses, the last descendant of the family of the Claudii, who had been deprived of their inheritance by Nero, was murdered by the degenerate Emperor's hired bravoes.

Though the Church sought to incorporate as many of the pagan festivals as possible into Christian celebration, she set her face resolutely against any incorporation of the *Saturnalia* and *Bacchanalia,* finding the licence which had become traditionally associated with the pagan festivals of winter something that no religious purifying could ever render innocent enough for Christians to patronize.

It is obvious, though, from the various edicts made by the Church authorities against "dressing up" and other pagan customs, that the *Saturnalia*—even if under another name, or under no name at all—did continue to be celebrated long after the official establishment of Christianity as the sole religion of the western world. That we still use masks and paper hats at our innocent Christmas revels shows that the Church, in the early days of Christianity, did not succeed in imposing a complete ban on Bacchanalian and Saturnalian practices.

Yet for all that these practices survived, the official disfavour with which the Church viewed them had inevitably the effects of "driving them underground"; of restricting their indulgence to the humbler folk. (Bear in mind that both "pagan"—a Latin word—and "heathen"—its Anglo-Saxon literal translation—mean "rustic," as opposed to "civilized," which means "in the manner of men who live in towns.")

There are many reasons why ancient customs, kept alive only among the country people and in the submerged masses of the towns, should have come, as it were, to the surface, around the middle of the fourteenth century, and so become once more acceptable to the higher orders. Not one of these reasons is quite clear; but it is possibly the fact that the Church had long since ceased to fear a pagan reaction which made the religious authorities tolerant of habits which had lost their original religious significance centuries before.

We have an example of this acquired tolerance in modern times. Fifty years ago, in Britain, "Guy Fawkes' Day" was a celebration which had a strong anti-Papal bias in its elements. The children, wheeling a "guy" around and cadging pence for their bonfire, used to call their activities "poping," and in towns with a big Roman Catholic population—such as Liverpool and Glasgow—the police were called out in force to prevent the flare-up of religious animosities.

All that has passed today, and it would never occur to the most strictly religious of Roman Catholic parents to forbid their children to let off fireworks on Guy Fawkes' Night—at least, not for purely religious reasons.

Later we shall see that "Guy Fawkes' Night" is a festival which celebrates something a great deal older than Guy Fawkes's attempt to blow up the Houses of Parliament.

But to return to the Lord of Misrule, coming shyly out of the neglected condition of a thousand years, like some hitherto poor relation whose value has rather belatedly been conceded by his important connexions.

An important point: the revels over which the Lord of Misrule was once again to preside appear to have preceded the restoration of their king. We find, in the records, details of expensively elaborate mummings a century or more before the Lord of Misrule—or Abbot of Misrule, or King, Prince, Emperor of Christmas (he had many names)—makes his reappearance.

For a mumming of 1348 there were provided "eighty tunics of buckram, forty-two visors, and a great variety of other whimsical dresses . . . for the disguising of the Court at the Feast of Christmas."

Stubbes, the Puritan Mr. Misery of Elizabeth's reign, whom just to remember that anyone had made himself happy drove nearly insane with anger, recalls for us that a certain Captain John Gladman rebuked the mummers for their folly in 1440. Gladman—if indeed he is no fiction of Stubbes' (and his name sounds suspiciously non-genuine)—did not incur the narrow Puritan's anger, seeing that the Captain appears to have been a sort of fifteenth-century Stubbes himself, though considerably more human.

"One Captain John Gladman, a man ever true and faithful to God and the King, and constantly sportive, made public disport with his neighbours at Christmas. He traversed the town on a horse as gaily caparisoned as himself, preceded by the twelve months, each dressed in character. After him crept the pale, attenuated figure of Lent, clothed in herring-skins, and mounted on a sorry horse, whose harness was covered with oyster-shells. A train, fantastically garbed, followed. Some were clothed as bears, apes and wolves; others were tricked out in armour; a number appeared as harridans, with blackened faces and tattered clothes, and all kept up a promiscuous fight. Last of all marched several carts, whereon a number of fellows, dressed as old fools, sat upon nests, and pretended to hatch young fools."

It seems that these mummings—Fosbroke says that the word is derived from the Danish *mumme* or Dutch *momme*[1]: disguise in a mask—were originally given in dumb-show; but at some time within the latter half of the fifteenth century words had come to attach themselves to the mumming, and there is a "pleye" of the reign of Edward IV in which the Nine Worthies take part.

Here are some sample lines:

ECTOR DE TROYE: Thow Achylles me in bataly me slow,
Of my worthynes men speken I now.
ALISANDER: And in romaunce often am I leyt,
As conqueror gret thow I seyt.
JULIUS CAESAR: Thow my cenatoures me slow in collory,
Fele londes byfore by conquest wan I.

[1] And both words are obviously derived from an original root which is found in the dialect phrase, "to keep mum," since *mask* is equated with *gag* even in the idiom of modern, polished usage.

JOSUE: In holy Chyrche *y*e mowen here and rede,
Of my worthynes and of my dede.
DAUIT: After y slayn was Golyas,
By me the sawter than made was.
JUDAS MACABEUS: Of my wurthynesse *y*yf *y*e wyll wete,
Secke the byble, for ther it is wrete.
ARTHOUR: The round tabyll I sette wp Knyghtes strong,
*Y*yt shall I come a*y*en, thow it be long.
CHARLES: With me dwellyd Rouland Olyvere,
In all my conquest fer and nere.
GODEFRY DE BOLEYN: And I was Kyng of Jherusalem,
The crowne of thorn I wan fro hem.

The importance that the "pleyes" or "disports"—which word was subsequently shortened to our modern "sports," even by the time of Holinshed (*temp.* Elizabeth)—had gained by the time of Henry VII is shown by a description of a banquet at Christmas, 1492, that the King gave for the Mayor and Aldermen of London.

After the Christmas banquet—which was eaten as Columbus's ships were making landfall—the King entertained his guests with various rich spectacles, "which sports, *being ended in the morning*, the King, Queen and Court sat down at a table of stone[1] to 120 dishes, placed by as many knights and esquires, while the Mayor was served with twenty-four dishes and abundance of wine.

"And finally the King and Queen, being conveyed with great lights in to the palace, the Mayor, with his company in barges, returned to London by break of the next day."

To sit the clock round twice, to see "pleyes" and "disports," shows how important the new diversions had come to be considered!

The fact that the hundred and twenty dishes were served by as many knights and squires is highly significant. It shows clearly that Henry Tudor was pursuing the same method as that by which Louis XIV was later to break the power of the nobles for independent action. One hundred and twenty knights and squires—apprentice-knights, in effect—under the King's eye at Westminster Hall, were one hundred and twenty fewer ambitious men less in places where their ambitions might lead them to plot against that national stability that Henry, for all his personal greed, did most

[1] One may justly interpret this phrase to mean a table with a top inlaid with coloured marbles (called *pietra dura* in Italian). Henry employed many Italian artists and craftsmen.

genuinely desire to confer upon the land that he had conquered.

Indeed, his known congenital parsimoniousness was such that we must accept Henry's ostentation in the matter of his dresses and his hospitality as something more than an indulgence of his ideas of what was due to a man in his position. He felt, it is certain, that he was raising the prestige, not only of his crown but of his kingdom, in living as a great prince should live; and that his extravagances, his *fantaiseries,* his sometimes apparently childish fopperies were not dictated by idle vanity, we may see in the fact that, for the first time, Henry's exchequer was under the strict duty to see that the national budget was balanced; that Henry's splendid living was *paid for.*

He left a fortune of four million pounds, it is true, but he left his country solvent as well. The nation, seeing their king so splendid in his court, and seeing all around the signs of growing prosperity marching equally with the signs of growing political stability, could not help but connect prosperity with peace; and to connect both with the luxury that the King affected.

When Henry died, in 1509, he left a kingdom to his son which was prosperous and secure: qualities which were the achievement of one man, More: in the twenty-four years of Henry VII's reign, England, in a peace that Henry had striven jealously to keep, had entered the ranks of the great nations; acquiring, among the really important states, a dominant position which had never been gained by England's many interventions of a warlike character.

Before we go on to tell of the sumptuous feasts which were to be a striking characteristic of the life, not only of the next king, Henry VIII, and of his great nobles, but of his lesser subjects (notably his lawyers) as well, let us consider for a little the kind of food which was served up at these banquets which so fascinated the historians of other days.

Different as the ways of the Middle Ages seem to us, we can yet feel that, were we by some magic to be transported back to those days, we should find more which was familiar to us than irreconcilably foreign. We should, we feel, soon become used to the strangeness of the dress, to the broad vowels of fifteenth-century speech, to the absence of motor-cars and electric lamps and the telephone.

After all, we think, it would only be like going to live in a rather primitive country district at a time when the inhabitants had put on fancy-dress for the celebration of some festival. We should feel ourselves (we reflect) no more strange than the visitor to Andorra today must feel, when he comes into that remote little anachronism, as the inhabitants of Andorra-la-Vella are dancing the Bal Plà.

Yet it is safe to say that, were we to take our place at one of the banquets of the time—say, at that given on the installation of John Stafford as Bishop of Wells, in 1425—we should not recognize as familiar *one* of the dishes put before us; and that *most* of them we should find positively inedible, if not downright disgusting.

Let us suppose, for instance, that the reader, caught in a warp in the space-time continuum, found himself sitting down to the banquet[1] which was given after the coronation of Henry VI in St. Peter's, Westminster, 6 November, 1429. What would he or she make of the feast, which is described thus:

"After that solempnyzacion in the sayd churche fynysshed, an honourable feest in the great halle of Westmynster was kepte, where the kinge, syttinge in his astate, was servyd with .iii. coursys, as hereunder ensureth (ensueth). Frument with venyson, Viand royall plantyd losynges of golde. Bore hedes in castellys of golde and enarmed. Beef with moton boyled. Capon stewyd. Signet rosted. Heyroun rostyd. Great pyke or luce. A rede leche with lyons corvyn therin. Custarde royall with a lyoparde of gold syttynge therein, and holdynge a floure delyce. Frytour of sunne facion, with a flour delyce therein. A sotyltie[2] of Seynt Edwarde and Seynt Lowys armyd, and upon eyther his cote armour, and a scripture passynge from them both, sayinge: 'beholde .ii. parfyght kynges under one cote armour,' and under the fete of the sayd seyntes, was wryten this balade:

"Holy seyntes, Edwarde and seynt Lowyce
Concerve this braunche, born of your blessyd blode,
Lyve among Christen, moste soveraygne of pryce.
Inherytour of the flour delyce so gode:
This sixte Henry to reygne and to be wise,
God graunte he may, to be your mode
And that he may resemble your knyghthode and vertue
Pray ye hertely unto our Lorde Ihesu.

[1] So called from the "banquets," or benches, on which the guests sat. Chairs were reserved for the very highest personages. Even bishops sat on "banquets."

[2] Or "subtlety."

"Viand blank barryd with gold. Gely party, wryten and noted with *Te Deum Laudamus*. Pygge endored. Crane rostyd. Byttore."

And so on, for what would take three pages of this book.

The list ends:

"A sotyltie[1] of our Lady, syttynge with her childe in her lappe, and she holdynge a crowne in her hande. Seynt George and Seynt Denys knelynge, on eyther syde, presentyd to her Kynge Henryes fygure, berynge in hand this balade, as foloweth."

We may dispense with the "balade." The golden age of British poetry was as yet far off.

Three-quarters of a century later the fashion had changed only in respect of its increased hold upon the national taste: the feast which marked the enthronement of Archbishop Warham was of the same character as that which marked the coronation of Henry VI, save that the later feast was considerably more elaborate.

"Before the serving of the first course, a huge 'warner,' a sort of subtlety, was brought in representing in the first stage a battlemented castle with eight towers, all made of flowers, with a beadle displaying his staff on each tower; then the King sitting in Parliament with his lords about him in their robes, and St. William like an archbishop sitting on the right hand of the King: then the Chancellor of Oxford, with other doctors, presenting the said Lord William kneeling in a doctor's habit unto the King with Latin verses, to which the King responds in the same tongue."

This feast—it had its usual excess of complicated and fancifully-named dishes, of course—exhibits the lengths to which ritualization had been carried in the period following the accession of Henry VII.

"The said Archbishop was solemnly served with Wafers and Ipocras, and immediately after the Sewer with the two Marshals, with great solemnitie from the Ewrie board, the Sergeant of the Ewrie pliking and foldyng it with great diligence, brought the Surnappe through the Hall to the hygh boorde, and the said Surnappe so brought well pliked to the boorde, one of the Marshals without hande laying thereto drew it through the boorde with great curiositie, after the old courtesy: and so the said Lord washed and said grace standing. And after this, standing at the void, the said Lord Archbishop was served with Consertes, Sugar plate, Fertes and other subtilties, with Ipocras. And so departed to his chamber."

[1] Or "subtlety."

I said just now that the modern reader, transported by some magic to that distant past, would not recognize *one* of the dishes served.

This statement may be repeated and emphasized, in spite of the apparent familiarity of such dishes—that we saw served at the coronation feast of Henry VI—as "beef with moton boyled," "capon stewyd," "signet rostyd," "heyroun rostyd," "custarde" and—at Archbishop Warham's feast—"wafers."

The names certainly are familiar enough, but it was the delight of the medieval cook so to disguise his ingredients by mixing them up that no one flavour could hold out against the combined tastes of perhaps thirty flavours.

"Herbs" and spices were added to every sort of food—*without* exception. And, as though the addition of cinnamon, pepper, ginger, mace, cloves and the rest were not enough to disguise the original flavour of the meat, fish or fruit which gave its name to the dish, the "main item" itself was cut up small and then pounded to a paste in a mortar.

The reason for thus "braying" the food was that the fork—that seemingly indispensable tool—was not introduced into England from Italy before the reign of James I; and the difficulty of cutting meat armed only with a knife was solved by reducing most of the food either to what we should now call a "mince," or to a paste or "purée," in which condition it could be eaten with a spoon or scooped up with the fingers.

Perhaps the most revealing directions in the fourteenth-century cookery-book, *Le Ménagier de Paris,* are those for making beef taste like venison or bear's flesh, or sturgeon taste like veal. As Mead so rightly points out, "the highest aim of the medieval cook seems to have been to transform food of one sort into something quite different."

To show, for instance, what a medieval cook could serve as a "wafer," let us observe what the old recipe instructs:

"Take the belly of a pike and seethe it well, put it into a mortar, add cheese thereto, and grind them together. Then take flour and white of eggs and beat together; then take sugar and powder of ginger, and put all together, and look that the eggs be hot, and lay thereon thy paste, and then make thy wafers and serve therein."

So much for "wafers"! Now see what the same cookery could

make of what, to us, is that eminently simple dish, stewed beef.

"Take fair ribs of the beef of the fore-quarters, and smite in fair pieces, and wash the beef in a fair (i.e., clean) pot.

"Then take the water that the beef was sodden in, and strain it through a strainer and seethe the same water and beef in a pot, and let them boil together. Then take cinnamon, cloves, grains of parise (ginger), cubebs, and onions minced, parsley, and sage, and cast thereto, and let them boil together. And then take a loaf of bread, and steep it with broth and vinegar, and draw it through a strainer, and let it be still. And when it is near enough (i.e., done) cast the liquor thereto, but not too much, and then let (it) boil once, and cast saffron thereto in quantity. Then take salt and vinegar and cast thereto, and look that it be poignant (piquant) enough, and serve forth."

This is comparatively simple for a medieval recipe, and—except that the meat has been triturated, pounded, brayed—as you will—into a paste, the dish bears a family resemblance to our modern "jugged hare," which is a curious culinary survival from medieval cooking.

Veal, chicken or kid was treated in a similar fashion. "Boil in clean water or in fresh broth, and cut into pieces, and pick them clean (i.e., remove the bones). Then draw the same broth through a strainer and cast thereto parsley, sage, hyssop, mace, cloves, and let (it) boil till the flesh be (done) enough. Then set it (away) from the fire and mix it with raw yolks of eggs, and cast thereto ginger, verjuice[1], saffron and salt, and then serve it forth for a good meat."

One would have thought that a grilled steak must be the simplest dish in the world; but not to the medieval chef!

"Take venison or beef and slice and grill it brown." So far, so good! But: "Then take vinegar and a little verjuice and a little wine, and put powdered pepper thereon enough and powdered ginger. And at the dresser strew on powdered cinnamon enough, that the steaks may be all covered therewith, and but a little sauce. And then serve it forth."

Almonds were used in enormous quantities by the cooks of the Middle Ages, though never—as far as I have been able to trace—in the form of "marzipan." A favourite product of almonds was almond-milk:

[1] Verjuice was the juice of any fruit, fermented or unfermented.

"To make a Cold Milk of Almonds, put fair water in a pot with sugar or honey clarified so that it be douce (sweet), then salt it and set it on the fire, and when it is at boiling, skim it, and let it boil a while. Then take from the fire and let it cool. Then blanch your almonds and grind them, and temper them with the same water into a good thick milk, and put (add) it to wine that it may have a good flavour thereof, and serve it. Then cut bread and toast it, and baste it, and toast it again, that it be hard (i.e., make 'toast Melba') and serve them in one dish and the milk in another dish."

But almonds were used in innumerable other ways, and entered into the combination of all sorts of dishes, in which their potent flavour would have served only to kill all others.

Mead reckons that, of 258 recipes in *Two Fifteenth-century Cookery Books,* no fewer than 83—or near a third of the total—contain almond as an ingredient.

One last recipe, to show what the medieval cook could do with his materials: that stand-by of the modern tea-shop—Poached Eggs on Toast.

"Take eggs, break them, and seethe them in hot water. Then take them up as whole as thou mayest. Then take flour and mix with milk and cast thereto sugar or honey and a little powdered ginger, and boil all together, and colour with saffron[1]. And lay thy eggs in dishes and cast the broth above, and cast on powder enough. Blanche powder is best."[2]

Several theories have been advanced to account for the lavish and universal use of spices in the Middle Ages. It has been suggested that the meat was too rarely fresh not to have needed strong flavours to hide the "high" taste of the meat. Or some others have suggested that spices were credited with so sovereign a medicinal value in those days that no dish was felt to be "safe" without the addition of ginger and the rest. Or—very much the same thing—the people of the past made such a habit of over-eating that, without the digestive virtues of ginger, cardamoms, and so forth to aid, they would all have perished of hyper-acute dyspepsia. Some say that the use of spices was developed simply because spices—brought from

[1] *Saffron* is the pollen of the *Crocus sativa,* and its production was once a great Essex industry; hence the name "Saffron Walden."

[2] According to the English lexicographer, Cotgrave, this was a mixture of cinnamon, nutmeg and ginger, "in use among cooks."

the East—were most costly, and that a rich man's vanity was flattered in proportion as his dishes contained the rarest and the most costly ingredients.

My own opinion is that we must look for the reason for the universal spicing of the dishes not to one cause, but a combination of causes, and that the main cause of the spicing is to be found in the monotony of the diet. It may be argued that no monotony more complete could have been achieved by the cooks in adding the same mixture of spices to every dish, from purée of apples to mashed porpoise, and that this must have been so it is impossible to deny.

But I do feel that spices were introduced into cooking in the desire to add, as we say, a "spice" to plain food, and that other considerations led later to the unrestricted use of spice. For it is commonly forgotten how many of the foods that we now not only take for granted, but consider absolutely indispensable, were missing from the dietary of the Middle Ages.

*The Forme of Cury*—the fourteenth-century cookery book that I mentioned earlier—gives, as the vegetables in use then, only onions (by far the most used in the recipes), leeks, cabbage, and a few other plants that we should now call "herbs."

The *Household Book* of Richard de Swinfield (1289-90) mentions only onions, leeks, garlic,[1] peas, beans and potherbs, while the *Roll* of the Countess of Leicester mentions only dried peas and beans, parsley, fennel, onions, green peas, new beans.

It was no better in the period just before the discovery of America. Dean Kymer of Salisbury, Chancellor of Oxford University, gives, as the vegetables then eaten, only cabbage, lettuce, spinach, beetroot, trefoil, bugloss, borage, celery—cultivated and wild—thyme, hyssop, parsley, a species of wild turnip and "pearl" onion. The Dean tells us that these "vegetables" were commonly boiled up with the meat, but he also says that they were used to make salads, dressed with olive oil and spices.

*The Forme of Cury* gives a fourteenth-century recipe for a salad. "Take parsley, sage, garlic, chibollas (young onions), onions, leek, borage, porrectes (small onions), and cresses, rue, rosemary, purslain. Lave and wash them clean. Pick them, pluck them small with thy

[1] The word "garlic" means "spear-plant" (from the shape of its leaf), and the ancient English name that it bears shows how long it has been an article of household use.

hand and mix them well with raw oil. Lay on vinegar and salt and serve it forth."

In the reign of Henry VII there was no brandy, whisky, gin or champagne. There were no potatoes, tomatoes, rhubarb, currants, gooseberries, apricots, bananas, raspberries, pineapples, musk-melons, water-melons. There was neither tea nor coffee. And there was, of course, no tobacco to end a meal, if not to flavour its dishes.

Limited to what was available at home—for only the smallest, most lasting and costliest products of foreign lands could be imported over the long and hazardous trade-routes of those days—the medieval chef sought for variety in his preparations among home products. And it is for this reason that we find the chefs using not only the animals and game which are now commonly eaten, but beasts of strangely inedible qualities.

Thus crane, cormorant, peacock, thrush, sparrow, porpoise, whale, lamprey, swan figure in the medieval menus.

"*Item,* a Warraunte to be servide oute Yerelie at Michalmes for twentie *Swannis* for th'Expencis of my Lordis house; As to saye for Cristynmas daie V—Sainte Stephins daie two—Sainte John daie two—Childremas daie ij—Sainte Thomas daie ij—Newyere daie iij—and for the xijth daie of Cristynmas iiij Swannes."

Columbus, though he did not discover America—in the strict sense of the word—did open up the New World to general trade; as Bartolommeo Diaz and Vasco da Gama opened up the sea route to the Far East. Within a few years the limits of Europe's horizon were to roll back like a spring-blind let go with a snap.

The most distant lands were to send their exotic fruits and flowers, their silks and lacquers, their porcelain and intoxicating herbs.

All were to effect the most profound changes in European taste.

## CHAPTER SEVEN

# THE AGE OF ELIZABETH

APART from the very few years covering the brief reigns of Edward VI and "Bloody" Mary, the sixteenth century was shared between Henry VIII and his daughter, Elizabeth. They shared, indeed, something more than may be reckoned in terms of a calendar: between them they brought the land that they ruled out of the Middle Ages into modern times. They were not responsible for the historical events which changed the world—Henry was not even responsible for the Reformation—but they influenced, by their peculiarly strong characters, the manner in which world events and world trends were to shape the pattern of British—and thus of American—existence.

Yet both father and daughter were fundamentally medieval in their outlook: they remained themselves unaffected by the changes that they controlled; and their influence is not discernible until we study the times following Elizabeth's death.

I repeat what I said earlier: that the Middle Ages ended with the accession of Edward IV. What I add now is that the manners and customs of the Middle Ages were to survive the *political and economic* division between ancient and modern times until at least the reign of James I. In spirit, both Henry VIII and Elizabeth belong to the age of the Wars of the Roses, rather than to the age of the Civil War.

Indeed, in so much as Henry VIII had a personal predilection for what seems to us pure buffoonery, he is, in that respect at least, much more medieval than his father, and this love of buffoonery was fully shared by his masculine daughter, "the Virgin Queen."

I have said that the sixteenth century was to see the introduction of many of those luxuries which have come to be accepted by the poorest of us as the very necessities of everyday life; unfortunately, the pioneers who brought back gold and silver, turkeys and potatoes, cocoa and quinine, to Europe, were destined also to bring back a disease which claimed Henry VIII—among hundreds of thousands —as a victim.

This disease is now curable, but its effects, in the first years of its introduction to Europe, were almost invariably fatal; though unfortunately death did not come until the mind had become gravely affected, and much of the eccentricity which marked the conduct of Henry in his latter days may be attributed to the effects of this then-incurable ailment.

But the illness was not contracted until Henry had been some years a king, and when he came to the throne he was a handsome, amiable, generous youth, whose abounding energy and cheerfulness found their most frequent vent in harmless practical jokes.

He had a natural dignity, and the typical Tudor sense of the importance of his position, but this did not prevent his wishing to dress himself up in any odd costume which took his boyish fancy, nor from selecting even the ambassadors of foreign countries as the victims of his impudent impostures.

It will be understood, then, that the Lord of Misrule attained to immense importance as a public figure in the reign of this joke-loving monarch. Thus, though the payments to the Lord of Misrule had never exceeded £6 13s. 4d., Henry immediately raised the payment to £8 6s. 8d., and soon after to £15 6s. 8d. This affection of the King's for the Lord of Misrule went hand-in-hand, understandably enough, with a deep love of mummery and "disgysings." In the accounts for Henry's first year of rule is a payment of £451 12s. 2d.—an immense sum of money for those days—to a certain Rob. Amadas, "upon his bill for certain plate of gold stuff bought of him for the disguisings."

William Buttry received, at the same time, £133 7s. 5d., "upon his bill for certyn sylks bought of him for the disguisings."

Five years later we find Leonard Friscobald receiving £247 12s. 7d. for "divers velvets and other sylks, for the disguisings," and Richard Gibson accepting payment of £137 14s. 0½d. for certen apparell . . . for the disguysing at the fest of Cristemes last."

Several later payments are recorded to the same Gibson, in connexion with an entertainment called a "Maskelyn" in the accounts; and there are entries relating to payments in respect of the gentlemen and children of the King's chapel.

The gentlemen received £13 6s. 8d. "for their good attendance at Xtemas"; the children a little less than half that sum. "Mr. Cornisse for playing affore the King upon newyeres day at nyght with the children—£6 13s. 4d."

Cavendish, the biographer of Cardinal Wolsey, has much to tell of the King's liking for the magnificence that his ambitious subject—the son of an Ipswich butcher—knew so well how to command.

"The banquets," says Cavendish, in speaking of Wolsey's hospitality, "were set forth, with masks and mummeries, in so gorgeous a sort, and costly manner, that it was a heaven to behold. There was all kind of music and harmony set forth, with excellent voices both of men and children. I have seen the King suddenly come thither in a mask, with a dozen of other maskers, all in garments like shepherds, made of fine cloth of gold and fine crimson satin, paned,[1] and caps of the same, with visors of good proportion of visnomy;[2] their hairs and beards either of fine gold wire or else of silver, and some being of black silk; having sixteen torchbearers, besides their drums, and other persons attending upon them, with visors, and clothed all in satin, of the same colours."

On one occasion the King, disguised as Robin Hood, with some of his noblemen attired as various friends of Robin, came unexpectedly into the Queen's private room, "whereat," says Holinshed, "the Queen and her ladies were greatly amazed, as well for the strange sight as for the sudden appearance."

Henry VIII was extremely fond of tournaments, and in this he was following the example of many previous kings. But he was responsible—if not as actual inventor, then certainly as principal patron—of a type of mock-battle eminently fitted for indoor entertainments.

The inspiration of the tournaments had already passed from the mythical achievements of King Arthur to the even more mythical activities of the gods of Greece and Rome; chivalry, no less than every other branch of human business in the early sixteenth century, was coming under the influence of classical culture. At the tournament following the coronation of Henry VIII the contestants assumed "the name and devices of the knights or scholars of Pallas, clothed in garments of green velvet, carrying a crystal shield, on

[1] *Paned:* made up of particoloured strips sewn together, in the manner in which *panes* (same word as "panels") are put in a window.

[2] That is, covering most of the face.

which was portrayed the goddess, Minerva, and had the bases and barbs of their horses embroidered with roses and pomegranates of gold; those of Diana were decorated with the bramble-bush, displayed in a similar manner. The prize of valour was the crystal shield...."

There is a singularly modern touch in the remark that "night closed upon the joyous scene; but before its approach the King, perceiving that the ardour of the combatants had become intemperate and dangerous, wisely limited the number of strokes, and closed the tourney."

The tournament had, indeed, become a pageant, as the emphasis of its theme tended to shift from combat pure and simple to combat rendered innocuous and decorated by elaborate theatrical trappings.

At Christmas, 1516, the pageant took place indoors—in the great hall of the Royal Palace of Richmond.

"Against the twelfe daie, or the daie of the Epiphanie, at night, before the blanket in the hall at Richmond, was a pageant devised like a mounteine, and set with stones; on the top of which mounteine was a tree of gold, the branches and boughes frised with gold, spreading on everie side over the mounteine, with roses and pomegranates, the which mounteine was, with vices,[1] brought up towards the king, and out of the same came a ladie apparelled in cloth of gold, and the children of honour called the henchmen, which were freshly disguised, and danced a morice before the king; and that done, re-entered the mounteine, which was then drawen backe, and then was the wassail or blanket brought in, and so brake up Christmasse."

The progress of these pageants—or "interludys"—towards excessive elaboration was speedy. In the following year, when the King "kept his Christmasse at Greenewich," the chronicle tells us that there "was such an abundance of viands served to all comers of anie honest behaviour as hath beene few times seene.

"And against New Yeeres night was made in the hall a castell, gates, towers and dungeon, garnished with artillerie and weapon, after the most warlike fashion: and on the front of the castell was written *Le forteresse dangereux,* and within the castell were six ladies cloathed in russet sattin, laid all over with leaves of gold,

[1] Or, as we should say, "windlassed" or "winched" in.

and everie one knit with laces of blew silke and gold. On their heads, coifs and caps all of gold. After this castell had beene caried about the hall, and the queene had beheld it, in came the king with five other, apparelled in coats, the one half of russet sattin, the other halfe of rich cloth of gold; on their heads caps of russet sattin embrodered with works of fine gold bullion.

"These six assaulted the castell. The ladies, seeing them so lustie and couragious, were content to solace with them, and upon fuerther communication to yeeld the castell, and so they came downe and dansed a long space. And after, the ladies led the knights into the castell, and then the castell suddenly vanished out of their sights. On the daie of the Epiphanie at night, the king, with eleven other, were disguised, after the manner of Italie; called a maske, a thing not seene before in England; they were apparelled in garments long and broad, wrought all with gold, with visors and caps of gold.

"And after the banket done, these maskers came in, with six gentlemen disguised in silke, bearing staffe torches, and desired the ladies to danse: some were content and some refused. And after they had dansed, and communed togither, as the fashion of the maske is, they tooke their leave and departed, and so did the queene and all the ladies."

Royal examples were quickly and flatteringly aped. An entry, of date 1512, in the Household Book of the Earl of Northumberland, refers to the Almoner as a "maker of Interludys," and it appears that he had a servant "to the intent for writynge the parts."

The Earl paid the players twenty shillings to perform a Play of the Nativitie "uppon Cristynmes day in the mornnynge in my lords chapell befor his lordship."

Lord Northumberland had a duly appointed Master of the Revels, but it is obvious that any of his senior household servants were liable to be called upon to aid the theatrical entertainments. The earl's chaplain, for instance, received 13s. 4d. "for makyng an Enterlued to be playd this next Christenmas."

These "enterlueds" were not confined to the festivities of the upper classes. All classes, according to Strutt, practised "mummeries" at Christmas-time, and where masks were not procurable—usually for reasons of cost—it was the custom, apparently, to daub the face with soot and other pigments—as children "collecting for the Guy" do now in the period round about 5 November.

Alexander Barclay, in his translation of Brant's *Ship of Fools,* says, of this custom:

> The one hath a visor ugley set on his face,
> Another hath on a vile counterfaite vesture,
> Or painteth his visage with fume in such case,
> That what he is, himself is scantily sure.

Horse-play undoubtedly added itself to these "mummeries" in Tudor, as it had in Roman, times. And—seeing how earthy an age it was—the horse-play must have been of the rudest kind; sufficiently rude, indeed, to have justified an Act, passed in the 3rd Henry VIII, prohibiting persons going about as "mummers," or in visors or in any "disguised apparrel," under pain of three months' imprisonment. Even the keeping of "visors" in the house was punishable under the Act by a fine of twenty shillings.

But, like the edicts against smoking issued by Tippelskirch, Governor of Berlin in the early part of the nineteenth century, these Tudor edicts against popular customs—there were plenty of other edicts besides that against "mumming"—were little more than the expression of pious hopes. In any case, it was at the horse-play which accompanied the mumming—horse-play which was probably too often disguised begging or even intimidation ("Penny for the Guy, Mister!")—rather than at the mumming itself, that the Act was directed. Laws against "tables, tennis, dice, cards, bowls, clash, coyting, logating or any other unlawful game" were equally unsuccessful. For one unlucky culprit made to pay the penalty exacted by the statutes a hundred went scot-free.

So with the mumming, which was to be found through every grade of society, from literally the highest—the Court—to the sweepings of the burrows and rat-holes around Whitefriars and the Bedlem Hospital.

The sixteenth century was to see the New World opened up. It was to see the creation of vast new empires, and a tide of wealth diverted to Europe of dimensions never before dreamed of, even in the airy fancies of *The Thousand and One Tales*.

Tobacco was to be introduced to add a new desire and a new solace to human existence. Turkeys and tomatoes and pineapples and potatoes were to give luxurious variety to the hitherto monotonous dietary of the Middle Ages. With new things to be bought there was to be an awakening, in all classes of society, to the need for money to buy those new things, and a scramble for wealth infected the whole population.

Old and new ports on the Atlantic thrived on the new trade with the Far West, and commercial activities on a modern scale are first recorded in our history books. Ships had to be built bigger and stronger to make the voyages to the West economically feasible, and the wonderful invention of insurance—that the Roman shippers had used—was revived to help the merchants of Elizabeth's day to bear the grave risks then inherent in all sea-ventures.

Unsuccessful in the first scramble for the prizes of the West—for where Spanish Pizarro was capturing Golden Peru for his king, Sebastian Cabot sailed from Bristol only to add chilly Labrador to the British Crown—the English adventurers ("little better than pirates," says Count Corti) strove desperately to make up later what they had missed in the beginning.

There was no one then to prophesy that the "plantation" of Virginia—a sickly growth, indeed, it seemed to be—would one day grow into an empire greater in wealth and political power than the splendid possessions of the Spaniards in the New World. Yes . . . and greater than the empire of the land from which the first Virginian colonists came.

All this activity—piratical or not—meant trade, and trade meant the rise of great commercial houses, and the rise of great commercial houses, with the trade that they handled and the wealth that they brought into the country, meant the rise of a new class of lawyer: the commercial attorney, freed from that curious ecclesiastical flavour which marked the lawyer of the earlier ages, managed the new wealth, developed it, shared in it—and finally learnt himself how to create it.

The sixteenth century in England saw the rise of that phenomenon of modern life: the "business man"—and in the times of the Tudors he first appears as merchant and lawyer.

A new aristocracy appeared: the aristocracy of business men; nobles who were neither soldiers nor churchmen, the two classes which had previously supplied the nobility of Europe. The professional lawyers accounted for a considerable proportion of the ranks of the new nobility, and the legal corporations—the Honourable Societies of the Middle Temple, the Inner Temple, and all the rest of them—waxed as wealthy as powerful; strong, and conscious of their strength, in being united in a society where individualism, though often paying wonderful dividends, yet sometimes had to bear its own losses.

Before the end of the century the Law had infiltrated into—one might almost say amalgamated with—the Court. Lawyers had been ennobled, and they were helping the Crown to grow rich. Royal patronage, in consideration for the loyal support of the gentlemen of the long robe, was extended to the legal profession, and the benchers of the various Inns of Court gave Christmas entertainments which first rivalled, and then exceeded in splendour, those of the Court.

It was in these legal entertainments that the Lord of Misrule achieved the perfection of his glory; and though the coming of the Commonwealth dealt him a blow which was to prove mortal, his reign—while it lasted—was splendid indeed.

The colleges of the two universities were other places in which the Lord of Misrule enjoyed considerable homage. The Christmas Lord of Magdalen College was styled *Rex Fabarum* or *Rex Regni Fabarum*. St. John's College, Oxford, yearly elected a Christmas Prince.

Another Christmas "character," who fell into disgrace as "Popish" after the reign of Mary Tudor, as the Lord of Misrule was to fall into disgrace for a similar "reason" during the Commonwealth, was the Boy Bishop, chosen from among the choristers and invested, by custom, with some very real authority during his brief spell of office.

Later ages have attempted to explain the Boy Bishop by making him a symbol of the Holy Innocents, but this explanation would be more convincing had the Boy Bishop's prelacy begun and not ended—as it did—on Holy Innocents' Day, 28 December.

The children of other times had reason to remember Holy Innocents' Day, for it was the custom to whip children on that feast, in remembrance of the massacre of the Innocents by King Herod, "that the memory of this Murther might stick the closer, and, in a moderate proportion, to act over again the cruelty in kind."

In 1683 the Rev. John Gregorie published a little pamphlet, entitled *Episcopus Puerorum in die Innocentium* (The Boy Bishop on Innocents' Day), which tells us the facts of this curious character.

"The *Episcopus Choristarum* was a Chorister Bishop chosen by his Fellow Children upon St. Nicholas Day. . . . From this Day till *Innocents' Day* at night (it lasted longer at the first) the *Episcopus Puerorum* was to bear the name and hold up the state of a *Bishop*, answerably habited with a *Crosier*, or *Pastoral Staff*, in his hand, and a *Mitre* upon his head; and such an one, too, some had, as was *multis Episcoporum mitris sumptuosior* (saith one), very much richer than those of the Bishops indeed.

"The rest of his Fellows from the same time being were to take upon them the style and counterfeit of Prebends, yielding to their Bishop no less than Canonical obedience.

"And look what service the very Bishop himself with his Dean and Prebends (had they been to officiate) was to have performed. The very same was done by the Chorister Bishop and his Canons upon the Eve and Holiday."

The full office of the day, according to the Sarum Rite, was said by the Boy Bishop, and it was provided, "that no man whatsoever, under pain of *Anathema*, should interrupt, or press upon these Children at the Procession spoken of before, or in any part of their Service in any ways, but to suffer them quietly to perform and execute what it concerned them to do.

"And the part was acted yet more earnestly, for *Molanus* saith that this Bishop, in some places, did receive Rents, Capons, etc., during his year; and it seemeth by the statute of *Sarum* that he held a kind of *Visitation*, and had a full correspondency of all other State and Prerogative. . . . In case the Chorister Bishop died within the Month, his Exequies were solemnized with an answerable glorious pomp and sadness. He was buried (as all other Bishops) in all his Ornaments, as by the Monument in stone spoken of before, it plainly appeareth."

Hone says that "the ceremony of the Boy Bishop is supposed to have existed, not only in collegiate churches, but in almost every parish in England. He and his companions walked the streets in public procession. A statute of the collegiate church of St. Mary Overy, in 1337, restrained one of them to the limits of his own parish. On 7 December, 1229, the day after St. Nicholas' Day, a Boy Bishop in the chapel at Heton, near Newcastle-on-Tyne, said vespers before Edward I on his way to Scotland, who made a considerable present to him, and the other boys who sang with him."

A Boy Bishop who sang before King Edward III on Innocents' Day received nineteen shillings and sixpence—a very great sum for the times.

The founder of St. Paul's School—which numbers, among its *alumni*, G. K. Chesterton and Field-Marshal Montgomery—expressly laid down in the statutes that the scholars should attend each year a service, to be held on Childermas Day (Innocents' Day), at which the Boy Bishop should preach. Colet enjoins that they "come to Paulis Churche, and hear the Chylde Bishop's Sermon; and, after, be at hygh masse, and each of them offer a penny to the Chylde Bishop; and with them, the maisters and surveyors of the Scole."

Henry VIII abolished the Boy Bishop in 1542—owing to his "Romish" flavour!—but he was restored by Henry's daughter, Mary, before whom, in one year, a Boy Bishop sang a flattering song, in which the plain, bigoted little Queen was compared (and certainly not to Mary's disadvantage) with Judith, Esther, the Queen of Sheba, and the Virgin Mary!

It would appear that the ceremony of the Boy Bishop was one of those popular customs only partly to be affected by governmental decree; for, though his office was abolished by a proclamation of 1542, we still find, in the accounts of St. Mary at Hill, London, for 1549 and 1550, charges for the Boy Bishop. The permission, then, given by Mary for the revival of the Boy Bishop would seem to have been in the nature of a legal concession to a right already exercised by the common opinion.

The curious fact is that, without any action taken against him by Elizabeth, he seems to have died away fairly rapidly after the death of Bloody Mary.

The day on which his reign came to an end—Childermas, or Innocents' Day—was always reckoned to be the most unlucky of the year, and just as sailors used to refuse to begin work on a Friday, so the ordinary person used to refuse, if possible, to begin any new undertaking on Childermas Day. Especially was it held disastrous to marry on Childermas, and King Louis XV of France held the day in such fear that he could not be persuaded to start any new business, or even to discuss his affairs, on Innocents' Day.

King Edward IV of England actually postponed his coronation from a Sunday to a Monday, as the former, that year, was Childermas.

Soured as Mary was to grow in after-life, it appears that no efforts were spared, in her girlhood, to give her the love of conviviality which so marked the character of her much-married father.

Cardinal Wolsey had established a "household" for the "Lady Mary, then being Princess of the Realm," and there is a letter, written to the Cardinal by "the household," in 1525, asking directions and leave of His Eminence to celebrate the Christmas ensuing, in a manner then thought fitting for a Princess of the Realm. The letter gives a clear picture of a fashionable Christmas of the early sixteenth century.

"Please it youre Grace for the great repaire of straungers supposed unto the Pryncesse honorable householde this solempne fest of Christmas, we humbly beseche the same to let us knowe youre gracious pleasure concernyng as well a ship of silver for the almes disshe requysite for her high estate, and spice plats, as also for trumpetts and a rebek to be sent, and whither we shall appoynte any Lord of Misrule for the said honorable householde, provide for enterluds, disgysyngs, or pleyes in the said fest, or for banket on twelf nyght. And in likewise whither the Pryncesse shall sende any newe yeres gifts to the Kinge, the Quene, your Grace, and the Frensshe Quene, and of the value and devise (nature) of the same. Besechyng yowre Grace also to pardon oure busy and importunate suts to the same in suche behalf made. Thus oure right syngler good lorde we pray the holy Trynyte have you in his holy preservacion. At Teoxbury (Tewkesbury), the xxvij day of November.

"Youre humble orators,

John Exon
Jeilez[1] Grevile
Peter Burnell
John Salter
G. Bromley
Thomas Audeley."

"To the most reverent Father
in God the Lord Cardinall
his good Grace.

[1] Jeilez=Giles!

Whether orderly feelings or something warmer prompted the show of affection on Princess Mary's part for her royal step-mother, Jane Seymour, we shall never in all probability know; most probably the former; but it is the fact that Mary spent much time with Queen Jane at Richmond, though the death there of the Queen, on 14 October, 1537, did not prevent the Princess's spending the following Christmas in that place.

The younger Mary, out of whom developed "the cold Queen of England," appears to have been a person not at all devoid of some very human characteristics. She loved gambling, especially at cards, and she kept a female "fool" named—in cynical reference to her step-mother?—Jane.

There is an item in her household book: "For shaving Jane fooles hedde, iiiid"—though why the shaving was carried out, whether for punishment, or for sanitary reasons, we do not know.

It was at Christmas, four years earlier than that entry that Henry VIII and his minister, Thomas Cromwell, decided to make the break with Rome, and at the Christmas-tide of two years later, the Queen next in succession to Jane Seymour, who died in childbed, landed in England, at Deal.

Henry, to do him justice, married Anne of Cleves, the lady whom he ungallantly called, "a great Flemish mare." The wedding took place on the Feast of the Epiphany, the last day of Christmastide, 1540; but the marriage was one hardly more than in name. Queen Anne retired to her charming mansion at Hever, in Kent, and the person whom Henry held responsible for deceiving him in the matter of the lady's charms was dealt with in the typically severe and final Tudor manner.

But Henry's reign was not simply one long record of capricious beheadings, even though it has served various vested prejudices to maintain that the rule of Bluff King Hal was a period of unrelenting tyranny, in which the scaffold echoed with the death-cries of "Merrie England."

No colder-hearted tyrant than Thomas Cromwell ever had the destinies of the English people in his hands; yet his tyranny was not extended to make miserable the lives of the ordinary people. In the scramble for power at the very top of the social ladder, quarter was neither given nor asked. There were no martyrs, in the Court of Henry VIII, to honourable causes; those who lost their heads were but paying the penalty of failure in a game where only greed was the stimulus of effort, and power over others the reward to be achieved.

The Christmas festivities continued without more than an occasional interference from above; but we have seen how the Order against the institution of the Boy Bishop failed to affect the custom. St. John's College, Oxford, had its Christmas Prince, and Trinity College, Cambridge, its Emperor—*Praefectus Ludorum, qui Imperator dicitur*—and Lincoln's Inn had its King of Cockneys, who held his court on Childermas Day, when he sat "and had good service; and that he and all his officers should use honest manner and good Order, without any wast or destruction making, in wine, brawn, chely, or other vitaills."

The functions of the "Imperator" of Trinity College were laid down in the statutes, when the college was founded in 1546, and they may serve as the general pattern for the powers and behaviour of all sixteenth-century Lords of Misrule, however their title varied.

Under the Imperator's "direction and authority," Latin Comedies and Tragedies are to be exhibited in the hall at Christmas. With regard to the peculiar business and office of Imperator it is ordered that one of the Masters of Art shall be placed over the juniors, every Christmas, for the regulation of their games and diversions at that season of festivity. At the same time, he is to govern the whole society in the hall and chapel, as a republic committed to his special charge by a set of laws which he is to frame in Latin and Greek verse.

His sovereignty is to last during the twelve days of Christmas, and he is to exercise the same power on Candlemas (2 February, the Feast of the Purification of the Virgin).

His fee amounted to forty shillings; but this sum was not a standard payment, the rewards of the Lord of Misrule varying with the wealth and generosity of the company over which he was elected to rule. We have seen that Henry VIII authorized a payment of £15 6s. 8d. to *his* Lord of Misrule, against Trinity's two pounds to *theirs*; and the various Inns of Court, as the century progressed, were to prove exceedingly liberal in their payments to the Christmas Kings.

At the other end of the scale there must have been payments even less than the Earl of Northumberland—the Percy family were a notoriously tight-fisted lot—paid to his "Almonar," for, as Stow points out, there was a similar functionary to be found in those times "in the house of every nobleman of honour or good worship."

To the same social impulse which called for an occasional brief reversal of the social order, and which was symbolized in the figure of the Lord of Misrule, belonged the "fool," a hired critic, attached to most households of any standing, whom custom permitted what to us seems an extraordinary licence. We have seen that the Princess Mary had her female "fool," Jane, and Mary's father had his "fool," too: Will Somers, whom the King held in high esteem, even to the extent of having Somers introduced into the superb royal family group that Holbein painted for Henry.

The "fool" as an institution survived well into the nineteenth century, though only among the country aristocracy, and not at Court. He was, of course, not by any means a fool, despite his name, and though it was held an advantage if he were a dwarf or a cripple, he had to be possessed of a shrewd understanding and a ready wit. The primitive element in the mentality of even the highest of those times found great pleasure in "freaks," and it was accounted genius on the part of the Duke of Buckingham that, at the dinner that he gave in honour of Charles I and his newly wed bride, the Duke should have arranged that his dwarf, Jeffrey Hudson, should come to table under the crust of a pie, out of which the little fellow stepped, brandishing his tiny sword.

The licence that old-established custom permitted to the "fool" —and that his employers paid him to indulge—was certainly not extended to some other wits. The autocrats of the sixteenth century were as touchy, as ready to see "disloyal" allusions in jokes, as their successors of the twentieth century, all of whom have "banned" music-hall jesters or literary comics for too-broad comments on the current regime.

The rules for conducting the grand Christmas pageants at the various Inns of Court, as described by Sir William Dugdale, forbid "Jack Straw" to be one of the characters represented in the Christmas revels; a fine of five pounds to be levied "on every fellow hapning to offend against this rule."

"Jack Straw"—his name survives in the name of a public-house at Hampstead, a few miles out of London—was the traditional personification of the Ordinary Man—without birth, money, patronage, influence or power, but certainly not without a clear perception of the greed and folly which masqueraded as "quality." He was a character peculiarly obnoxious to the King and his ministers, and the stiff fine imposed by the Benchers on those playing "Jack Straw" shows as much the dislike that the King bore the character as the eagerness of the Benchers to please their Sovereign.

Gray's Inn put on a play at Christmas, 1527—the first play on record to have been performed at an Inn of Court—which deeply ruffled the false dignity of the puffed-up Wolsey.

The plot of this play showed how Lord Governance, falling under the evil spell of Dissipation and Negligence, was inspired to divorce his wife, Lady Public Weal. Wolsey, promptly recognizing himself in the principal character, and not having the tact to conceal the recognition, promptly disbarred its lawyer-author, Sergeant Roe, and sent him to prison, together with the actor who had played the offending part. The two men were released only when they had concocted an "explanation" of the plot sufficiently improbable to be able to restore the greedy cardinal's injured pride.

But the revellers usually contrived to keep their pageants free from offensive qualities—at least in the political sense—and the Lord of Misrule attained a position of great dignity, so that the banned "Jack Straw" was soon forgotten.

There was a London merchant, Henry Machyn by name, who kept a diary from July, 1550, to August, 1563. Machyn, born in London in 1498 or thereabouts, was a liveryman of the Company of Merchant Taylors, but he seems to have made his money as a furnisher of funerals. He was a devout Catholic, but his tact (and very likely his commercial standing) kept him from falling foul of the authorities, despite his rigid adherance to the "old faith." His diary gives us the character of a man, well described as the sixteenth-century Pepys, who enjoyed life and who had a perennial interest in anything and everything which came before his interested view. Machyn, like most of the Londoners of his day, was a staunch supporter of the street entertainments. Here is his picture of a procession of the Lord of Misrule, at Christmas-tide, 1551-2:

"The iiij day of Januarii was made a grett skaffold in chepe,[1] hard by the crosse, agaynst the kynges lord of myssrule cummyng

[1] i.e., The London street now called "Cheapside." "Chepe" is the old English word for "trade" or "commerce." "Chapman" means, thus, a "trader."

from Grenwyche and (he) landed at Toure warff, and with hym yonge knyghts and gentyllmen a gret nombur on hosse bake sum in gownes and cotes and chaynes abowt ther nekes, and on the Toure hyll ther they went in order, furst a standard of yelow and grene sylke with Saint George, and then gounes and skuybes (squibs) and trompets and bagespypes, and drousselars and flutes, and then a gret company all in yelow and gren, and docturs declaryng my lord grett, and then the mores danse, dansyng with a tabret. . . ."

This Lord of Misrule was a person of consequence, indeed, and by no means the hired buffoon and Aunt Sally that some historians have found him to appear. Even Sir Thomas More, when attached to the suite of Cardinal Morton—of Morton's Fork notoriety—thought it not beneath his dignity to "stepp in among the players" at the Christmas revels; and the saintly Latimer, even lying under the charge of heresy which was soon to lead him to a martyr's death, wrote: "I intend to make merry with my parishioners this Christmas, for all the sorrow, lest perchance I may never return to them again."

For, if the Puritans were later to develop a rabid hatred of Christmas, the leaders of the Reformation bore no such prejudice against the Saviour's Nativity. Luther, indeed, may be said to have been the founder of the modern Christmas, in that he took a pleasing ordinariness into the purely ecclesiastical feast of former times. The people had for long had their own simple interpretations of the Bible stories, and their acted representations, known in France and England as "mysteries," were to have, as I shall show in a later chapter, an important effect upon the dramatic art of the West.

It was Luther's happy thought to "democratize" the feast of Christmas, by uniting the purely churchly elements in it with that grosser, earthier element which was the peculiar prerogative of the people. Luther's theology was of a simple kind, and he looked at things—right and wrong as he could be—from the point of view of the common man. He could interpret theological concepts in terms of the man-in-the-street, and he could bring the man-in-the-street's refreshing simplicity into the too often musty repositories of ecclesiastical thought.

For him Christmas was a time of joy—*the* time of joy. Luther believed in Hell—a hell as picturesquely savage as any ever imagined by an Hieronymus Bosch; and the consideration of final judgment used often to drive him into a state of frenzied fear.

But he did believe in Heaven, too; and he held that God's mercy was every whit as much to be relied upon as God's rebuke. The modern Christmas owes much to Germany, as Germany has much owed her Christmas to Luther. Perhaps the fact that Germany was almost the last of the European peoples to be Christianized accounts for the fact that the German Christmas seems simpler, fresher, than the feast in lands converted earlier to the Christian faith. If, in the German Christmas, we are nearer to paganism, we are none the less nearer (we feel) to the primitive simplicity which is at the root of all things; that primitive simplicity from which all later complications have developed.

It was Luther's peculiar virtue to interpret the feast of Christmas in terms that any man might comprehend. The angels had brought tidings of great joy: Luther it was who pointed out this fact to all Christendom. It was joy, he emphasized, that the Nativity brought to mankind—not death and judgment.

He held that the darker forces of Nature, even the seeming cruelty inherent in the Godhead, were powerless at Christmas; and others after Luther preached the truth that he had maintained.

Shakespeare, in *Hamlet,* tells us that:

> Some say that ever 'gainst the season comes,
> Wherein our Saviour's birth is celebrated,
> The bird of dawning singeth all night long:
> And then, they say, no spirit dares stir abroad;
> The nights are wholesome; then no planets strike;
> No fairy takes, nor witch hath power to charm,
> So hallowed and so gracious is the time.

But if Luther and Latimer and Shakespeare had a liking for Christmas and Christmas things, the feast was not without its enemies: enemies—or their descendants, rather—who were to effect an almost total, even if only temporary, triumph over the ancient feast.

Philip Stubbes, the Puritan, had very little sympathy for Christmas, or for those who made the feast an excuse for celebration of one sort or another.

Especially did Philip dislike the Lords of Misrule, or, as he called them, Christmas Lords. He says:

"The name, indeed, is odious both to God and good men, and such as the very heathen people would have blushed at once to have named amongst them. And, if the name importeth some evil, then, what may the thing itselfe be, judge you? But, because you desire to know the manner of them, I will showe you as I have seen them practised myself."

The fact that, elsewhere, Stubbes points the resemblance of the Christmas Lords and their pranks to the *Bacchanalia* and *Saturnalia* of those same heathens who "would have blushed" to hear the name of the Christmas Lord, hardly argues for Stubbes's consistency. But small inconsistencies do not worry him any more than the other Puritans of his time: his abiding prejudice against all forms of joy make him proof against self-examination.

"First," he continues, "all the wilde-heds of the parish, conventing together, chuse them a graund-captain (of all mischeefe) whom they in-noble with the title of my Lord of Misrule, and him they crowne with great solemnitie, and adopt for their king. This king anointed chuseth forth twentie, fortie, three score, or a hundred lustie guttes, like to him self, to waight uppon his lordlie Majestie, and to guarde his noble person. Then everie one of these his men, he investeth with his liveries of green, yellow, or some other light wanton colour; and as though they were not gaudie enough, I should say, they bedecke them selves with scarfs, ribons and laces, hanged all over with gold rings, precious stones and other jewels; this doon, they tye about either leg xx or xl bels, with rich handkerchiefs in their hands, and sometimes laid a crosse over their shoulders and necks, borrowed for the most part of their pretie Mopsies or looving Besses, for bussing (kissing) them in the dark."

Sad goings on! But worse is to follow.

"They have, also, certain papers, wherein is painted some babblerie or other, of imagery woork, and these they call my Lord of Misrule's badges; these they give to every one that will give money for them, to maintain them in their heathenrie, devilrie, whordom, drunkenness, pride and what not. And who will not be buxom with them, and give them money for these their devlish cognizances, they are mocked at and flouted not a little."

They *were,* probably, a bit of a nuisance in the streets, but not more so than some flag-day sellers, "ex-Servicemen's bands," and other importuners that we have all encountered.

"And, so assotted are some, that they not only give them monie, to maintain their abhomination withall, but also wear their badges and cognizances in their hats and caps openly. But," says Stubbes, "let them take heede: for these are the badges, seales, brands and cognizances of the devil, whereby he knoweth his servants and clyents from the children of God; and so long as they wear them, *Sub vexillo diaboli militant contra Dominum et legem suam,* they fight under the banner and standard of the Devil against Christ Jesus and all his lawes.

"Another sorte of fantasticall fooles bring to these helhounds (the Lord of Misrule and his complices) some bread, some good ale, some new cheese, some olde, some custards and fine Cakes, some one thing, some another; but if they knew that as often as they bring anything to the maintenance of these execrable pastimes, they offer sacrifice to the devil and Sathanas, they would repent and withdraw their hands, which God grant they may!"

Without taking quite so exaggerated a view of the revellers as Stubbes did, some of Stubbes' contemporaries could still hold the Lord of Misrule and his "complices" in some dislike.

The Bishops of Norwich, Lichfield, London and Oxford, and the Archbishop of York, all issued, at sundry times, injunctions against the Lord of Misrule's entering churches and "disporting" there.

Parkhurst, Bishop of Norwich, issued the following injunction: "Item, that no person or persons calling themselves lords of misrule in the Christmas tyme, or other vnreuerent persons at any other tyme, presume to come into the church vnreuerently playing their lewd partes, with scoffing, iesting, or rebaldry talke, and, if any such haue alredy offended herein, to present their names to the ordinary."[1]

The brief reign of the youthful king, Edward VI, was mostly passed in bitter political controversy, disguising itself as religious disputation. It saw another would-be dictator, another "Guardian of the People's Liberties," of an only-too-familiar type, led to the end which ought to await all dictators.

[1] The ecclesiastical courts of the day had considerable powers, not excluding those of fine, imprisonment and even death. In 1785 York ecclesiastical court sentenced a woman to six weeks' imprisonment for loose conduct. These powers were not taken away from the ecclesiastical courts until 1827.

But the execution of his uncle, Somerset—it is not without significance that the headquarters of the British Inland Revenue department stands on the site of his splendid palace—did nothing to cheer the royal boy, nor halt the progress of that wasting disease, unfortunately inherited from his father, which was to carry off the precociously learned, precociously aged—if, indeed, he had ever been young—king, before he was seventeen.

Pawn of forces that he did not understand, much less have the desire or the strength to combat, the weakly Edward yet reigned over a period whose importance seems astonishingly disproportionate to its length. Even the will that they forced the dying boy to sign led to minor civil war and the death by execution of guilty and innocent, the latter including the gifted "Nine Days Queen"—Lady Jane Grey.

Yet Edward, for all the grim atmosphere of politico-religious intrigue in which he passed the years of kingship, was not denied all the diversions both of his years and of his rank.

Though the sinister "Council" which used him as a puppet saw to it that every document that he signed had been drawn up to serve one or the other of their own dark ends, the "Council," in half-contemptuous gratitude for the young king's involuntary assistance, appointed a certain George Ferrers to be the King's Lord of Misrule. Ferrers's commission came to him by the title of "Master of the King's Pastimes," as Holinshed tells us.

"Which gentleman so well supplied his office, both in show of sundry sights and devices of rare inventions, and in act of diverse interludes, and matters of pastime plaied by persons, as not onlie satisfied the common sort, but also were verie well liked and allowed by the Councell, and other of skill in the like pastimes; but the best of all by the young King himselfe, as appeered by his princelie liberalitie in rewarding that service."

"Christmas," adds Holinshed, "being thus passed with much mirth and pastime, it was thought now good to proceed to execution of the judgment against the Duke of Somerset."

The Duke's head was, accordingly, taken off on 22 January, 1552; and some idea of the mirth and pastime which had been enjoyed during the Christmas intervening between the Duke's judgment and execution may be gathered from the bills that Ferrers, "Master of the King's Pastimes," presented after the holidays.

Ferrers himself received £100 in fees, out of a total cost for the royal festivities of more than £700—and the Lord Mayor of London[1] entertained Ferrers after Christmas.

The Court Fool was John Smyth, and with his assistance Ferrers provided a first-class entertainment, Smyth being new-dressed for the occasion, with a long fool's coat of cloth-of-gold, trimmed with white, red and green velvet.

The prices paid are not without interest for us in these costly days. The velvet for Smyth's dress cost £2 a yard; the plain cloth-of-gold costing only 33s. 4d. a yard. His hood and buskins, which took two and a half yards of figured gold, cost £5. The total for Smyth's outfit was £26 14s. 8d.

Ferrers spent almost exactly double that sum on his own festal attire: £52 8s. 8d. The Lord of Merry Disports was not the one —"wise gentleman and learned" though he was—to neglect himself in looking after the comforts of all.

He wore, in virtue of his office as Lord of Misrule, "a robe of rich stuff made of silk and golden thread containing 9 yards at 16s. a yard, guarded with embroidered cloth of gold, wrought in knots, 14 yards at 11s. 4d. a yard; having fur of red feathers[2] with a cape of camlet thrum. A coat of flat silver, fine with works, 5 yards at 50s., with an embroidered garb of leaves of gold and coloured silk, containing 15 yards at 20s. a yard. He wore a cap of maintenance, hose buskins, panticles of Bruges satin, a girdle of yellow sarsenet with various decorations."

Nothing so clouds the judgment as religious controversy, and persons who identify themselves with—or, perhaps only by chance, are identified with—the leadership of religious groups must never expect to receive unbiased criticism at the hands of those who differ from them in points of theology.

Mary Tudor, by making an earnest effort to restore the Church of Rome to the position that it held in the days before the Reformation in England, was obviously inviting the harshest judgment from

[1] The first mayor was Henry Fitz-Alwyn, who was appointed in 1188 and held office for twenty-four years.

[2] This was almost certainly of Aztec work. Similar feather-work was sent by Cortes to Spain, but I cannot trace any other mention of it in English historical records.

those who resented her attempts to re-establish the Roman hierarchy in England.

But though it seems that she *was* an earnest bigot—though we must bear in mind that bigotry was very much the fashion of her times—she was certainly not the utterly humourless, inhumanly frigid creature that passionate enmity had made her out to be.

Courage is an essentially human quality, and persons of a high courage are not usually found deficient in all other human qualities. And the Queen's handling of the grave disturbances which followed the visit, at Christmas, 1554-5, of an embassy from the Emperor Charles V showed not only that she possessed the traditional courage of her family, but that, almost alone among the Catholic party, she possessed courage.

This embassy, consisting of the Counts Egmont and Lalain, the Lords of Courrières and Nigry and a splendid train, had come to England in order to arrange the marriage between Mary and her cousin, Philip of Spain. The prospect of this marriage infuriated certain sections of the English "die-hards," and the men of Kent, thinking that the Count of Egmont was Philip—the intended husband of their Queen—"rose in a fury, and would have killed him if they could have got at him."

The whole country was in a ferment, and the insurrection led by Sir Thomas Wyatt was of so formidable a character that only the Queen did not see in it the certain overthrow of her realm. The lawyers pleaded in Westminster Hall with coat-armour under their gowns, and Dr. Weston, preaching in Whitehall Chapel on Candlemas Day, wore mail under his vestments.

All the same, there was a tumbler who came on after the Queen had reviewed the pensioners in Greenwich Park who made her Majesty laugh heartily, and though Mary Tudor thought it prudent to imprison her sister, Elizabeth, at Hatfield House, she visited the prisoner, and "next morning, after mass, a grand exhibition of bear-baiting was made for their amusement, with which, it is said, 'their highnesses were right well content.' "

It was Mary who rescued the Boy Bishop from the ban under which an ordinance of Henry VIII had put him.

She ordered the Bishop of London on 13 November, 1554, to instruct the clergy of his diocese to appoint a Boy Bishop to each parish; and in the following year, on St. Nicholas' Day and

Childermas Day, "the child Bishop of Paules Church, with his company" came into the Queen's privy-chamber to sing before her.

Mary, with her husband, Philip, kept the Christmasses at Richmond-on-Thames, and masques, after a foreign pattern, were provided for the entertainment of the sovereigns and their guests. The "scriptwriter" employed for these masques was a London schoolmaster, Nicholas Udall, a pedant of grossly dissolute life, whose least offensive fault was that he liked to thrash his scholars with unbridled severity.

Yet Udall holds a most important place in the history of the English stage. He was the author of the first comedy to be written in the English language, and the masques that he prepared for Mary and Philip set a new standard in theatrical entertainment. They were sophisticated in an astonishing degree, and were as far advanced beyond the childish "pleyes" of Henry VIII's time as Udall's own works were far behind the masques of Ben Jonson and Milton and the comedies of Shakespeare.

There are some odd references in the list of these masques: one reference in particular makes us wish to know more of the masque concerned. It is "a masque of covetous men with long noses."

Other masques mentioned are "of six Venuses, or amorous ladies, with six Cupids, and as many torch-bearers," "of eight Mariners, of cloth of gold or silver, and six pairs of chains for the galley-slaves," "of six Hercules, or men of war, coming from the sea with six Mariners to their torch-bearers," and so forth. The influence of the classic culture, which was coming to England from Constantinople, via Italy, France and Spain, is most apparent in the themes of the masques.

The Christmas of 1557—the last of Mary's life—was spent at Hampton Court, and to the festivities had been invited the heiress-apparent, Elizabeth, who sat at table with King Philip[1] and Queen Mary, but retired before the "revels, maskings and disguisings took place." We are not told whether this was by her own choice or by her sister's command.

On 29 December, the King, Queen and Princess watched a grand tournament—a "justing"—in which two hundred knights, half-dressed in the Spanish style, half "accoutred in the Almayne fashion" took part.

[1] He was, of course, not King of England.

This was the last Christmas that Mary was to see. She died on 17 November, 1558, and the following Christmas was the first of Elizabeth's reign, which was marked by the new Queen's magnificent state-entry in London. The bishops met her at Highgate, where they offered her their allegiance, and gave her formal invitation to assume the crown.

Elizabeth had made no secret of the fact that her sympathies lay, not with the Old Religion, but with the New, and she made her intentions abundantly clear at the very beginning of her reign when, at Highgate, she received graciously all the bishops but Bonner, who had been her sister's principal agent in the attempted restoration of Catholicism.

But it was to Elizabeth rather as the saviour of the English way of living than as the saviour of a "reformed" faith that the people looked. It was not so much Protestantism that they preferred to Catholicism, as Elizabeth—a Welsh princess—to Philip—a Spanish king.

Elizabeth's first Christmas was principally spent in preparations for the coronation, which was fixed to take place on 15 January following; and in the pageantry displayed on that occasion—pageantry which included a water-procession from Westminster to the Tower of London, and a state-procession by road on the return journey—the loyal citizens of the metropolis had an earnest of the magnificence which was to mark every aspect of Elizabethan life.

The print, published in 1633, is of interest as showing a seventeenth-century backgammon board, precisely identical with those in use today.

Commerce flourished in her reign, and the vast increase in trade was reflected in the growing wealth (and proportionate importance) of the City livery-companies, which now began to rival the Inns of Court as patrons of extravagantly costly pageants.

The Age of Elizabeth—the Golden Age of English Literature—has been so often described that there is no need here for me to do more than to mention that, during the half-century that it covered, English writers and dramatists progressed from fumbling, childish beginnings to the evolution of a consciously perfect technique: what began with the elementary clowning of a Udall ended with the mature wisdom of a Shakespeare; what began with the halting and insecure descriptions of a Henry Machyn culminated in the splendid precision of the Authorized Version.

Great patronage makes great art; but it is a fact that the great patrons are rarely great artists. Elizabeth, by her encouragement, not only of artists, but of all whose efforts seemed to make for the greater glory of the Queen and her realm, inspired a nation to give of its best. And what a best that was! Even today some of the most successful films use Elizabethan scripts; and the best seller of all is an Elizabethan work: the Authorized Version of the Bible—for it is Elizabethan, even though King James's name appears in the dedication.

Elizabeth herself was no demure miss out of *Patience*. She knew herself better than did any of her contemporaries, and out of this knowledge she well described herself when she said: "Though I have the body of a weak woman, yet have I the heart of a man."

She had many of the tastes of a man, too. And of an Elizabethan man, with a taste for coarse pleasures well developed among the mass of likings which made up her essentially masculine character.

Nothing perhaps better illustrates the rougher tendencies of a woman for whom Spenser wrote his *Faerie Queene* than this extract from a letter written by Christopher Playter to Mr. Kytson of Hengrave Hall in 1572:

"At Chris-time here were certayne ma$^{rs}$ (masters) of defence, that did challenge all comers at all weapons, as long sworde, staff, sword and buckler, rapier with the dagger: and here was many broken heads, and one of the ma$^{rs}$ of defence dyed upon the hurt which he received on his head. The challenge was before the quenes Ma$^{tie}$ who seemes to have pleasure therein; for when some of them would have sollen a broken pate, her Majesty bade him not to be ashamed to put off his cap, and the blood was spied to run about his face. There was also at the corte new plays w$^{h}$ lasted almost all night. The name of the play was huff, suff and ruff, with other masks both of ladies and gents."

The first English comedy was, we have seen, written for a Christmas festival of Mary and Philip. The first English tragedy, too, was first written to be performed at Christmas: *Gorboduc*. Its authors were two young members of the Inner Temple: Thomas Norton, twenty-nine, and Thomas Sackville, twenty-five; and *Gorboduc* was first played at the Inner Temple's "Grand Christmas" of 1561-2.

Robert Dudley, afterwards Earl of Leicester, was the Constable-Marshal that year. On Boxing Day—then known as St. Stephen's Day—Dudley presented himself in Inner Temple Hall, "in gilt armour, with a nest of feathers of all colours on his helm, and a gilt pole-axe in his hand; with him sixteen trumpeters, four drums and fifes, and four men armed from the middle upwards."

The Constable-Marshal and his escort marched three times "about the hearth,"[1] and then Dudley knelt before the Lord Chancellor, asked for admission into the Chancellor's service, delivered up his naked sword, and "was solemnly seated."

For the occasion Dudley assumed the name of Palaphilos, Knight of the Honourable Order of Pegasus,[2] to preside over a twelve days' entertainment which would make the drab legal circles of these times rub their eyes in astonishment, were the Benches to decide upon its revival.

Nichols, in his *Progresses of Queen Elizabeth*, gives in meticulous detail the programme of the Christmas festivities, which, elaborately sumptuous as they were, were matched, in a greater or lesser degree, in all "houses of worship" throughout the kingdom.

The Lord of Misrule was an important figure at these legal junketings, for all that an Act of Common Council, passed in the reign of Mary Tudor, forbade—on the grounds of national economy—the Lord Mayor or Sheriffs to keep any Lord of Misrule in their houses. This would seem, by implication at least, to have forbidden

[1] In the halls of ancient English houses (as still at Penshurst Place, in Kent) the hearth was in the centre of the room, the smoke escaping through louvres in the roof.

[2] Pegasus, the winged horse of Bellerophon, is the badge of the Inner Temple.

the same to the Benchers of the various Inns of Court and similar bodies: but the ordinance (like that applying to the Boy Bishop) was one obviously more honoured in the breach than in the observance.

Sheriffs, indeed, and presumably many other "worshipful persons," certainly kept their Lords of Misrule until the outbreak of the civil war, and if we regard the "fool" as being of a cousin-relationship to the Lord of Misrule, then we may say that this ambiguous character did not finally depart from us until our own day.

Certainly, the Lord of Misrule reigned over the Inns of Court feasts in all his old splendour and with all his old power.

It must be borne in mind by the reader that, though the Lord of Misrule was a temporary character, elected as part of a Christmas festival, his powers, sanctioned by custom and carefully codified, were *real*. He had a numerous court, with *functionaries* whose duties corresponded with those normally to be expected in the courts of more permanent sovereigns, and over his temporary kingdom the Lord and his dignitaries exercised true authority. And again, he was greeted with great and sincere respect. Until we can realize that the Lord of Misrule was not a joke, we cannot begin to understand the important part that he played in the lives of our ancestors of the Renascence.

All the sonorous ritual of medieval pageantry was called upon to assist these functions to be as impressive as possible: a faint shadow of their splendour is to be found in such occasions as the opening of Parliament or the opening of an Assize; but to read the "Order of Service" of the Inner Temple Christmas of, say, 1561, is to realize how far we have progressed on the road to universal and total drabness.

The realization becomes even more poignant when, at the end of a detailed account of the grand manner in which the meal is to be announced, served and eaten, there is this brief remark:

"A repast at dinner is 8d."

On Christmas Day itself the revels, as may be expected, achieved the summit of magnificence. A boar's head was served, "upon a silver platter, with minstralsye"; and one understands that "a repast at dinner is 12d., which strangers of worth are admitted to take in the Hall; and such are to be placed at the discretion of the Marshal," was a bargain indeed.

There was much elaborate ceremony on Boxing Day; and it was on this day that the Constable-Marshal, in full coat-armour, mounted, made his state-entrance into the Hall, and made submission to the Lord Chancellor.

There also were the Master of the Game, in green velvet, and the Ranger of the Forest, in green satin, with their hunting horns, upon which, together, they blew "three blasts of venery" as they paced three times around the hearth.

"This ceremony also performed, a Huntsman cometh into the Hall, with a fox and a purse-net; with a cat, both bound at the end of a staff; and with them nine or ten couple of hounds, with the blowing of hunting-hornes. And the fox and the cat are by the hounds set upon, and killed beneath the fire. This sport finished the Marshal placeth them in their several appointed places."

It was not until nearly three centuries later that the Royal Society for the Prevention of Cruelty to Animals came into being: the treatment accorded to "our dumb friends" in the sixteenth century being strictly divided into the treatment to be accorded to those which were pets and to those which were not.

"At Supper, the Hall is to be served in all solemnity, as upon Christmas Day, both the first and the second course to the highest table. Supper ended, the Constable-Marshal presenteth himself with drums afore him, mounted upon a scaffold, borne by four men; and goeth three times round about the harthe, crying out aloud, 'A Lord, a lord,' etc. Then he descendeth and goeth to dance, etc. And after he calleth his Court every one by name, one by one, in this manner:

"Sir *Francis Flatterer* of *Fowlehurst,* in the county of *Buckingham.*

"Sir *Randle Rackabite,* of *Rascall-Hall,* in the county of *Rakehell.*

"Sir *Morgan Mumchance,* of *Much Monkery,* in the county of *Mad Mopery.*

"Sir *Bartholomew Baldbreech,* of *Buttocks-bury,* in the county of *Brekeneck.*

"This done the Lord of Misrule addresseth himself to the banquet; which ended with some minstralsye, mirth and dancing every man departeth to rest.

"At every mess a pot of wine allowed.

"Every repast is 6d."

It was not until the very end of the century that a new pleasure was to be found added to all the old ones; but it was a pleasure which was to prove a social force rivalling, if not perhaps over-topping, the more ancient forces of love and wine as a swayer of human destinies: tobacco.

With the death of Mary, and the coming of Elizabeth to the throne of England, the seamen-adventurers of the type of Raleigh, Frobisher and Hawkins felt themselves free to harry the Spanish commerce; capturing the plate-ships of His Most Catholic Majesty and sacking the rich towns which already had sprung up along the coastline of the Spanish Main.

England had been late in the race for colonial possessions, and jealousy, as much as "patriotism," we may accept, was the stimulus of the Elizabethan sea-rovers' attacks upon the commerce of a nation which had gained the reward proverbially credited to the early bird.

Between them the Spaniards and the Portuguese had carved up all of America south of California, Mexico and Florida, inclusive, and the French and the British were forced to look for "plantations" in the northern parts of North America.

To Sir Walter Raleigh[1] had been assigned by his queen the privilege of exploration and "plantation" in North America; and moving up the east coast of North America to a point distant about equal from the Spanish "plantation" of Florida and the English possession of Labrador, Sir Walter landed and claimed the land in the name of his royal and virgin mistress, calling it, after her, Virginia.

Raleigh brought back glowing accounts of the new English land, but two of his fellow-captains, Amadas and Barlow, caused more excitement than did Sir Walter's stories by their bringing home with them three "Indians." The red-skins had brought with them their pipes and tobacco, and from them Sir Walter learnt the art and pleasure of smoking: they say that he was the first Englishman to do so; and as proof there is the historic anecdote of the servant who emptied a bucket of water over his master, thinking that Raleigh had caught alight—an anecdote which has been told of other pioneer smokers in other lands.

In 1585 Raleigh sent his cousin, Sir Richard Grenville, to Virginia, to organize the "plantation," and Grenville, returning to

[1] Sir Walter always spelt his own name "Raleghe."

England after some successful pioneer work, left Captain Lane behind with one hundred and seven men: a tiny beginning for so great an enterprise!

Thomas Hariot, a mathematician, was one of those entrusted by Raleigh and Grenville to "survey" the new colony, and among the matters which caught Hariot's interest was the habit of smoking, as practised among the "Indians."

Hariot, on his return, made a lengthy written report to Raleigh on the subject—a report which was afterwards printed.

"We ourselves," said the author, "tried their way of inhaling the smoke, both during our stay in Virginia and after our return, and have had many rare and wonderful proofs of the beneficial effects of this plant, which to relate in detail would require a whole volume to itself."

The first attempt at colonizing Virginia having proved a failure, Drake, who had gone to the colony in 1586 to render what assistance he might, took the colonists back to England.

The survivors of the original Virginian expedition had spent eighteen months in America, in constant touch with the natives, and had, in that period, become thoroughly addicted to the habit of smoking. This habit, together with the material means of satisfying its cravings, they brought back with them to their homeland. It was not long before the amusement or disgust that the sight of their pipes caused gave way to a desire to imitate the smokers, and before the end of the century the habit had become sufficiently widespread for that odd person, James I, to launch a violent protest against tobacco in a book published as early as 1603.

That tobacco, in twenty years, had laid a firm hold upon the nation, James does not deny. He affirms that

> many in this kingdome have had such a continuall use of taking this unsavourie smoke, as now they are not able to forbeare the same, no more then an olde drunkard can abide to be long sober, without falling into an incurable weaknesse and evill constitution: for their continuall custome hath made to them, *habitum, alteram naturam*: so to those that from their birth have been continually nourished upon poison and things venemous, wholesome meats are onely poisonable.

Queen Elizabeth delighted to honour the Christmas entertainments given by her lawyers, especially when those entertainments included plays—in the modern, rather than in the early Tudor, sense of the word. But she did not rely on others to provide her diversions, and at Hampton Court and Greenwich the Queen kept up superb Christmasses, at which she could indulge her favourite pleasures of dancing and dicing—all the Tudors, especially the women, were passionate gamblers.

The Queen's liking for dicing was further gratified by her consistent good fortune—a good-fortune which was the harder to escape seeing that the Virgin Queen invariably played with loaded dice!

National calamities and acts of God were never considered sufficient reasons, or reasons at all, for not keeping up Christmas in royal state.

Lord Shrewsbury writes in 1568 to his Countess: "The Plage is disposed far abrode in London, so that the Queene kepes hur Kyrsomas her, and goth not to Grenwych as it was mete." "Her" was Hampton Court. "If ye would," wrote Sir Thomas Smith from the same place in 1572, "what we do here, we play at tables, dance and keep Christmas."

Theatrical entertainments were a constant source of pleasure to the Queen, and it was she herself who, by organizing the presentation of plays, brought the modern stage into being. She did not write plays herself, but she did not content herself with mere patronage. She, like the true Tudor that she was, did things herself.

In 1569 she formed the children of the Chapel Royal into a theatrical company, under the personal control of Richard Edwards, poet, musician and playwright, who had already written and produced two comedies, *Damon and Pythias* and *Palamon and Arcite*. These two comedies were often played before the Queen, both in London and at Oxford.

A second company of players was formed soon afterwards by the Queen, and these she called "The Children of the Revels." Salathiel Pavy, a child-actor who "specialized" in the playing of old men, was a member of this company at the end of the century, and his death at the age of thirteen inspired Ben Jonson to write a beautiful epitaph on the gifted lad.

"The Children of the Revels" performed many plays by the age's most famous playwrights: Lyly, Ben Jonson and Shakespeare; but there is a legend that Shakespeare himself acted in his own plays before the Queen, shining especially in the part of the ghost in *Hamlet*.

The glory of the Elizabethan stage we doubtless owe to the masterpieces which were written for it, but to Elizabeth's active interest in the theatre we doubtless owe the fact that those plays were acted in circumstances which brought them to the notice of the world.

There was much complaint in the latter half of the sixteenth century that the landed gentry were forsaking their country seats in order to spend their time nearer the Court: the result, of course, of the policy which had been deliberately devised by King Edward IV for the breaking of the power of the "independent" barons; and a policy which had been continued by Henry VII.

The complaints, naturally, came from the country, where those who formerly might look forward to being entertained at the Lord of the Manor's expense now felt themselves woefully neglected—and this at a time when, for all the expenditure upon war, the country was enjoying a period of unexampled prosperity. Again, the dissolution of the monasteries had caused an army of workless vagabonds to be let loose: paupers who had formerly been employed, or at least fed, by the rich monastic foundations that Henry VIII had seized for himself and his supporters. The traditional Christmas largesse represented, for these people, the last vestige of the charity upon which they had once lived all the year round, and they deeply resented the fact that there were no Christmas feasts for them, since the nobles and county gentlemen spent their holidays in London.

The printing-press, during the hundred years that it had been established in England, had provided a means of airing every sort of discontent. The Elizabethan age was the age of the pamphlet and the broadsheet; and some of these were plain to the point of being considered seditious. Many an author was to give his pen too much freedom in the sacred cause of grumbling, and to lose his ears and his nose for a punishment.

In the Roxburgh Collection of Ballads in the British Museum is one with the title: *Chrismas's Lamentation for the losse of his acquaintance; showing how he is forst to leave the country and come to London.*

Christmas is my name, far have I gone,
Have I gone, have I gone,
without regard,
Whereas great men by flocks there be flown,
There be flown, there be flown,
to London-ward;
Where they in pomp and pleasure do waste
That which Christmas was wonted to feast,
Welladay!
Houses where music was wont for to ring,
Nothing but bats and owlets do sing.
Welladay! Welladay! Welladay!
where should I stay?

It is not unlikely that the Queen herself read this particular ballad: she was no idle autocrat, but one who exercised power by a constant, active supervision of even the most seemingly trivial aspects of the social life.

At any rate, she must have been aware of the discontent that this doggerel summed up; and, being Elizabeth, she did something to put matters right.

The day had gone when the ambitions of the country nobles were to be feared by the Crown. Under Elizabeth the nation had become united; and the provinces now needed a strong nobility to preserve the order that the seat of government had established.

So, by the Queen's command, the great lords and gentlemen were sent back to the country mansions and palaces before Christmas, "to repair to their counties, and there to keep hospitality amongst their neighbours."

Thus, Lord Berkeley at Caludon and the Sidneys at Penshurst —where, one Christmas long ago, the Black Prince and the Fair Maid of Kent passed a pleasant holiday—revived the ancient tradition of hospitality.

As Ben Jonson, who was often a guest at Penshurst, wrote:

Where the same beer and bread, and self-same wine,
That is His Lordship's, shall be also mine.

CHAPTER EIGHT

# CHRISTMAS UNDER SCOTTISH KINGS

JAMES I was a hater of witches and tobacco, but he loved Christmas; and since he was no mortifier of the flesh, he liked the material joys that tradition had come to associate with the feast of Christ's Nativity.

His own Scots annoyed him by taking a chill, Calvinistic attitude towards Christmas, calling it "Papist," "heathen," "idolatrous," "blasphemous," and worse (though it is difficult to see on what grounds even Calvinism could defend the policy of ignoring the one fact—that of Christ's birth—which is common to the belief of every sect of the Christian Church).

But, justifiable or not, their attitude of condemnation was one to which they stuck, and their stubborn reluctance to treat the greatest festival of the Church as anything but a revival, or continuation, of the Roman *Saturnalia* angered James exceedingly, who, though no Roman Catholic, was yet very far from leaning towards Calvinism.

In 1617 the King decided to visit the northern part of his kingdom in order to enforce upon the Scots compliance with the rules of the Church of England, that he proposed to establish as the state church of Scotland.

The King expressed his will in the famous Five Articles, one of which ordained that "the festivals of Christmas, Good Friday, Easter, Ascension Day and Whit Sunday should be observed in Scotland just as in England."

On this issue the Scots—the common people being just as pigheaded as their king—were quite prepared to defy the royal wish.

They flatly refused to celebrate the obnoxious "pagan" feasts, and three years later James succeeded in obtaining parliamentary sanction, in the form of an Act, to enforce the Five Articles. Supporting the King in his attempt to enforce conformity on the Scots was Archbishop Laud, whose officious proselytizing on behalf of his own brand of Protestantism was destined to have some grave effects, twenty years later, not only on the House of Stewart, but also on his own career.

The English part of the United Kingdom, united for the first time under the son of Mary Stewart, needed no legal enactments to cause them to keep their Christmasses in the old style; but James had need to pay attention to their Christmas-keeping for all that.

Like his predecessor on the throne, James I was of the opinion that his crown did not need the support of absentee landowners gathered about him at Whitehall. He decided that they were of far more use to the social stability of the kingdom on their own estates, and he expressed himself firmly on the subject.

Addressing the Council of the Star Chamber, he said: "And therefore, as every fish lives in his own place, some in the fresh, some in the salt, some in the mud, so let every one live in his own place—some at Court, some in the city, some in the country; specially at festival times, as Christmas, and Easter, and the rest."

Considering that the expression of opinion is not alone enough to enforce the royal will, James issued a proclamation, ordering the landed gentry to return to their estates at Christmas.

John Chamberlaine, writing to Sir Dudley Carleton, on 21 December, 1622, mentions the ordinance.

"Diverse Lords and personages of quality have made means to be dispensed withall for going into the country this Christmas, according to the proclamation; but it will not be granted, so that they pack away on all sides for fear of the worst."

The "worst" was no idle fear, either; James had his compliant and ruthless Star Chamber to enforce his wishes; and the fines imposed by the Star Chamber formed an important proportion of the royal revenue.

James needed money; he was what the Americans call a "big spender," and he had known sufficient hardship as a boy to make him take to self-indulgence, when he had the opportunity, as a duck takes to water. He had also the advantage of living in an age when kings were not expected to conform to the moral standards of the most righteous of their subjects, and James's vices were of the sort which cost their possessor a great deal of money to indulge.

But even in his normal enjoyments the King was most extravagant. Chamberlaine, writing to Carleton, says: "On the Twelfth-eve there was great golden play at Court. No gamester admitted that brought not £300 at least. Montgomery played the King's money and won him £750, which he had for his labour. The Lord Montegle[1] lost the Queen £400. Sir Robert Cary, for the Prince, £300; and the Earl of Salisbury, £300; the Lord Buckhurst, £500; *et sic de caeteris*. So that I heard of no winner but the King and Sir Francis Wolley, who got above £800."

The Queen—Anne of Denmark—was as extravagant as her lord; but her pleasures were less offensive to morality, even if not to good book-keeping. The masque, which had been introduced into England in the reign of Mary Tudor, had reached its perfection as an art-form in the early years of the seventeenth century; and the Queen poured out money, as the writers and the stage-designers poured out their genius, to keep up a constant supply of this exquisite form of entertainment.

Combining the features of the old-fashioned pageant or "disguising" with some of the features of the modern stage-play, yet adding to the combination of both a quality which is distinct from either, the masque reached perfection over an astonishingly brief period, and enjoyed that perfection for a period even briefer.

Never before or since do we find a situation similar to that which obtained in England at the beginning of the seventeenth century: where riches in the hands of patronage, and genius in the power of men able to supply what patronage so enthusiastically welcomed, combined to achieve a glory which had never been matched.

What a day it was! When the masques were written by such authors as Milton and Ben Jonson, when the music was supplied by such men as Byrd, and when the stage-sets were designed by such artists as Inigo Jones.

Not even in the great days of the eighteenth century can there have been such an assemblage of talent and genius as in those parties which used to gather at the Mermaid Tavern in Friday Street, hard by the church of St. Mary le Bow: that tavern to which came Jonson and Shakespeare, Beaumont and Fletcher, Donne, Selden, Cotton, Carew, Massinger, and others too numerous to mention.

[1] It was the anonymous warning to this peer which betrayed the "Gunpowder Plot."

And as for patronage . . . "The Queen hath likewise a great Mask in hand against Twelfth-tide, for which there was £3,000 delivered a month ago."

Extravagance on the part of the Royal Family not unnaturally found imitation among lesser persons.

The grossest imitation—which, they say, is the sincerest form of flattery—was to be found in the legal circles of the time; and the Inns of Court outdid the King and Queen in the sumptuousness and the costliness of their entertainments.

There is a hint, to be sure, of something other than strict loyalty to the Throne in the description of a Middle Temple Christmas of date 1635; for the "prince" that the Benchers "set up . . . in great state" was the son of a man whose father had been fined three years before by the Star Chamber. And the hint is underlined when we read that this "prince," Mr. Vivian, let fall his glass as he was drinking the King's health, "which much defaced his purple satten suit."

But anger over his father's treatment did not prevent Mr. Vivian spending £2,000 out of his own pocket for the honour of acting as the Christmas Prince.

The colleges of the two unversities, now that the Boy Bishop had fallen into discard, elected a Christmas Prince, as did now the various Inns of Court. The Christmas Prince of St. John's College, Oxford, for the Nativity of 1607-8, was a clergyman, Thomas Tucker, who was afterwards canon of Bristol.

Mr. Tucker's reign was of the most magnificent description, and the titles by which he was greeted on his "coronation" ring with the sonorous grandeur of the age.

"The most magnificent and renowned Thomas, by the favour of Fortune, Prince of Alba Fortunata, Lord St. Johns, High Regent of the Hall, Duke of St. Giles, Marquis of Magdalens, Landgrave of the Grove, Count Palatine of the Cloisters, Chief Bailiff of the Beaumonts, High Ruler of Rome, Master of the Manor of Waltham, Governor of Gloucester Green, Sole Commander of all Tilts, etc."

The titles have reference to places in or near Oxford.

The complete record of the reign of Thomas Tucker affords a striking example of the solemn mummery which used to accompany the elevation of anyone to the dignity of Christmas Prince; and to read the mock-heroic speeches of the officers of the Court is to realize why the masque had such a great attraction for its time.

Oxonian Christmas Princes were able to discharge their excess of energy in fantastic masqueradings; the Lords, Princes—or, as they were sometimes called, Lieutenants—of the Inns of Court Christmasses found relief from the pressure of their emotions in antics far less dignified than those which marked the Christmasses of dons and scholars at Oxford.

Even the judges were supposed, by custom, to watch the members of the Bar dance before them at Christmas, and in the reign of James I the under-barristers were put out of Commons, by decimation, because they did not dance before the judges, according to the ancient usage of the Honourable Society.

The Lords of Misrule and the Lieutenants were even more lively than the dancing barristers. Firearms had a peculiar attraction for them, though they did not despise the charms of naked swords.

There is an amusing story of "the Gentlemen of Graye's Inn," deciding to end Christmas-tide in a suitable fashion, fetching four cartloads of "chambers" (small signal cannons) from the Tower of London, and letting them off all at once. They made such a din that "the King, awakened with this noise, started out of his bed, and cryed, 'Treason, treason,' etc., and that the Cittie was in an uprore, in such sort (as it is told) that the whole court was raised and almost in armes, the Earle of Arundell running to the Bedchamber with his sworde drawne as to rescue the King's person."

In the following reign—that of James's son, Charles I—the law-students and under-barristers made it clear that they regarded themselves as having the right to pass Christmas in their own fashion, "as ancient custom ordained."

In 1627 "the Temple Sparks had enstalled a Lieutenant, which we country folk call a Lord of Misrule. The Lieutenant had, on Twelfth eve, late in the night, sent out to collect his rents in Ramme Alley and Fleet Street, limiting five shillings to every house. At every door they winded their Temple horn, and if it procured not entrance at the second blast or summons, the word of command was then 'Give fire, gunner.'

"This gunner was a robustious Vulcan, and his engine a mighty smith's hammer. The next morning, the Lord Mayor of London was made acquainted therewith, and promised to be with them the next night; commanding all that ward, and also the watch, to attend him with their halberds. At the hour prefixt, the Lord Mayor and his train marched up in martial equipage to Ramme Alley.

"Out came the Lieutenant with his suit of Gallants, all armed *in cuerpo*. One of the Halberdiers bade the Lieutenant come to my Lord Mayor. 'No,' said the Lieutenant, 'let the Lord Mayor come to me.' But this controversy was soon ended, they advancing each to other, till they met half way; then one of the Halberdiers reproved the Lieutenant for standing covered before the Lord Mayor. The Lieutenant gave so crosse an answere, as it begat as crosse a blow, which, the Gentlemen, not brooking, began to lay about them; but in fine the Lieutenant was knockt down and sore wounded, and the Halberdiers had the better of the swords. The Lord Mayor being master of the field, took the Lieutenant, and haled rather than led him to the Counter, and with indignation thrust him in at the prison gate, where he lay till the Attorney General mediated for his enlargement, which the Lord Mayor granted upon condition he should submit and acknowledge his fault.

"The Lieutenant readily embraced the motion; and the next day, performing the condition, so ended this Christmas Game."

The Scots King's own peculiar tastes had, naturally, an effect upon the contemporary fashions in Christmas celebrations: at least, in the court circles. James was something of a monomaniac on the subject of witches and wizards, and would never accept a natural explanation while his erratic fancy could produce a supernatural one. He even believed that any conjuring-trick above the simplest standard was done by infernal power, and in his great book on demonology he did not hesitate to affirm that only the "Divell" could perform the feats of the professional magicians. "The Divell," wrote James, in all seriousness, "will learne them many juglarie tricks, at cards or dice, to deceive men's senses thereby, and such innumerable false practiques, which are proved by over-many in this age."

James may not have been converted to the Scots view that Christmas was a blasphemous relic of paganism, but he shared in the Scots conviction that the Devil was a very real Person indeed, and that His agents were as numerous on this earth as they were as active for the destruction of the good.

The juggler, the sleight-of-hand exponent, the illusionist, were unpopular at Court in James's day, and were never included among the "turns" at the Christmas entertainments. James was a man of singularly coarse habits, but he had a surprising dislike of coarse spectacles; and his liking for tournaments we may explain by James's romantic notions of chivalry, and by the superb opportunity that it gave to James's eldest son, Henry, Prince of Wales, to display his agility, his courage and his excellent young figure.

James's three sons, Henry, Charles and James, were all exceedingly fond of display of a theatrical sort; Henry liking the masque as well as the tournament; and both the younger princes acted in masques on many occasions, as did the King and Queen.

Prince Henry was a brilliant boy and his father's especial pride. His early death, at the age of eighteen, was a source of infinite grief to his father, but who yet had, in the pain of losing a dearly loved son, the consolation of knowing that he had never quarrelled with that son, nor denied the lad any pleasure that the father might have given.

James had many faults, but failure to love his children was not among them.

One of the most magnificent tournaments of the reign was that which took place on Twelfth Night, 1610, at Whitehall, in which the Prince took a leading part.

The tournament was given partly as the usual Christmas entertainment, and partly in connexion with the forthcoming investiture of Henry as Prince of Wales.

"Strangely attired," Henry issued a challenge to all the knights of Britain, on New Year's Day, 1610, and the "barriers" were erected in Whitehall on 6 January, in the evening.

The King, Queen, their officials and the ambassadors of Spain and Venice were among the distinguished company which witnessed the feats of arms. Fifty-six earls, barons, knights and esquires, besides Prince Henry and the Duke of Lennox, took part, and the jousting went on from ten in the evening (which was a Saturday) until three on the Sunday morning; the speeches at the "barriers" being written by Ben Jonson.

The winners were the Earl of Montgomery, Sir Thomas Darcy and Sir Robert Gordoun.

Under James the country saw a revival of that pernicious rule of favourites which had blotted the reigns of Edward II and Richard II.

Kings, like lesser folk, must have their likes and dislikes, but the tactful monarch seeks to pursue the mean between excessive favouritism and excessive neglect of his subjects.

Good looks and that sort of gutter-impudence which was later to enchant George IV were, when found together, the certain passport to the favour of the King.

An impecunious young Scotsman named Robert Ker—or Carr—had the two qualities in a marked degree, and knowing the King's weakness for good-looking youths, especially of his own race, Ker set out to get himself noticed by James.

He contrived to become page to Lord Dingwall at a tourney, and had the exceeding good fortune to slip and break a leg when, as was a page's privilege, he was presenting his master's shield to the King.

James, struck with the youth's beauty, had him carried into a house, and sent the royal surgeon to attend to the Scots adventurer.

This was the first step in Ker's rise to fame and fortune: on Christmas Day, 1607, he was knighted by James—who could not bear to let Ker out of his presence—and made first gentleman of the Bedchamber.

"Such was his favour that every one pressed around him to obtain their suits with the King. He received rich presents; the ladies courted his attention; the greatest lords did him the most obsequious and disgusting homage"—things which always happen when the King rules through a favourite.

Cited as co-respondent by the Earl of Essex, Ker married the lady, upon which he himself was raised to the rank enjoyed by Lady Essex's former husband, being created Earl of Somerset.

Now this pretty blackguard added murder to his other crimes by poisoning, in collaboration with his wife, Sir Thomas Overbury: a murder so flagrant that not even the King's influence could save his favourite from being charged with the crime.

It is rarely, indeed, that a criminal is saved from paying the penalty of a monstrous crime by committing a worse; but Ker's luck was not to fail him even in the dangerous position in which he now found himself.

The consummate impudence which had earned him a title and immense riches now served to win him escape from a felon's death.

He . . . blackmailed the King! He sent a message to his royal patron saying bluntly that, if his judges were to proceed with the trial, Ker would be reluctantly forced to tell some very unpleasant truths concerning James's tastes.

The prisoners were accordingly reprieved; and, though compelled to serve a term of imprisonment, they were not hanged.

A more fortunate favourite was Buckingham, a person of origins no more distinguished than Ker's, and with impudence of the same type, but with much more intelligence and with a genuinely kind heart to make excuse for his childish greed. It is true that Buckingham was eventually killed by Fenton at Portsmouth, but he did not fall into the disgrace which awaited Ker, nor did he even serve a term of imprisonment.

"The King hath been at Theobald's," wrote Chamberlaine to Dudley Carleton, "ever since Wednesday, and came to town this day. I am sorry to hear that he grows every day more froward, and with such a kind of morosity, that doth either argue a great discontent in mind, or a distemper of humours in his body. Yet he is never so out of tune but the very sight of my lord of Buckingham doth settle and quiet all."

This was written a few days before Christmas, 1617, just after the King had returned, in a very bad temper, from dealing with his fractious and obstinate Scots subjects.

The rule of favourites is always bad, and in social systems where the king *is* the government their rule is exceptionally bad for the country's finances.

All the same, their rule was most beneficial for the arts. Each of them sought to keep up a Court rivalling in brilliance that of the man from whom they derived their riches. Each became a munificent, a lavish patron of poets, authors, playwrights, musicians, artists, painters and architects. The favourites, indeed, did considerably more for artists than did the King, since, not only were the favourites generally possessed of more taste than was James, but —as most of them contrived to be on good terms with Prince (afterwards King) Charles—their own taste was improved by the advice of the Prince, who was one of the soundest connoisseurs of art of his day, and the soundest, without doubt, ever to sit on the throne of Britain.

The Van Dycks and Rubens which hang on the walls of Windsor

Castle were brought there by Charles. The superb Raphael cartoons now in England were bought by him for £300—a rare bargain, but only to be had by a man possessing his unerring appreciation of true artistic values.

Vice may have flourished at the court of James I, but it was vice which lost half its grossness by being associated with such a flowering of artistic genius.

In the following reign the patron was to be the source of artistic inspiration as well as of the means to commission the artist's work. That this patronage was to lead to financial differences between the King and Parliament is a historical fact which hardly concerns us here, save in the effect that the Civil War which followed the quarrel was to have on the traditional celebrations of Christmas. What that effect was we shall see in a later chapter.

But until the Civil War put a temporary stop to all creative work by the artists they enjoyed a heyday of patronage under Charles I, whose associate was the magnificent Buckingham. For fifteen years, until the outbreak of the Civil War, the English Court—and the capital in which it was situated—enjoyed the reputation of being the most polished in Europe; artistic, cultured, civilized; not even excluding the Vatican.

## CHAPTER NINE

# STUART EXTRAVAGANCES

CHARLES I, loving the masque as much as his father had done, continued its use when he came to the throne in 1625.

Ben Jonson still continued to write the "scripts" for the masques, and Inigo Jones to supply the scenery and what we now call the "production," and it was in the reign of this selfish, treacherous, but art-loving king that the masque developed into the modern play, or perhaps it is juster to say that the modern stage then came into being as a development of earlier theatrical forms.

Extravagance was in the air: the King set an example that persons all over the country strove to imitate and, in some cases, to excel. The enactment that the landed gentry should spend their Christmasses on the estates, rather than at Court, was renewed—a sign that the earlier enactments had had less than the effect intended. But still sufficient of the nobility remained in London to present to the world the spectacle of a capital city apparently devoted only to the most costly self-indulgence.

The lawyers were making money—for commerce, while the nobles were spending their time in unproductive activity, was laying the foundations of our world-trade—and their entertainments were given upon the most magnificent scale.

At the end of the Christmas-tide of 1633 the four Inns of Court —the two Temples, Gray's and Lincoln's—combined to present the masque, "The Triumph of Peace," which cost them no less than £20,000!

The King cultivated friendly relations with the legal profession, in order to pursue his plan of creating an authority in the kingdom independent of Parliament, which had already—since the union of England and Scotland, with its consequent importation of a Scots (in those days, "foreign") king—shown disturbing signs of an unruly and somewhat anti-royal spirit. Elizabeth had, to all intents and purposes, ruled without a Parliament; yet her autocracy had been such that she had governed the country alone without needing to fight against the opposition of rival power-lovers. Like her great predecessor, Alfred the Unifier, she had seemed, to her people, so to symbolize the national character and the national ambitions; so to represent, in one fine mind, the aspirations of the millions over whom she ruled, and in whose name she spoke; that no other ruler was needed, no other voice than hers needed to be heard. Centuries later, another British queen—Victoria—was to become the symbol of every Briton's pride and hopes. Such monarchs need neither advisers nor assistants: certainly not in the people's view, though possibly that view may not be shared by ambitious politicians.

But in the space which intervened between Elizabeth's death and James's coming to the throne, Parliament, acting as "caretaker" of the realm, had tasted an authority which had never before been its to enjoy. For the first time in four hundred years of its existence Parliament had, even though for a short and strictly limited period, tasted supreme authority. The fact that the enjoyment of that authority was to be only temporary gave the Parliamentarians so strong a desire to have it for ever that they were prepared literally to fight to retain a hold upon a pleasure that chance had put into their hands when it seemed that they might sigh after it eternally. The fight had begun in the reign of James, whom the parliamentarians tried not to let forget that he "owed his throne to them." That this was not a fact, and that James would not, for one moment, accept it as fact, made no difference to their contending that James had behaved with ingratitude in not sharing his power with a group to whom he owed that power in the first place.

Charles I came to the throne to face a battle with a parliament already openly committed to a show-down between "The People" and the Crown. Perhaps, when all is said and done, the quarrel between a middle class jealous of aristocratic privilege and an aristocracy in no mood to extend its ranks had better have happened in England when it did than that it should have been delayed a further hundred and fifty years, as was the case in France. It is hard to see how the quarrel could have been altogether averted, and so it was probably better that it happened when it did.

Reformers are always in opposition; since, as soon as they acquire power, they cease to be reformers. Or, rather, critics in opposition are always reformers.

Parliament began its sniping by attacking the extravagance of the King and his friends; and, certainly, the extravagance was there to be attacked. On the other hand, the nation's wealth was increasing every day, and what the Parliament stigmatized as costly waste would now pass for estimable "public works."

Royal spending was not all unproductive: and many schemes were held up by Parliamentary unco-operation which would have been of assured and permanent value, such as the plan for a unified Royal Palace and Government offices in Whitehall.

This plan got no farther than the provision of the banqueting-hall (from Inigo Jones's designs) and the same architect's tiny Roman Catholic chapel in St. James's, which was built so that Queen Henrietta Maria could attend services there.

But any and every Royal expenditure was considered fair game by the Parliament; and the unfortunate effect of the Parliamentarians' carping was to convince the King that his royal dignity could be sustained only by disregarding *all* Parliamentary criticism, even where it was dictated, not by prejudice or animosity, but by common sense.

The details of the fight between King and Parliament belong to the history books, and do not concern us here; and the quarrel is of importance in this book only in that it caused the Royal entertainments to rise to new heights of lavishness.

It is easy to see the King giving all his attention to preparing masques, with the assistance of those two artists of genius, Ben Jonson and Inigo Jones, while the British people starved. Hollywood has made several successful pictures based on a similar supposed situation in France in 1780. It is astonishing that they have not rewritten the script to apply to the England of 1630.

The records of the time gave the lie to the contention of anti-royalist historians that the King's entertainments impoverished the nation, and made festivity something to be found only in the royal palaces and in the mansions of the great, who, says Dawson, lived like petty princes at this time, and in the arrangement of their households copied their sovereign—even to having liveried heralds at Christmas, to cry largesse thrice at the proper time.

But the poets of the day reveal clearly enough that pleasure was by no means the prerogative of the wealthy: there is, indeed, everywhere noticeable that rise of the middle class which was to

The Hobby-horse: an indispensable element of English "masquing." The horse was the totem of the Anglo-Saxons—it is because it still is that the modern British taboo against eating horse-flesh is so powerful. The image of the totem-animal at the "masquings" was held to ensure good luck.

Dragging in the Yule-log in medieval England. A youth rode the log into "the hall," the maidens dragging it. Ritual songs and drinking always accompanied the ceremony. The carol, *The Old Oak Bough,* is a part of the ancient song-cycle.

become the chief source of Britain's strength. And that middle class—by which we mean anything between the manual labourer and the nobleman—did itself well at all times—but especially at Christmas.

Herrick's poem, "A New Year's Gift, sent to Sir Simeon Steward," described no country shivering in the misery of royal neglect. The scenes of innocent merriment that he pictures are scenes from simple homes. Withers, again, sings the joys of the simple life:

> The wenches with their wassail bowls
> About the streets are singing;
> The boys are come to catch the owls,
> The wild mare in is bringing.
> Our kitchen-boy hath broke his box,[1]
> And to the dealing of the ox
> Our honest neighbours come by flocks,
> And here they will be merry.
>
> Now kings and queens poor sheep cotes have,
> And mate with everybody;
> The honest now may play the knave,
> And wise men play the noddy.
> Some youths will now a-mumming go,
> Some others play at Rowland-ho,
> And twenty other gambols mo,
> Because they will be merry.

Arthur Young, an English clergyman, made a tour through France just before the revolution of 1789. His description of the country would be unrecognized by Hollywood scriptwriters, for we meet no Belsen scarecrows in his sober, truthful pages.

So with the descriptions of the English scene in the years just prior to the Civil War. A country gentleman, in 1634, disregards the ordinance abolishing the Lords of Misrule, and carefully draws up "articles" for the guidance of his own Lord of Misrule.

The gentleman was Richard Evelyn—father of the famous diarist who acted as host to Peter the Great of Russia. The elder Evelyn was at that time Sheriff of Surrey and Sussex, and though Evelyn was not a "working man," he was not a member of the extravagant court circle. He was a country gentleman, in short, and his attitude towards life, on the very verge of the Civil War, well reflects the

[1] The Christmas-box was made of clay, and had to be broken to get at the contents.

average social attitude of the average man of his day.

"Articles made and appoynted by the Right Wo$^{ll}$ Richard Evelyn Esq., High Sheriffe and Deputie Leavetenaunt to the Kinge's Mat$^{ie}$ for the Counties of Surrey and Sussex.

"Imprimis. I give free leave to Owen Flood my Trumpeter, gent. to be L$^{od}$ of Misrule of all good Orders during the twelve dayes. And also I give free leave to the said Owen Flood to comand all and every person whatsoever, as well servants as others, to be at his comand whensoever he shall sound his Trumpet or Musick, and to do him good service as though I were present my selfe at their perills."

There follows what shall be done during the twelve days.

"If any man shall bee drunke, or drinke more than is fitt, or offer to slepe during the time abovesaid, or do not drinke up his bowle of beere, but flings away his snuffe (that is to say) the second draught, he shall drinke two, and afterwards be excluded.

"If any person shall come into the kitchen whiles meate is a dressinge, to molest the cookes, he shall suffer the rigour of his Lo$^{pps}$ law.

"If any man shall kisse any maid, widdow or wife, except to bid welcome or farewell, without his Lo$^{pps}$ consent, he shall have punishment as his Lo$^{pp}$ shall thinke convenient.

"The last article: I give full power and authoritie to his Lo$^{pp}$ to break up all lockes, bolts, barres, doores, and latches, and to flinge up all doores out of hendges to come at those whoe presume to disobey his Lo$^{pps}$ commaunds.

"God save the King."

As, among other offences, the "articles" drawn up for the reign of Evelyn's Lord of Misrule forbade swearing during the twelve days, the High Sheriff of Surrey and Sussex evidently looked to his Lord of Misrule to improve the manners of his household. The revellers of Blatherwick, however, at Christmas, 1637, had been guilty, in the opinion of the Commissioners for Causes Ecclesiastical, of sadly undermining morals at the holy feast.

One Saunders and his friends had appointed a Lord of Misrule to be the king over their frolics. The very appointment of such a dignitary was unlawful, but legalized by custom, and no one had anything to say against that.

What did bring down the condemnation of the Commissioners

was Saunders and Co.'s decision to have a wife for their Lord: what we may call a Christmas Lady.

They looked around and found what seemed to them a suitable bride in Miss Elizabeth Pitto, the daughter of the town's hog-herd. The young lady was conducted into the presence of Mr. Saunders, who had dressed himself as a parson, wearing a labourer's smock for a surplice. The Lord of Misrule was then married to the hog-herd's daughter, Mr. Saunders reading the service from the Book of Common Prayer.

"All the after ceremonies and customs," says Ashton, "then in use were observed, and the affair was carried to its utmost extent. The parties," he adds, "had time to repent at leisure in prison."

It is not easy now to tell whether the Puritans hated Christmas because the feast made most people a little happier then than they were at other times, or because Christmas had become associated in their minds with the Court, and so with the extravagance that they had made it their business to attack.

But it is clear enough that they added Christmas very early to their list of dislikes, and their criticism of the Nativity assumed the bitterest quality as the quarrel between King and Parliament mounted to its climax.

Nicholas Breton—no Puritan he!—after a description of Christmas joys—"It is now Christmas, and not a cup of drink must pass without a carol"—ends thus: "In sum, it is a holy time, a duty in Christians for the remembrance of Christ and custom among friends for the maintenance of good fellowship. In brief, I thus conclude it: I hold it a memory of the Heaven's love and the world's peace, the mirth of the honest, and the meeting of the friendly."

William Prynne, a Puritan lawyer—a very different sort of lawyer from those who spent £20,000 on a masque—was of another opinion. For him, 25 December was rather the Nativity of Satan than of the Saviour, and—following the same perverted line of thinking—the masques with which the Court and other centres of authority celebrated the feast were about as innocent as the Black Mass.

Mr. Prynne stated and elaborated these whimsical views in his book, *Histriomastix,* sub-titled, "The Scourge of Stage-Players." He roundly condemned masques, stage-plays, balls, "mummery" (naturally!), and even such—to our eyes—innocent customs as the decking of houses with evergreens.

"Against the Feast of Christmas, every man's house, as also their parish churches, were decked with holme, ivy, bayes, and whatsoever the season of the year afforded to be green." Thus says Stow, the historian of London; and calls attention to a custom which annoyed Master Prynne.

Perhaps even Prynne's malignant dislike of all rejoicing might not have got him into trouble had he not coupled the King and Queen with the "paganism" that he deplored. But, in attacking royal tastes, he laid himself open to disaster, and the Star Chamber called him before its judges. Prynne was fined £5,000, expelled from the membership of Oxford University, of Lincoln's Inn and, indeed, of the legal profession generally. He was also condemned to see his book burnt before his eyes by the common hangman[1]; to stand twice in the pillory, losing an ear each time; and to suffer perpetual imprisonment.

Green, noticing the matter of Prynne in *A Short History of the English People,* finds that the sentence "showed the hard cruelty of the Primate"—Archbishop Laud, who presided over the sittings of the Star Chamber.

The sentence was certainly severe, but not unduly so by the standards of the time, and within a few years the Puritans, in power, were to show with what kindness they treated *their* enemies. In any case, Prynne was the declared enemy of all which was innocent and gay; he was the atrabilious apostle of all uncharitableness and unkindness, and we need shed no tears for *him*.

Had Mr. Prynne really had the courage of his convictions—with which too many unthinking people have credited him—he would have accompanied his fellow joy-haters to America, in 1620. The "Pilgrim Fathers" would have provided a Christmas for Lawyer Prynne well in keeping with his austere views.

Here, for instance, is William Bradford's account of what happened at the Christmas following the landing of the "Pilgrim Fathers" at Plymouth Rock. In order to show their hatred and contempt of the Nativity, the "Fathers" ordered that all should work on Christmas Day.

"Munday, the 25 Day, we went on shore, some to fell tymber,

[1] Derrick—who has since given his name to the crane used on ships.

some to saw, some to riue, and some to carry, so that no man rested all that day, but towards night, some, as they were at worke, heard a noyse of some Indians, which caused vs all to goe to our Muskets, but we heard no further, so we came aboord againe, and left some twentie to keepe the court of gard; that night we had a sore storme of winde and raine. Munday the 25 being Christmas day, we began to drinke water aboord, but at night the Master caused vs to have some Beere, and so on board we had diverse times now and then some Beere, but on shore none at all."

The same glumness, according to Bradford, marked the "celebration" of the Christmas following.

"On ye day called Christmas-day ye Gov'r caled them out to worke (as was used), but the most of this new company excused themselves, and said it went against their consciences to worke on ye day. So the Gov'r tould them that if they made it a mater of conscience, he would spare them till they were better informed. So he led away ye rest, and left them: but when they came home at noone from their worke, he founde them in ye streete at play, openly; some pitching ye barr, and some at stoole ball, and such like sports. So he went to them and tooke away their implements, and told them that it was against his conscience that they should play, and others worke. If they made the keeping of it a matter of devotion, let them keepe their houses, but there should be no gameing or revelling in ye streets. Since which time nothing hath been attempted that way, at least openly."

Twenty years later than this drab Christmas, the Old Country was to have the privilege of experiencing for itself the joys of a Puritan Yule. America had already given us tomatoes and turkeys, cocoa and tobacco, pineapples and quinine: now it was to export a social habit—and not by any means for the only time in the history of the Mother and the Daughter Countries.

Of course, as no one in this world is ever altogether right, so no one is ever completely wrong; and there were not lacking some cogent arguments to support the Puritans' contention that Christmas feasting was bad for the national morale.

For instance, they might have cited, in favour of their opposition to the traditional celebration of Christmas, the events which inspired the Lords Commissioners of the Navy to write to the Duke of Buckingham on 13 January, 1626, that "they have received information from persons who have been on board the *Happy Entrance* in the Downs, and the *Nonsuch* and *Garland* at Gore-end, that for these Christmas holidays, the captains, masters, boatswains, gunners and carpenters were not aboard their ships, nor gave any attendance to the service, leaving the ships a prey to any who might have assaulted them.

"The Commissioners sent down clothes for the sailors, and there were no officers to take charge of them, and the pressed men ran away as fast as the Commissioners sent them down. If they had beaten up and down, they might have prevented the loss of two English ships taken by the Dunkirkers off Yarmouth."

On 15 January, following the time-honoured practice of shutting (and bolting) the stable door *after* the horse has escaped, the Duke wrote to Sir Henry Palmer on the subject of the general desertion of the King's ships at Christmastide, and called upon Sir Henry "presently to repair on board his own ship, and to charge the officers of all the ships composing his fleet, not to depart from their ships without order."

It is about this period that a new and fundamentally important element enters into the composite of factors which make up the modern Christmas. The printing-press had, for a century after its introduction into Europe, undergone little improvement; but at the end of the sixteenth century the Dutch printers had effected some astonishing progress in the design of the presses, while the paper-makers, by improved techniques, had successfully attempted to lower costs. The improvements in presses and papers meant that printed matter was now brought within reach of the shallowest pockets.

Ballads were hawked in the streets, and chap-books came to be found among the presents commonly given by the people at Christmas-tide. By means of the pamphlet the Man With An Idea could reach thousands, whereas before his speeches could get his Idea over to only hundreds—provided that the Watch did not move him on before he had finished his harangue.

The advantages of the pamphlet, indeed, were so obvious to all that anyone with an argument to expound rushed into print; and so it is that the seventeenth century is the great age of the pamphlet. The age of argument by printing-press, rather than argument by lung-power, had arrived; and the pros and cons of Christmas were, with a host of other matters, discussed in the broadsheets and pamphlets of the day.

Sang one ballad-monger whom I have already quoted:

> Christmas is my name, far have I gone,
> Without regard, without regard.
> Whereas great men by flocks there be flown,
> To London-ward, to London Ward.
> There they in pomp and pleasure do waste
> That which Old Christmas was wonted to feast,
> Well a day!
> Houses where music was wont for to ring,
> Nothing but bats and owlets do sing.
> Well a day, Well a day.
> Well a day, where should I stay?

But, as so often happens in history, the supporters of old customs were not one-tenth as noisy as those who attempted to overthrow them; and for every broadsheet and pamphlet which appeared in the reign of Charles I in praise of Christmas, there were dozens to argue against its propriety and even morality.

## CHAPTER TEN

# PURITANS AND THE PRESS

IN THE last chapter I mentioned the growing power of the printing-press in affecting public opinion by the dissemination of new ideas —or of very old ideas, polished up to look like new. But ballads and broadsheets and pamphlets were not the only vehicles of propaganda. The printing-press gave birth to a force for propaganda much more potent than these. It created the newspaper: that powerful instrument of rule that men have rightly christened The Fourth Estate.

The first quarter of the seventeenth century saw the establishment of the newspaper; and it has been too often forgotten, in deciding just how Cromwell's ideas triumphed temporarily over those of the House of Stuart, that the Puritans had control of the Press of that day.

There were royalist newspapers, of course, and some which, while not supporting the King, were yet far from supporting the totalitarian principles of Cromwell. But the majority of the papers supported the Roundheads—and it was the Roundhead idea which was to triumph.

In 1642 the Civil War broke out, for reasons which hardly concern us here; and one of the first official acts of the rebel Parliament was to "modify" the traditional celebrations.

Plays were ordered to be suppressed, and it was seen that it would not be long before Christmas—against which so many Puritan writers had raved—would follow plays into the list of things forbidden to "godly" men.

Unsure of the extent of its power to impose a complete break with the past, it was not until 3 June, 1647, that the Cromwellian Parliament came out openly against Christmas; and felt itself strong enough to announce that the feast of the Nativity of Christ, and all other religious festivals, must no longer be observed; the free time formerly enjoyed by scholars, apprentices, servants and others on those festivals to be enjoyed in future on the second Tuesday in the month.

So that this ordinance of June should be borne in mind as Christmas approached, the town-crier went around, as he did at Canterbury by order of the Mayor, to warn the citizens that Christmas was now abolished—and therefore forbidden. This ordinance produced some memorable riots—particularly at Ealing and Canterbury, for, as Richard Kentish told the House of Commons; "The people of England do hate to be reformed; so now a prelatical priest, with a superstitious service book, is more desired, and would be better welcome to the generality of England, than the most learned, laborious, conscientious preacher, whether Presbyterian or Independent. These poor simple people," the plain-speaking (and, in his fashion, honest) Roundhead added, "are mad after superstitious festivals, after unholy holidays."

Kentish's fellow-members of Parliament agreed with him that the "poor, simple creatures" of England were mad to celebrate their traditional holidays, but they were fiercely determined to wean the poor, simple creatures—if necessary by force—from their traditional madness.

The Anglican Prayer Book had been abolished by Act of Parliament, and religion put into the hands of a "Directory." The first Christmas to come after the establishment of the "Directory"—1645—fell on a Thursday, and the new rulers, believing that example was every bit as good as precept, showed their own view of Christmas by going to business, either in the House of Commons, or in the "Assembly" which had replaced the House of Lords.

All the same, the legislators had to close their eyes to the fact that, despite their "progressive" ordinances, most of the shops were closed on that day, as an M.P. named Whitelock, a godly zealot, observed in his memoirs.

One of the Government newspapers, the *Mercurius Academicus,* in the Christmas number of 1645, carried the news that General Browne, a Puritan leader, proclaimed the abolition of Christmas at Abingdon, and ordered people to go to work as usual on that day.

Another Government newspaper, *The Weekly Account,* announced the abolition of Christmas by inference, in recording that "The Commons sate in a Grand Committee" on that day; but *The Kingdome's Weekly Messenger* is a little more explicit:

"Thursday, Decemb. 25, vulgarly known by the name of Christmas Day, both Houses sate."

The City of London newspaper, *Mercurius Civicus,* explained to its readers the foolishness of keeping Christmas Day, and urged every good citizen to disregard the ancient superstitions, while it advanced a more constructive argument against Christmas-keeping by suggesting that it was more probable that Christ was born in September than in December, and quotes "a late reverend minister's" revival of an ancient heresy to the effect that "God did conceal the time when Christ was borne, upon the same reason that He tooke away the body of Moses, that they might not put an holinesse upon that day."

The horrible unimaginativeness of *all* reformers never showed more clearly than in the *Mercurius Civicus's* advice to its readers that, if they wanted a holiday, "let them keep the fifth of November, and other dayes of that nature, or the late great mercy of God in the taking of Hereford, which deserves an especiall day of thanksgiving."

"Many people," the newspaper remarked severely, "in these times are too much addicted to the superstitious observance of this day, December 25th, and other saints' days, as they are called." That earnest zealot, the editor, declared himself scandalized by the manner in which the people, despite the opinion and act of Parliament and the Assembly, continued to celebrate Christmas.

"Hardly," he remarked, "forty shops were open within the lines upon that day. The State hath done well to null it out of respect (i.e., abolish Christmas Day) as Moses did the Brazen Serpent."

A curious pamphlet of the time is entitled, *The Arraignment Conviction and Imprisonment of CHRISTMAS on St. Thomas Day last. And How he broke out of Prison in the Holidayes and got away, onely Left his hoary hair, and gray beard, sticking between two Iron Bars of a Window. With An Hue and Cry after CHRISTMAS, and a Letter from* Mr. Woodcock, *a Fellow in Oxford, to a Malignant*[1] *Lady in LONDON. And divers passages between the Lady and the Cryer, about Old Christmas: And what shift he was fain to make to save his life, and great stir to fetch him back again. With divers other Witty Passages. Printed by* Simon Minc'd Pye, *for* Cissely Plum-Porridge; *and are to be sold out by*

[1] Malignant—the Puritans' general term for their opponents.

Ralph Fidler, *Chandler, at the signe of the* Pack of Cards *in* Mustard-Alley, *in* Brawn Street. *1645*.

The tone of the pamphlet, if it be not evident to the reader in the laboured "wit" of the lengthy title, is evident enough in the remark (which has been taken from the context) that "the wanton Women dote after him; he helped them to so many new Gownes, Hatts, and Hankerches, and other fine knacks, of which he hath a pack on his back, in which is good store of all sorts, besides the fine knacks that he got out of husband's pockets for household provisions for him."

"Whosoever," says the writer, "can tel what is become of (Christmas), or where he may be found, let them bring him back againe into England, to the Crier, and they shall have a Benediction from the Pope, an hundred oaths from the Cavaliers, 40 kisses from the Wanton Wenches, and be made Pursevant to the next Arch Bishop. Malignants will send him a piece of Braune, and every Prentice boy will give him his point[1], next Holy Thursday, the good Wives will keepe him in some corner of their mince pies, and the new Nuncio Ireland will return him to be canonized the next Reformation of the Calender.

"AND SO POPE SAVE CHRISTMAS."

All the same, one feels, in reading through *The Arraignment of Christmas,* that the author is airing opinions in which he does not altogether believe: that, in short, he is writing for propaganda. One feels, too, that there is a sentimental longing for the old ways—even though he seeks to banish their charm by laboured sneers.

Parliament, by consistently sitting on every Christmas Day, from 1644 to 1656, did its best to "officialize" Christmas out of existence; but how poorly they succeeded in imposing their grim will in those parts of the country where time-servers and lick-spittles were prepared to enforce Puritan policies for the advantages that support of the Government would bring is implied in Gervase Markham's *English Housewife,* published in 1653.

Gervase Markham describes what he calls "a moderate dinner"; and it seems a dinner very little different from those that we

[1] Ashton suggests that this may mean "a pint of wine," but this explanation is improbable, not to say nonsensical. "Give his his point" obviously means "give him his favour"; "will support him."

encounter in former—and less officially austere—periods of our history. It shows, indeed, that while the Man of God, Noll Williams (*alias* Oliver Cromwell), was privately having coins struck by a French engraver; coins which showed "Oliver, by the Grace of God, Protector of England, Scotland, France and Ireland," laurel-crowned on one side, and the arms of Britain, charged with the arms of Cromwell, *crowned with the Imperial Crown of the Holy Roman Empire*, on the other; the Lord Protector's loyal subjects were paying just about as much attention to Puritan principles in their own lives as the Protector was in his.

"Now," says *The English Housewife,* "to these full dishes may be added sallets, fricases, *quelque choses,* and devised paste, as many dishes more, which make the full service no less than two and thirty dishes, which is as much as can conveniently stand on one table, and in one mess. And after this manner, you may proportion both your second and third courses, holding fullness on one half of the dishes, and show in the other, which will be both frugal in the splendour, contentment to the guest, and much pleasure and delight to the beholder."

The Latin motto beneath the coat-of-arms of the ancient city of Canterbury reads, in English, *Hail Mother of England*!—a reference to the fact that the first Christian see was established at Canterbury in the year A.D. 600. Here was—and still is—the small Roman brick building which was a Christian church before the Saxons came—and before that was the temple, perhaps, of Mithra, the god of the Roman legionary.

In the city Rome, driven out by the blond pirates from the shores of the Baltic Sea, had re-established her power: but a rule of faith, this time, rather than of force. From the first simple cathedral had grown the splendid edifice that even the bombs of the German aviators have not yet been able to destroy.

Dimly, doubtless, but none the less strongly, they realized these things, the citizens of Canterbury. They, like us, had been introduced to the blessings of totalitarianism—and they preferred the older, less "progressive" world. But, unlike us, they had the courage of their convictions. So that when, on Wednesday, 22 December, 1647, the "Cryer" of Canterbury, "by the appointment of Master *Major*[1], openly proclaimed that Christmas Day and all other super-

[1] i.e., Mayor.

stitious festivals should be put downe, and that a Market should be kept upon *Christmas day*, they rose in revolt.

". . . they continued in arms till Tuesday morning: There are none as yet dead, but diverse dangerously hurt.

"Master *Sheriffe* taking *White's* part, and striving to keep the Peace, was knockt down, and his head fearfully broke; it was God's mercy his braines were not beat out, but it should seem he has a clung (tough) pate of his own.

"They also went without *St. George's* gate, and did much injury to Mr. *Lee*.

"As I am credibly informed, the injuries done are these.

"They have beat down all the windowes of Mr. *Major's House*, burnt the Stoups at the comming in of his dore, Master *Reeves'* Windowes were broke, Master *Page*, and Master *Pollen*, one *Buchurst*, Captaine *Bridge*, Thomas *Harris*, a busie prating fellow, and others were sorely wounded.

"It is Ordered that *Richard White* and *Robert Hues*, being in fetters, be tryed according to the Law, and upon faire Composition, the multitude have delivered their Armes into the Hands of the City, upon engagements of the best of the City that no man shall further question or trouble them."

In London, where the seat of so-called government had been established, the citizens enjoyed their totalitarianism at the source, as it were.

"Parliament, on Sunday, December 25th, commonly called Christmas Day, received some complaints of the countenancing of malignant ministers in some parts of London, where they preach and use the Common Prayer Book, contrary to the order of Parliament . . . upon which some were taken into Custody."

"Mr. Harris," we read, "a Churchwarden of St. Martins, (was) ordered to be committed for bringing delinquents to preach there, and to be displaced from his office of Churchwarden."

The rulers attempted to win over adherents by bribery.

Sir Thomas Gower, writing to John Langley three days after the Christmas Day of 1652, says:

"There is little worth writing, most of the time being spent in endeavouring to take away the esteem held of Christmas Day, to which end, order was made that whoever should be protected by the State; yet I heard of no more than two who did so, and one of them had better have given £50, his wares were so dirtyed[1] and secondly, that no sermons should be preached, which was observed (for aught I hear) save at Lincoln's Inn."

Evelyn, the diarist, a staunch Episcopalian, had to suffer for his faith; his heart sickening as he saw the gradual suppression of the religion in which he had been brought up. He saw sermons banned, Church of England ministers prohibited from teaching in the schools; and he was unpleasantly surprised, on leaving Exeter Chapel on Christmas morning, 1657, to find himself surrounded by soldiers, and—with the rest of the congregation—arrested, and examined, singly, by a committee consisting of Colonel Whalley, Goffe and some others.

Those readers who think that "grilling" is a modern horror will note with a painful sense of familiarity that the panel of "examiners" sent from Whitehall first took down John Evelyn's name and address before they cross-questioned him.

"When I came before them, they took my name and abode, examined me why, contrary to the ordinance made, that none should any longer observe the superstitious time of the Nativity (so esteemed by them), I durst offend, and particularly be at Common Prayers, which they told me was but the Mass in English, and particularly pray for Charles Stuart, for which we had no Scripture. I told them we did not pray for Charles Stuart, for which we had Scripture. I told them we did not pray for Charles Stuart, but for all Christian Kings, Princes and Governors. They replied, in doing so we prayed for the King of Spain, too, who was their enemy, and a Papist, with other frivolous and ensnaring questions and much threatening; and finding no colour to detain me, they dismissed me with much pity of my ignorance. These were men of high flight and above ordinance, and spake spiteful things of our Lord's Nativity. As we went up to receive the Sacrament, the miscreants held their muskets against us, as if they would have shot us at the Altar, but yet suffering us to finish the Office of the Communion, as, perhaps, not having instructions what to do, in case they found us in that action. So I got home the next day: blessed be God!"

Cromwell, like all the other dictators whom history has known, was a great stickler for legal forms, and professed himself to be

[1] Shops, in those days, had no display windows. They were closed by shutters, which were removed in the morning.

bound by all the laws he had caused to be passed—unless he wished not to be, in which case he had another law passed, abrogating the law that he did not care for.

Thus when, just before Christmas, 1657—the last of the Protector's life—he was asked to send soldiers "to repress . . . some Congregations being met to observe this day, according to former solemnity," he did not immediately do so, but recalled that such an action (done, of course, already many times!) would be contrary "to the *Liberty of Conscience* so much owned by the *Protector* and his friends."

Of course, the arch-hypocrite was moved by no considerations of justice—or even of consistency—in thus advancing an objection to persecuting his enemies. He merely wished to asked his lick-spittle advisers to justify his prejudices by an appeal to the "law" that he had devised out of his own hatred of mankind.

They did what he wished. They told him that they understood how noble the Protector was being in his wish to let the "malignants" have their services. But . . .

". . . It being contrary" (they pointed out) "to Ordinances of Parliament, that these days should be so solemnized, the *Protector* gave way to it, and those meeting were suppressed by the Souldiers."

Christmas, indeed, has never known a bitterer enemy, since King Herod, than Oliver Cromwell; but Christmas has outlasted both.

The Protector died, leaving the crown-stamped coins—sample coins—in his cabinet, to testify to his unrealized ambition to wear the Imperial Crown of the Holy Roman Empire: his ambition being no less than that.

His amiable, unambitious son inherited the ramshackle "system" that Oliver had created, and it took less than a year to collapse. The Stuarts returned, in the person of that Prince Charles who hid in Boscobel Oak from Cromwell's soldiers.

The people welcomed him back to the throne of his fathers, for, no matter what historians say, the judgment of the people was sound. A system which arrests people for celebrating Christmas Day is an inferior system to that which permits people to celebrate in innocent, harmless fashion this ancient feast. So that Charles Stuart was to be preferred to Oliver Cromwell.

No Puritan was Charles, and with his return Christmas came back—or, rather, emerged from hiding.

"Had a pleasant walk," wrote Pepys in 1662, "to White Hall, where I intended to have received the Communion with the family, but I came a little late. So I walked up into the house, and spent my time looking over pictures, particularly the ships in King Henry VIIIth's voyage to Bullaen [Boulogne]; marking the great difference between those built then and now. By and by to the Chapel again, where Bishop Morley preached upon the Song of the Angels, 'Glory to God on high, on earth peace, and good will towards men.' Methought he made but a poor Sermon, but long, and reprehending the common jollity of the Court for the true joy that shall and ought to be on these days; he particularized concerning their excess in plays and gaming, saying that he whose office it is to keep the gamesters in order and within bounds, serves but for a second rather in a duell, meaning the groome-porter. Upon which it was worth observing how far they are come from taking the reprehensions of a bishop seriously, that they all laugh in the Chapel when he reflected upon their ill actions and courses. . . . I walked home again with great pleasure, having there dined by my wife's bed side with great content, having a mess of brave plum-porridge and a roasted pullet for dinner, and I sent for a mince pie abroad, my wife not being well, to make any herself yet."

Christmas had returned into British social life.

CHAPTER ELEVEN

# AFTER THE RESTORATION

ENGLAND under the Totalitarians was not entirely subdued to "progressive" ways of thought: as under more recent dictatorships, the opposition proved itself bravely—and astonishingly—vocal. The "underground" had its own printing-presses, and the British Museum has many examples of pamphlets, produced at the very zenith of Cromwell's ascendancy, pouring scorn and hatred on the Puritans' "zeal." The opposition even had its own newspapers, and it would appear that these—defying the extreme touchiness which characterized the Puritans (as it does all other reformer groups)—were sold more or less openly.

And, of course, since the Puritans had selected Christmas to be as it were the symbol of their opposition to "malignancy," so the "malignants" professed, in an exaggerated adherence to Christmas, their hatred of Christmas's enemies.

Number 37 of the newspaper, *Mercurius Democritus*, of date 22 December, 1652, has the following lines on Christmas, in reference, doubtless, to the fact that the editor had heard that the Protector was about to make a further "abolition" of the feast:

> Old Christmas now is come to town,
> Though few do him regard,
> He laughs to see them going down,
> That have put down his Lord.

And, in the following year, *The Vindication of Father Christmas* is explicit upon the qualities of Christmas in a manner which could only have been considered grossly disloyal by the Lord Protector and his under-strappers.

But just as history teaches us that no revolution, however brutal and "total," ever succeeds *completely*, so it teaches us that no reaction, however total, ever succeeds *completely* in reversing the effects of the revolution.

Doubtless the people of England looked forward to the end of Cromwell's dictatorship as to a time when all would once more be as it had been; when such "pagan" joys as Lords of Misrule, plum-porridge, Yule logs, boar's-heads, and the rest, would once again be theirs to enjoy; when the dour rulers would no longer be in power to call *"Verboten!"* to every single pleasure.

But, unrealized by those who had so strongly resented the Puritans' "reforms," the Commonwealth had had its effect upon them, no less than upon those who had supported the reformers. Christmas came back, indeed, but he came back wearing something of the sober manner of the men who had temporarily driven him out. Old Christmas, in the twenty years that he had been officially outlawed, had lost much of his former jauntiness. It was a quieter Christmas who came back with the Merry Monarch—who cared himself for Christmas very little more than had Oliver Cromwell; though Charles did not forbid his subjects to revive the ancient celebrations.

Indeed, when the Duke of Norfolk spent £20,000 on the first of the post-Restoration Christmasses, Charles was most displeased. So much so that Charles refused to celebrate his own Christmas, so strongly did he disapprove of His Grace's ostentation. "The Duke's munificence," says the Rev. John Ward, a contemporary diarist, "gave great offence at Court."

Charles had known actual poverty while an exile in Holland, and though he was to show himself capable of lavish spending, it was rather on others (mostly his mistresses) than on himself that he spent it. The King was an amiable person, who disliked unpleasant relations with anyone, but he had a pronounced streak of meanness in his character, and he hated to disburse sums on what we may call "anonymous" hospitality. He liked to make presents to certain chosen friends; not to a chance-collected mob.

Thus the Christmas spectacles which had proved such costly items in previous reigns were altogether missing from the budgets of Charles II, even though Parliament granted the restored king the largest civil list granted to any English king up to that time: the even to us vast sum of £1,200,000 a year. There were no more tournaments, no more "disguisings," no more masques, and Christmas and Twelfth Night revels at the Inns of Court. There were only plays; but they were no more elaborate than any to be seen by buying a ticket for Drury Lane or the Duke's Playhouse in Salisbury Square.

True, the great nobles went eagerly about restoring *their* old splendour; but the national Christmas had somehow grown less aristocratic. The strange thing is that Cromwell only pretended to be a man of the people: his dreams and secret ambitions were concerned, not with true democracy, but with the wearing of an imperial crown. Yet, for all his hypocritical attachment to democracy, his effect upon the nation had been to do the very thing to which he had given, as he thought, only lip-service.

With the Restoration, Christmas had become more the property of the people than of the rulers. In the simpler ways, however, Charles celebrated Christmas; it was only in the more ostentatious details that his Christmasses differed from those of his royal predecessors.

He suffered, for instance, to be revived the pleasant custom of the King's getting presents from his loyal subjects:

"This day" (says Pepys), "I was told that my Lady Castlemaine hath all the King's Christmas presents, made him by the Peers, given to her, which is a most abominable thing."

His own Christmas Pepys spent in modest charity: "Being a fine, light, moonshine morning, home round the city, and stopped and dropped money at five or six places, which I was the willinger to do, it being Christmas day."

Christmas, indeed, from the end of the Commonwealth onwards, loses, in our eyes, its medieval aspect, and so becomes the more familiar to us. There is a description of Christmas aboard an English man-of-war given in the diary of the Rev. Henry Teonge, a naval chaplain, which may be compared with some of the descriptions of Christmas in earlier chapters of this book.

"Dec. 25, 1675.—Crismas day wee keepe thus. At 4 in the morning our trumpeters all doe flatt their trumpetts, and begin at our Captain's cabin, and thence to all the officers' and gentlemen's cabins; playing a levite[1] at each cabine door, and bidding good morrow, wishing a merry Crismas. After they goe to their station, viz., on the poope, and sound 3 levitts in honour of the morning. At 10 wee goe to prayers and sermon; text, Zacc. ix. 9. Our Captaine had all his officers and gentlemen to dinner with him, where wee had

[1] The same as "reveille"—"levite" being a Latin and "reveille" a French word.

excellent good fayre: a rib of beife, plumb-puddings, minct pyes, &c., and plenty of good wines of severall sorts; dranke healths to the Kinge, to our wives and friends, and ended the day with much civill myrth."

Christmas had quietened down, too, in the Inns of Court, where once the benchers had spent £20,000 on the revels. The Lord of Misrule, banished *de facto* as well as *de jure* by the Lord Protector, had crept back. But how changed he was from what he had been in his heyday!

In 1682 Mr. Richard Gipps, of Gray's Inn, on promising to fill the role of Master of the Revels during the ensuing period of Christmas, was to be admitted a barrister without payment of the customary fees: a change indeed from the days when the person acting as Lord of Misrule or Master of the Revels was expected to dip deeply into his pocket to pay for the expenses of his retinue!

Retrenchment—which is a pleasanter word than "meanness"—was in the air; and the custom of the Court was not without its effect upon the general manners of the nation. Ostentation was foreign to Charles's nature, and people were not induced to make a splash in emulation of their king. Charles, indeed, was the first of the "middle-class kings" who have come to be held the ideal of British monarchy. It may seem regrettable to our way of thinking, but his own subjects could find themselves sympathizing with the royal point of view which held it to be more sensible to squander a fortune on a good-looking woman than on a tournament or a masque. There were plenty of Puritans, of course, to complain of the King's morals—or lack of them—but the very attacks of the Puritans made for the King's popularity with other classes of the people, since the Puritans (like the Russians of today) seemed to have an itch to make themselves as detested as possible.

Charles, then, seemed to the less puritanical of his subjects to exemplify the healthier, least pretentious, of English virtues. Horse-racing, cards, moderate drinking and feasting, and a somewhat less moderate fondness for the society of pretty women: there was nothing in all this which seemed abnormal or even particularly reprehensible to the average Englishman of the day.

Royal magnificence, indeed, left the Court for the princely mansions of the great nobles. Not even Hampton Court's Wren-designed annexe rivals the splendour of the mansions built for the Duke of Marlborough, for Lord Fitzwilliam, for the Earl of Leicester. It is a fact which has not had sufficient attention from the historian: the decision—made consciously or instinctively, it is hard to say—to ally the Crown, for its own support, with the People, rather than with the Aristocracy. It was Charles who first of the English kings turned from the nobility to the middle class for his support, and it is from his time that we may trace the rise of Tory Republicanism.

The age of Charles II is noteworthy for the care with which the ordinary person recorded the ordinary facts of his ordinary life: some superb diaries of the time are still extant; and from their pages we may reconstruct the life of the period. Pepys, Evelyn, Sydenham, Newton, Ward are but a few of those whose recorded experiences, made day to day, paint for us an accurate picture of a time which has a curious aspect of modernity in that, like our own, it appears to be an age of averages: there are no violent extremes, such as are to be found in all earlier and even in some later times.

To compare the Christmasses of one age with the Christmasses of lesser folk of another age is absurd as a guide to changing manners, but something of the really profound change which had overtaken English society in the years between the outbreak of the Civil War and the Restoration may be appreciated in considering differences between the Christmasses of Richard Evelyn, High Sheriff of Surrey, and of Sir John Reresby, Lord of the Manor of Thrybergh. We have seen with what formality Mr. Evelyn set out the functions and the rights of his Lord of Misrule; Sir John Reresby's Christmas, though no less lavish, was of an obviously far less pretentious sort.

On Christmas Eve and Christmas Day, Sir John invited some of his poorer tenants to a celebration; on St. Stephen's (Boxing) Day he invited the farmers and the more substantial tenants—fifty-four of them. On St. John's Day forty-five of the chief tenants sat down to dinner at their landlord's table; and so on, in an ascending scale of social degree; until Twelfth Day, when seven gentlemen and tradesmen sat down together.

Sir John did his guests handsomely: it is recorded that Mr. Belton, "an ingenious clergyman," did himself more than merely handsomely, since the host observes, a little critically, that Mr. Belton was "too much of a good fellow," on the occasion.

"The expense of liquor," Sir John noted, "both of wine and others, was considerable"; and the expense, two years later, must have been even higher, since no fewer than three hundred were entertained on New Year's Day, "so that whole sheep were roasted and served up to feed them. For music," the generous host adds, "I had four violins, besides bagpipes, drums and trumpets."

Another great landowner of the period, Sir William Hollis, of Houghton Chapel, Northamptonshire, kept open house during a "Christmas" that the knight kept up from 1 November until 2 February: three months in all! It was the amiable habit of Sir William to welcome any man who presented himself at Houghton, and to permit him to stay three days "without being asked who he was, or from whence he came."

There is no lack of hospitality discernible in these post-Commonwealth Christmasses, but the old formality, the old ritual, has obviously departed. The Lord of Misrule, if he is not yet quite dead, is dying, and only the pale ghost of him is to linger in the Inns of Court, army-messes and boys' schools, until, somewhere in the nineteenth century, he makes his quiet and unnoticed exit.

The Commonwealth killed him, for a sufficient reason. Kings could permit, and even encourage, a parody of royalty, *so long as royalty remained invulnerable as an idea: as a social concept.*

In the past no one had doubted the idea of kingship, and no king had doubted it himself. Kings had been killed, yes. Deposed and killed; even imprisoned and subjected to the most degrading indignities. But all these things had been offered to *persons*: it was not until Cromwell came along that insults were offered, not so much to a man wearing the crown, as to the crown itself, and all that it stood for.

It was more than a revolution in British politics when the Parliament voted in favour of the execution of Charles I: it was a revolution in human ways of thought—and whatever else kinghood was to retain in the counter-revolution, it was never to recapture that mystic quality which was implied in the phrase, "King, by the Grace of God."

There was a general feeling, after the Restoration, that kingship had been dealt so dangerous a blow by Cromwell that it might not be able to withstand further corrosive assaults of laughter and parody.

Thus the Lord of Misrule's long life came to an end. He had had the misfortune to be violently attacked by the Puritans and put quietly away by the Royalists. No custom could have been expected to survive attack by both sections of the nation.

In the *Cronia* of Lucian, the Latin poet, "Cronosolon," priest of Cronos, lays down the rules for the festival of *Saturnalia*; and included in those "laws" is the rule that "all men shall be equal, slave and free, rich and poor, one with another"—a rule whose application gave rise, among many things, to the Lord of Misrule, however variously named.

He did not die altogether at the Restoration, and lingered on, the pale shadow of his former self, in out-of-the-way corners; as the Tudor fashion in military uniforms lingers in the costume of the Yeomen of the Guard.

The headmaster of Downside College kindly supplied me with the following note with regard to the "Christmas King": "The custom disappeared at Downside in 1878, as boys then went home for Christmas."

I can trace no later survival of a custom for whose origins the historian must search in the mists of our race's pre-history.

For the people, Christmas began to assume that universal character which has made it the feast, not only of the year, but of the world. And it acquired this character by losing some of its more extravagant features, so that even the very poorest could join with the very richest in celebrating it.

All the same, Christmas does not outlaw unhappiness, much though human nature would make it do so, and bad fortune may fall as well on Christmas Day as on any other. It would be hard to say whether or not James II, fleeing from England, found himself safe at Ambleteuse, in Brittany, on Christmas Day, 1688; but there can be no doubt of William III's sentiments when they brought him the news of his wife's death, of smallpox, on 28 December, 1694. And certainly not the least shadow of doubt concerning the sentiments of Sir John Fenwick, the Jacobite, on his learning that an Act of Attainder, carrying the death-penalty, had been passed at Christmastide, 1696.

Peter the Great of Russia spent a much more pleasant Christmas in the following year. Peter, deciding to westernize his more than half-Oriental state, had come to the West to learn for himself what he wished his subjects later to know.

He wanted a navy, and as a first step in getting himself one he studied shipbuilding at Deptford, on the Thames, staying at near-by Sayes Court, a pleasant country-house that he had rented of Evelyn, the diarist. Evelyn was an ardent collector of rare herbs and flowers, and how the Czar and his entourage destroyed their landlord's valuable herbal-garden by leaping on to it out of the first-floor windows may be read in fuller detail elsewhere, as may the account of the Muscovites' drinking-habits—startling even in that age of hard drinking.

Peter, especially, astounded the English with his habit of lacing a pint of neat brandy with a handful of red pepper, and draining the mixture in one long gulp. We may be sure that there was no lack of brandy—or of red pepper, either!—at Sayes Court, Deptford, at Christmas, 1697.

The death of William III on Candlemas Day, 1702, and the consequent accession of Queen Anne—last of the Stuarts to wear the crown of Great Britain—did nothing to diminish the pace with which England moved towards the Industrial Revolution.

This Revolution, which has changed the face of the world, which has altered the fundamentals of human destiny, did not begin in the towns. It began in the country, and it originated almost entirely in the work of one man: a gentleman-farmer named Jethro Tull.

This Tull had an inquiring mind, and a certain inventive faculty. He studied land-productivity in relation to manpower, and then invented mechanical contrivances by which the number of men necessary to work the arable land was enormously reduced, while the productivity of the land was enormously increased. The effect of Tull's inventions was to reduce the price of corn (and thus to lessen the wealth, and so the political power, of the farmers) and enormously to lessen the need of agricultural workers at the same time as vastly cheapened food made for an astonishing rise in the population. So a condition favourable to the creation of the factory-system was established through a gentleman-farmer's invention of the mechanical dibber, by which seeds, instead of being scattered lavishly in the wind, to sprout where they fell, were planted in the ground, safe from wind and birds. Seed used in ounces in Tull's dibber raised more crops than pounds scattered broadcast and haphazard by the sower.

The displaced farm-workers flocked for work to the towns; and in the towns, living mostly on cheap gin and cheap bread, they multiplied like the rabbits on the untended land that they had abandoned.

Mechanical contrivances were applied to other things than agriculture, and factories sprang up all over the country, manned by the depressed thousands who could no longer find a living on the land.

Slums grew, but so did wealth; and the country habits were brought into the towns, while the distinguishing marks of the old country life gradually faded away. Customs, owing to the shifting of people, tended to become less parochial: men kept their festivals in the same way, whether in Manchester or in London. Only in those parts of the country untouched by the deep changes of the Industrial Revolution—such as Cornwall and Lincolnshire—did the old country ways survive hardly modified by the universalizing tendencies of the economic change which had overtaken the nation. Doubtless the change is clearer to us than it was to those who were contemporary with its beginnings.

It must, indeed, have seemed the same sort of world to Queen Anne as it had to Charles II when she splendidly entertained the new King of Spain at Windsor, just after the Christmas of 1703-4. His Majesty showed the traditional Bourbon tact—and recognition of the *real* importance of persons—by paying compliments to the Queen's favourite, Sarah, Duchess of Marlborough.

And it can hardly have occurred to Queen Anne that the welcome that she extended at Christmas, 1704, to the Duke of Marlborough, returning victorious from his costly triumphs, was extended to the practitioner of a form of warfare which was already doomed, and that the new industrial century just beginning would see outmoded as finally as the war-technique of Queen Boadicea.

No, destiny is visible only at a distance, and Marlborough came home to spend his Christmas, doubtless thinking himself as important as he was famous; as indispensable as he had been successful.

"But perhaps the most palpable triumph of Marlborough was the transferring of the military trophies which he had taken, from the Tower, where they were first deposited, to Westminster Hall. This was done by each soldier carrying a standard or other trophy, amid the thunders of artillery and the hurrahs of the people; such a spectacle never having been witnessed since the Spanish Armada. The Royal Manor of Woodstock was granted him, and Blenheim Mansion erected at the cost of the nation."

The tournaments, mummings, "disguisings," masques and revels of the previous reigns have gone completely: Queen Anne's Christmasses are as "modern" as Queen Victoria's. The theatrical element, which, in earlier times, was as important a factor of Christmas as the element of eating, is now altogether missing. At least, it is missing in the Court Christmasses, though traces of it linger in the Christmasses of humbler folk, especially in the country districts.

A more intimate entertainment is to take the place of the costly shows of other days: an entertainment very, very cheap in itself—and one that rich and poor alike may enjoy—but one which can, and often does, lead to the expenditure of vast sums. Playing-cards are to become, before the century is a decade on, the craze of the upper classes. And the eighteenth century, even if some know it as The Age of Reason, should accurately be known as The Age of Cards.

Addison and Steele paint faithful, even if slightly over-coloured, pictures of the country life of their time; and in Sir Roger de Coverley's attitude towards Christmas—"I love to rejoice their poor hearts at this season, and to see the whole village merry in my great hall"—we may see, not so much the author's, but every middle-class Englishman's ideal of the true Christmas sentiment; and often we find the pages of *The Spectator* breathing sentiments which may be described only as purely Dickensian.

So much for the country, where fashions change more slowly, and, save in exceptional times, food is more easily come by; and so appetites, by habit, larger. The old family games, which will be described in a later chapter, were played about the Yule log or its anaemic descendant, and that element of mysticism which united Christmas present with Christmas pre-Christian was not missing, as the maids cast their simple spells to ensure luck through the coming year.

In the towns pleasures were more sophisticated, as they always have been; and imports from a foreign world now almost completely opened up to trade made for new standards of luxury among the middle class. The mechanical improvements which had been applied to many trades had not given the art of printing the miss, and now the novel came to be added to Christmas pleasures; heavy both in bulk and in manner though it sometimes was.

Gin was the vice and the curse of the early eighteenth century, in whose London could be seen grog-shops advertising their wares by a placard: "Drunk for a Penny; Dead-drunk for Twopence!" Gross though they are, Hogarth's etchings are, we feel, not too exaggerated in their presentation of the delirious madness which followed in the train of cheap gin.

Gin was for the lower orders. It had, indeed, risen a little in the social scale when Dickens could make Sairey Gamp pour it out from her little brown tea-pot[1]. But the middle and upper classes also developed a fondness for strong drink as the century progressed, even if not for such poison as grog-shop gin. Favourable trade-treaties with Portugal brought port to every Briton's table able to afford eighteen-pence for a bottle of crusted Lisbon. And jealous of the trade that Portugal was doing with Britain, France—not letting the intermittent warfare interfere with trade—negotiated with Britain to let in her clarets and burgundies, her champagne and brandy, on favourable terms.

The cookery-books of the day show the change in manners: where the Middle Ages put spice into every dish, the eighteenth century put some form of alcohol; a habit which survives with us only in our plum-pudding, our trifle, our mincemeat and Christmas cake.

Cards, then, came into fashion in the eighteenth century, along with a taste for other sorts of alcohol than the traditional beer and ale which were still, in those days, brewed at home, save in the biggest of the towns.

But there was a third pleasure to come into fashion, which was calculated to give more innocent pleasure to more people than even innocently played cards did.

This was the pantomime, a form of entertainment which, though it has a Greek name and may be traced back to pre-Christian times, has somehow come to be accepted as the one peculiarly English contribution to Christmas. No other nation has yet succeeded in imitating the English pantomime; and as it was in England, in

[1] This, and some other "Dickensian" inventions, were lifted from the ingenious and immortal Henry Fielding.

the reign of George I, that the comic pantomime was first introduced in its perfected form, so in England—or Britain, rather—it has remained. It is one of those home-products which do not bear export, even for dollars!

On 26 December, 1717, Rich, who was the licensee of the theatre in Lincoln's Inn Fields, produced *Harlequin Executed,* the first of the innumerable series of English pantomimes. "To retrieve the credit of his theatre," says Davies, "Rich created a species of dramatic composition, unknown to this, and I believe to any other country, which he called a pantomime; it consisted of two parts—one serious and the other comic. By the help of gay scenes, fine habits, grand dances, appropriate music, and other decorations, he exhibited a story from Ovid's *Metamorphoses,* or some other fabulous writer.

"Between the pauses or acts of this serious representation, he interwove a comic fable; consisting chiefly of the courtship of Harlequin and Columbine, with a variety of surprising adventures and tricks, which were produced by the magic wand of Harlequin; such as the sudden transformation of palaces and temples to huts and cottages, of men and women into wheelbarrows and joint stools, of trees turned into houses, colonnades to beds of tulips, and mechanics' shops into serpents and ostriches."

This classic description of the first of our pantomimes could very well serve—making allowances for some archaisms—for a description of any modern pantomime, so well did Rich make his pattern to serve for all time, and so little has that pattern changed with the changing years.

From the date of the first pantomime until his death in 1761—a period of forty-five years—Rich produced one successful piece after another, so that "the credit of his theatre" was certainly saved, and a new pleasure added to the traditional English Christmas.

"No other style of entertainment," Ashton adds, "was ever so popular. Garrick tried spectacular drama, and failed."

Walpole, writing to Lady Ossory, 30 December, 1772, says: "Garrick has brought out what he calls a *Christmas tale,* adorned with the most beautiful scenes, next to those in the Opera at Paradise, designed by Loutherburg. They have much ado to save the piece from being sent to the Devil. It is believed to be Garrick's own, and a new proof that it is possible to be the best actor and the worst author in the world, as Shakespeare was just the contrary."[1]

Yet though Garrick, as Walpole reported, "failed in spectacular drama," there was a play which had become the customary stock offering on Boxing Day, and which threatened, for a time, to outdo the Rich pantomime in popularity as the traditional Christmas theatrical entertainment.

This was the play, *George Barnwell,* or, to give it is full title, *The London Merchant; or the History of George Barnwell,* which was first acted at Drury Lane in 1731, and was revived, as a curiosity, only a few months ago in London.

It is not easy for the modern playgoer to understand the great success that this piece enjoyed for many generations, any more than he or she may account for the success of that other "winner," *Douglas,* which also was recently revived at Edinburgh.

*George Barnwell* is one of those highly "moral" melodramas in which our tougher—and so infinitely more sentimental—ancestors took such delight. The news of the play's success reaching the ears of Queen Caroline, she sent for a copy of the play to read. Hone, in his *Every-Day Book,* actually notes it as an extraordinary occurrence that "the representation of this tragedy was omitted in the Christmas holidays of 1819 at both the theatres for the first time."

"It was considered," says Ashton, "a highly moral play, and was acted for the particular benefit of apprentices, to deter them from the crime of theft, and from keeping company with bad women"; but in the end it was the pantomime and not the moral play which was to become the traditional fare in the British theatre at Christmas. In recent years, it is true, there has been a tendency in the opposite direction—such plays as *Treasure Island, Where the Rainbow Ends* and *Peter Pan* have been shown at some theatres as an alternative to the pantomime, but the pantomime still holds foremost place as the traditional Christmas entertainment.

It should not shock the reader to know that to discover the origin of the pantomime—as indeed of all our modern theatrical entertainments—we must look to the sacred offices of the Church.

There were theatrical representations before the birth of Christ; even before the building of the city of Rome; but with the collapse of the Roman civil culture, and the usurpation of Roman imperial

[1] This typically dogmatic opinion of Walpole's is not supported by those who actually saw Shakespeare act.

rule by barbarian invaders, the Church became the sole repository of learning, the sole guardian of culture, the sole patron of the arts and sciences.

Inevitably, then, all learning and art, if they were to find a patron, had to assume an ecclesiastical tone and colour; and long before the end of the Dark Ages, in which the lamp of civilization burnt with a dull, smoky flame, every human activity, save that of war, was bound up in some way with the usage and the policy of the Church—and even into warfare the influence of Rome had penetrated.

But though they were to prove themselves the faithful preservers of a civilization that, without their care, would have been altogether lost to Europe, the men of the Church were still men . . . and not gods. They suffered, like the laity, from the stringencies imposed by political and economic upset; and their intellectual level suffered a decline in common with that of the mass of the people.

The sophistication of Periclean Greece and Augustan Rome vanished from art; in its place came a sentiment almost primitive; certainly simple, in our eyes, almost to the point of childishness. The descent to primitivism had been quick; the way back to the intellectual levels of pagan Greece and Rome was to be a long and difficult achievement.

Art, then, had almost to begin anew. Sculpture, painting, literature had, as it were, to be mastered all over again; of all the arts, only architecture—oddly enough—continued to survive at a level higher than the essentially primitive; possibly because the builders' guild was among the few to remain organized, corporate bodies on the collapse of the Empire.

The beginnings, then, of our modern theatre were beginnings indeed, and Miles, in his well-known *Christmas in Ritual and Tradition,* is right when he says that "the medieval religious drama was a natural development from the Catholic liturgy, not an imitation of classical models."

At the beginning of Christianity the Church was strongly opposed to all forms of drama, "because of their connexion with heathenism and the licence towards which they tended"; but the love of spectacle, the love of a show, *the desire to use one's eyes,* in short, is fundamental in our human nature. And if the Church sought to repress that desire because she seemed to see that it was leading men to evil things, she was forced to recognize that the need could not be abolished, but must be turned to serve the good.

At the base of all religious ritual is drama: the priest is, in essence, *an actor*. At the beginning he was the only actor in the drama, but gradually his monopoly began to be shared; and Miles points out that "the offices of the Church are in great part *dialogues* between priest and people, or between two sets of singers." And he adds: "It was from this antiphonal song, this alternation of versicle and response, that the religious drama of the Middle Ages took its rise."

It became the practice to insert dialogue, question-and-answer, additions into the old antiphons. An example from the famous monastery of St. Gall in Switzerland, of the ninth century, gives one a good idea of the type. These antiphonal dialogues were called "tropes." The Christmas trope from St. Gall goes as follows (in the English translation):

> ALL SING:
> Today must we sing of a Child, whom in unspeakable wise His Father begat before all times, and whom, within time, a glorious Mother brought forth.
> QUESTION:
> Who is this Child whom we proclaim worthy of such great praise?
> ANSWER:
> This is he whose coming to earth was foreseen and foretold long ago by the foreordained and chosen sharer of God's secrets!

Now, though the St. Gall MS. does not actually say so, the "Question" and "Answer" must have been said by different persons or different choirs; for "it was from an Easter trope in the manuscript, the *Quem quaeritis* (Whom do ye seek?), a dialogue between the three Maries and the angel at the sepulchure, that the liturgical drama sprang. The trope" (says Miles), "became very popular, and was gradually elaborated into a short symbolic drama, and its popularity led to the composition of similar pieces for Christmas and Ascensiontide."

This Easter trope ran as follows:

> On the Nativity of the Lord at Mass, let there be ready two deacons, having on dalmatics, behind the altar, saying:
> *Quem quaeritis in praesepe, pastores, dicite?*—Whom seek ye in the manger, Shepherds? Say!

Let two cantors in the choir answer:

*Salvatorem Christum Dominum, infantem pannis involutum, secundum sermonem angelicum*—The Saviour, Christ the Lord; an infant wrapped in cloths, according to the angelic word.

And the deacons:

*Adest hic parvulus cum Maria, matre sua, de qua, vaticinando, Isaias Propheta: ecce virgo concipiet et pariet filium; et nuntiantes dicite quia natus est*—Here is the Little One with His Mother, Mary, of whom, in prophesying, Isaiah the Prophet said: Behold a Virgin shall conceive and bring forth a Son! And you: say you that He is indeed born!

Then let the cantor lift up his voice and say:

*Alleluia, alleluia, jam vere scimus Christum natum in terris, de quo canite, omnes, cum Propheta, dicentes: Puer natus est!*—Hallelujah, hallelujah! Now indeed we know that Christ is born on earth, of whom sing ye all with the Prophet, saying: A Son is born!

Miles significantly points out that the two deacons, in their "broad vestments," were doubtless intended to represent the midwives mentioned in the "Gospel of St. James"—now banished from Church usage. As he says: "The dramatic character of this is very marked."

From this early ritualization developed a Church office which was a true dramatic interlude: the Epiphany play known generally as the *Stella,* though it was also known as *Tres Reges* (Three Kings), *Magi* and *Herodes.* In the opinion of Chambers, the play centres around a dramatized Offertory, and he suggests that as it was the custom for Christian kings to present gifts of gold, frankincense and myrrh to the altar on Twelfth Day—the present King of Great Britain does it still by proxy, in the Royal Chapel of St. James's—the ceremony of the *Tres Reges,* or *Stella,* was devised for use when there was no actual king able to be present.

In the version of the *Stella* which was used in Rouen, three clerics, playing the part of the Three Kings, came into the church from the east, north and south, accompanied by their servants, who were carrying the Magi's gifts. The "king" from the east, pointing to the star with his wand, says:

*Stella fulgore nimio rutilat!* — The star glows with exceeding brightness!

The second king says:

"Father Christmas," officially abolished with other "heathenries" by the Commonwealth Government, reappears, after the restoration of the Monarchy, at the Yuletide feastings of Charles II.

This old print, of *circa* 1720, is entitled "Christmas Gambolls." It shows Cheapside with the spire of St. Mary-le-Bow in the middle distance. A town-constable is moving on an unlicensed eighteenth-century "barrow boy" to the interest of the crowd.

*Quae quem regem regum natum demonstrat!*—Which shows that the King of Kings is born!

While the third king adds:

*Quem venturum olim prophetae signaverant.*—Whose coming the prophecies of old had foretold.

Then the "Magi," kissing one another, sing:

*Eamus ergo, et inquiramus eum, offerentes ei munera: aurum, thus et myrrham.*—Therefore let us go and ask after Him, offering Him gifts: gold, incense and myrrh.

The play then continues the action until, at the invitation of the "midwives," who formed part of the medieval legend of the Nativity, the kings approach the Crib, and present their offering, in dramatically terse phrases:

*Suscipe, Rex, aurum!*—Receive, O King, this gold!
*Tolle thus, tu vere Deus!*—Take the incense, True God!
*Myrrham, signum sepulturae!* — (Take) myrrh, the symbol of burial!

These simple "interludes" gradually became less simple as characters began to be multiplied: some of them not always to be found in the Gospel narrative, save by inference. And some of these "co-opted" characters were destined to have a profound effect upon the play itself. Such a character was King Herod, whom the early dramatists had a tendency to equate with Satan, and whose unqualified wickedness made him a most popular character indeed with the people. Shakespeare's making Hamlet say that his uncle "out-Herods Herod" shows how great a popularity the character of the infanticide king had enjoyed, and as himself or as his numerous imitations Herod still holds the public attention, for he is the eternal villain; and he is the moustache-twirling rogue who forecloses on the mortgage and threatens the virtue of the paupers' daughter no less than he is the principal character in a melodrama on tour in 1950 called *Hitler's Mistress*!

"At first," says Miles, "Herod holds merely a mild conversation with the Magi, begging them to tell him when they have found the new-born king; in later versions of the play, however, his wrath is shown on learning that the Wise Men have departed home by another way; he breaks out into bloodthirsty tirades, orders the slaying of Innocents, and in one form takes a sword and brandishes it in the air. He becomes, in fact, the outstanding figure in the drama, and one can understand why it was sometimes named after him."

At Laon the actors even represented the slaying of the Innocents, and the character of Rachel ("weeping for her children!") was introduced into the Laon *Stella*.

The writers who prepared the scripts for the *Stellas* and *Herodes* had as honest a contempt for mere chronology as had Shakespeare. Their chief concern was with *effect,* and they would bring the most incongruous characters together in order to achieve that effect. Thus in the play—or the liturgical drama, rather—called the *Prophetae,* the Prophets, together with Virgil, Nebuchadnezzar and the Erythræan Sibyl—an odd collection, forsooth!—give their testimony to the Jews who refuse to accept Christ as the Messiah.

Later, as this drama became more popular, more prophets were added to the *dramatis personae,* and from the *Prophetae* sprang the various cycles of Old Testament drama which were one of the chief entertainments of the Middle Ages.

An early example of one of these play-cycles was the Anglo-Norman play of *Adam,* which, beginning with the Fall, continued through the story of Cain and Abel, and ended with the testimony of the Prophets.

These plays had all sprung from an elaboration of the established Church ritual, and at first—for many centuries, indeed—they were played nowhere save in church, and on no occasion save in connexion with a church ceremony. But these dramas becoming as elaborated in the number of the players as in the complexity of their themes, they came at last to be too elaborate for the church to hold, and they took themselves outside. At first in the precincts of the church, and later farther afield—by the market cross, before the city hall, and so on.

Thus was drama once more secularized; for though the stage long continued to present its plays with consistently religious themes, the characters which were added to the "stock" characters of Adam and Eve, Cain and Abel, Noah, Ham, Shem and Japhet, and so on, were anything but "religious" in their conception. A regrettable weakness of the audiences was to be seen in their decided preference for the Devil over the more respectable characters of the plays—"mysteries" was the English name for them—and especially their preference for the Devil in his guise of combined knock-about comedian and smart-Aleck. You will remember that Absalom, in Chaucer's *Miller's Tale,* used to play "Herod" in the local mystery.

As early as the eleventh century the elaboration of the liturgical dramas had taken them outside the church building, into the churchyard and even farther afield; and, owing to the large "cast," laymen as well as clergy had begun to act in these dramas. Another innovation which further secularized these originally ecclesiastical plays was the change-over from the use of Latin to that of the vulgar tongue. We find, no later than the twelfth century, an "Adam" in Norman-French, and a "Misterio de los Reyes Magos" in Spanish: the latter "a highly developed vernacular *Stella.*"

"The thirteenth and fourteenth centuries saw a progressive supplanting of Latin by the common speech, until, in the great cycles, only a few scraps of the church language were left to tell of the liturgical origin of the drama."[1]

Christmas was not, in northern lands, the best time for the presentation of outdoor shows, and so the outdoor plays tended to be given during the warmer months of the year. It was not, indeed, until the play went, as it were, indoors again that we find it making a part of the Christmas entertainment.

All the same, there are records of religious plays acted in England at Christmastide. One was given at Tintinhull, in 1451, and at Dublin, in 1528. The *Stella* apparently survived the Reformation, since it is found acted (in church) as late as 1579.

In the literal sense of the word, the play was popularized when its composition passed out of the hands of the clergy and into those of the layman. Medieval religion was no chill, formal thing; the man of the Middle Ages believed that, since he was created in the image and likeness of his Creator, the Creator must be remarkably like the man who worshipped Him. And this being so, we are struck by a naturalness in presenting sacred subjects which, until we have recollected the frame of mind of the writer, sometimes strikes us as disrespectful; though, of course, there was no intention of

[1] Miles: *Christmas in Ritual and Tradition.*

disrespect in the writers of the plays which went up to make the Chester, Towneley and "Coventry" cycles.

Take, for example, the handling of Mary and Joseph's arrival at the Bethlehem inn, where "there was no room." (I have modernized the medieval spelling, for clearness.)

JOSEPH: Hail, worshipful sir, and good day!
A citizen of this city ye seem to be;
Of lodging for spouse and me I you pray,
For truly this woman is full weary,
And fain at rest, sir, would she be;

We would fulfil the bidding of our emperor,
For to pay tribute, as right is our (i.e., as is our duty)
And to keep ourselves from dolour (trouble)
We are come to this city.

(Following the Gospel narrative, the Host tells the travellers that there is no room in his inn.)

Ah, sweet wife, what shall we do?
Where shall we lodge this night?
Unto the Father in Heaven pray we so,
Us to keep from every wicked wight!

The audience, listening to this simple phrasing, was able to identify itself, not only with the speakers' sentiments, but with the speakers themselves. Mary and Joseph were not, for them, semi-divine beings, robed in glory, but two bewildered human beings, in distress, and meeting—alas!—the too-common response to an appeal for aid.

In one of the plays of the York Cycle this enchanting dialogue ensues between Joseph and Mary. The husband has gone out, immediately after the Nativity, to fetch a light. On his return he says:

Say, Marie doghtir, what chere with the?[1]
MARY: Right goode, Joseph, as has been ay.
JOS.: O Marie, what swete thyng is that on thy kne?
MARY: It is my sone, the soth to saye,
that is so gud.
JOS.: Well is me I bade this day,
to se this foode! (being)

[1] So that the "Wot cheer, me 'ole darlin'!" of our Cockneys is less slang English than ancient English!

Me merueles merkill (marvels much) of this light
That thus-gates shynes in this place,
For suth it is a selcouth (wonderful) sight!

We have already seen, in an earlier chapter of this book, the medieval playwrights' handling of the scene where the Angels announce the Nativity to the Shepherds; some of the best writing of the sort is done with the Shepherds as the central characters; for these simple persons lend themselves to the most naturalistic descriptions. The Shepherds in the Chester Cycle refer to the local brew of ale, just as the musical-hall comedian today secures a laugh by some apparently unpremeditated reference to a local tavern.

The Chester Shepherds drink "ale of Halton" with their meal of sour milk, onions, garlick and leeks, green cheese, a sheep's head soused in ale, and other dainties. Their lad, Trowle, a butt for their humour and a mouthpiece for the political views of the author, is a type which has become established in the drama of the world. There is a bit of Trowle in Sam Weller and Sancho Panza, in Falstaff and Sam Costa, in every "stooge," indeed, who ever grew from a dramatist's pen.

They speak their mind, as "stooges" have the right. When they catch sight of Joseph, one exclaims:

Whatever this ould man that heare is,
Take heede how his head is whore (hoary),
His beirde is like a buske of breyers (a bush of briars),
With a pound of heaire about his mouth and more!

But their hearts are sound, for all their seeming impudence.

They give the Child presents, as simple as their thoughts and speech: a bell, a flask, a spoon to eat with, and a cape. Trowle has nothing to offer but a pair of his wife's "hosen"—old ones; but he offers those . . . and they are accepted. Four boys give a bottle, a hood, a pipe and a nut-hook.

THE FOURTH BOY

Nowe, childe, although thou be comon from God,
And be God thy selfe in thy manhoode,
Yet I knowe that in thy childehoode
Thou wylte for sweete meate loke.

To pull down aples, peares and plumes,
Oulde Joseph shall not nede to hurte his thombes,
Because thou hast not pleintie of crombes,
I geve thee heare my nutthocke!

The extraordinary quality of this simple art is never more strongly felt than at this point, where the gifts of the Shepherds, one feels, are so much more valuable than the gold, the frankincense and the myrrh which are to follow after.

Mak, in one of the two shepherd-scenes in the Towneley Play Cycle, is an immortal character: the amiable, quick-witted work-shy, who will venture his neck rather than do honest toil. The Eternal Fly-boy, the Immortal Spiv, with whom honest folk are always so bewitched, and for whom they feel, despite their own having chosen the way of honesty, an unconquerable sympathy and admiration.

But all the time, whether they are dealing with "comics" like Mak or Trowle or "straight characters" like the Shepherds, the writers consistently exhibit their own unique mixture of naïvety and reverence: a mixture which was as much the product of their age as of the plays' authors. Here is The Third Shepherd, in a play from the Towneley Cycle, addressing the Holy Child, as He lies in His crib:

Hail, derling dere,
    Full of godhede!
I pray thee be nere
    When that I have nede.
Hail! swete is thy chere (face);
    My hart wolde blede
To see thee sitt here
    In so poore wede,
With no pennys.
    Hail! put forth thy dall (hand)!
I bring thee bot a ball;
    Have and play thee with all,
And go to the tenis!

These plays—derived from earlier liturgical dramas—were to be found in every country of Europe, which, until the first quarter of the sixteenth century was over, shared a common religious belief. Yet the plays of each country, be they English, French, Italian,

Spanish or German, are the original products of their individual national sentiment. The plays are never translation, even though there is, of course, a unifying treatment and a common tendency to like the same characters and similar scenes. The comic Shepherds enter into the cast of the French "mysteries," no less than into that of the English. A character in the French "mysteries" corresponding to Mak in the Towneley Cycle is the Shepherd Rifflart, a true comic type.

Classicism, however, was felt in France earlier than in England: by about 1500 the Shepherds and similar characters cease to be mere French rustics, and become woodland creatures of classical mythology—as interpreted by the not-so-very classical writers of the time. A "mystery" printed in France in 1507 has nymphs and oreads among its minor characters. The transition from the "mystery" to the modern play was as gradual in France as elsewhere; the introduction of "classical" elements marked the beginning of the change.

Germany appears to have adopted the Christmas play very late—just as she retained paganism for centuries after the rest of Europe had been converted to Christianity. Indeed, the Christmas play appears in Germany only on the very eve of the Reformation. And, just as the Christmas play appeared in Germany on the verge of that religious revolution which was to prove such an enemy of such plays, so the Christmas play in Germany was to outlast its performance elsewhere.

Yet even in France, though the "mystery" was attacked both by Reformers and Catholics—for different, but sufficient reasons—it survived, in out-of-the-way places, all through the sixteenth, seventeenth, eighteenth, and even the nineteenth century, so there is a record of a "Herod" play having been performed at Dinan, in Brittany, as late as 1886; and right up to the end of the nineteenth century in England—and perhaps to an even later date—Christmas plays were being celebrated in the English country districts, notably in the neighbourhood of Leeds. The Leeds play had a character all its own, for its characters included not only the Seven Champions of Christendom—including a mysterious "St. Thewlis" (obviously derived from "Thule"), who was the "champion" of some northern kingdom—but the King of Egypt, his daughter, and his court-jester. The "action" of the play concerned the combat of the Seven Champions—who occasionally had a recruit in the shape of "St.

Peter of Rome"—for the hand of the King of Egypt's daughter. St. George always won!

In other parts of England the play was given with different characters, and was sometimes called "St. George and the Dragon," and included such personages in its cast as Father Christmas and the Turkish Knight.

If the plays are no longer given, it is only in comparatively recent times that their performance has been discontinued.

In the Saxon Erzegebirge the play still survives, as it does in certain of the remoter parts of Switzerland, France and Spain.

To this Christmas drama belongs the Christmas crib, which will be considered later. But here it should be pointed out that the crib—called *presepe* in Italy—is, in reality, a kind of static drama, a play arrested at one point, as though the wand of a magician had frozen the characters stiff at one supreme moment of their existence. To adopt a term from the cinema, the crib is a "still" of the whole drama of the Nativity.

The Italian "mysteries" were never as robust—as coarse, if you like—as their French and English and German counterparts, yet the odd thing is that their origin was not in liturgical practice. So that they should have been more, not less, earthy.

Where the "mysteries" of the more northern lands sprang from parts of the Church services which were "acted," the Italian "mysteries"—*divozioni,* they were called—were derived from the *laude,* recitatives in the vernacular, which were sung all over Italy by the wandering *Flagellants* or *Battuti*. These persons, who represented but one of the many outbreaks of the "dancing mania" in Europe, were inspired to their peculiar religious hysteria by the appalling conditions of an Italy ravaged with equal thoroughness by the plague and the robber barons—no one could say which was the more ferocious or the more exacting of toll.

The historian is surely justified in deciding that no one at that time of bloody anarchy—at least, no one who lived in a town or city or whose country lay within the orbit of the predatory warriors—was completely sane; and a vast number of persons were undeniably rendered at least temporarily mad by the horrors of everyday life.

Among these persons were many who, deciding that neither plague nor baron had wronged them sufficiently, went in bands, throughout the country, lashing each other until they bled, in remission for the sins which had brought such terrible punishment upon Italy.

These flagellants—who were bitterly persecuted by the civil power, and not at all smiled upon by the Church—used to chant stories from the Bible and the New Testament in the vulgar tongue. These chants resembled Negro "spirituals"; being, indeed, like those "spirituals," the spontaneous expression of a primitive mind's misery, expressing itself in religious "uplift."

These chants were simple in narrative, but, because they were sung by people constantly on the march, had a rhythm which made them popular long after the flagellant movement had died away, and that they were sung to words that even the humblest could understand, made them loved where the Church's Latin hymns could never be more than reverenced.

Out of the *laude*—as the flagellants' "spirituals" were called—came the *divozioni,* which were the narrative *laude* with acting added. The rustics turn up in the Italian plays of the Nativity, as they do in the French and the English plays, but there is what some may call a refinement, and some a dullness—a respectability is perhaps the most accurate phrase—in the Italian "mysteries" which prevents them from ever acquiring that earthy element which is present in the northern plays, and which, gradually displacing the purely religious element, produced the modern purely secular play, and so was the origin of the modern stage in all its aspects. There is nothing that I can trace in Italian folk-drama of the religious sort which can show such lines as these, for example, which come from the Bovey Tracey Mummers' Play:

> In comes I, the Turkish Knight,
> Come from the Turkish land to fight!

or

> Here comes I, Beelzebub,
> And in me hand I carries me club!

Yet the earthy element is very pronounced in the Provençal, Catalan and Basque plays, which are given to this day.

By growing nearer to Nature, and away from religious abstractions, the English and French "mysteries" laid the foundations of a great tradition of secular dramatic art. In Italy the development was all the other way: the flagellants' *laude*—"spirituals" sung in the tongue of the people—gave place to the dramatic *divozioni,* and these to the sumptuously presented *rappresentazioni* of the end of the fifteenth and beginning of the sixteenth century, whose nature is significantly betrayed by Machiavelli's description of a Florentine spectacle in 1466, as played "to give men something to take away their thoughts from affairs of state." This spectacle "represented the coming of the three Magi Kings from the East, following the star which showed the Nativity of Christ, and it was of so great pomp and magnificence that it kept the whole city busy for several months in arranging and preparing it."

It is not out of such splendid pageantry that a great national dramatic art is created. So that there was only the opera for Italy, where, eventually, there were the plays of Shakespeare and Molière for France and England.

This "dehumanizing" process also affected the Spanish "mystery": and thus Spain cannot show the living stage as England and France can. Simple at first, the "mystery" was elaborated into a formality which had no connexion with Nature. Artificial and insipid, the Spanish "mystery" remained a fashionable entertainment long after the "mystery" as such had descended to performance only by rustics for rustics. The great Spanish playwright, Lope de la Vega, filled his Christmas plays with strained allegory and classical conceits. They have a certain baroque magnificence, but there is neither fire nor simplicity in them to make them charm or dazzle. They are like the statues of Christ in Spanish churches: so dressed up in tinselled robes and gilt crowns that hardly anything of the image is to be seen. It is a far cry from the manger at Bethlehem to Lope de la Vega's conception of the scene. The clods of the Towneley Cycle, who offer the Child Jesus an apple, some worn hose and a nutcracker, are far nearer.

I have described the "maskings," the "disguisings," the "plays," which were the predecessors of our modern comedies and tragedies, our farces and our revues. All derived ultimately from the early dramatizations of the Church's liturgy—the *Stella*, the *Tres Reges*, the *Herodes* and the *Magi*.

The *Stella,* indeed, is still performed in various places in Europe, especially in Spain and in Italy. In Naples at Christmas they perform the *Cantata dei Pastori,* which is a play, in doggerel, of the Nativity story. The "plot" covers the period from the creation of Adam until the adoration of Christ by the Shepherds—the exact period covered by the Chester, York and Towneley "mysteries." There is a typical Neapolitan touch in the introduction of several devils—Lucifero, Satanasso, Belfegor, Belzebù, and others—who tempt Adam and Eve, and pester St. Joseph and the Virgin, until they are ordered off by an angel. There are two fictional characters as well, Razzullo and Sarchiapone, who are tempted by the devils, and assisted by the angels. This play is very crude, and represents—like the Christmas play in Sicily (called there *Il Pastorale*)—a survival into modern times of a medieval treatment.

In England, of course, the "mystery" vanished, save in the remoter country districts. As late as the middle of the last century the Christmas Mummers of Dorsetshire used to perform a Christmas play, which, by a lucky accident, was recorded on paper before the play vanished with the Mummers.

The *dramatis personae* of this simple play are as follows:

Old Father Christmas; St. Patrick; Colonel Spring; Room; Captain Bluster; Old Betty; Anthony, the Egyptian King; Gracious King; Doctor; St. George; General Valentine; and Servant-man.

The style of the "poetry" is sufficiently well indicated by this extract:

> Here comes I, Anthony, the Egyptian King,
> With whose mighty acts, all round the globe doth ring;
> No other champion but me excels,
> Except St. George, my only son-in-law.
> Indeed, that wondrous Knight, whom I so dearly love,
> Whose mortal deeds the world dost well approve,
> The hero whom no dragon could affright,
> A whole troop of soldiers couldn't stand in sight.
> Walk in, St. George, his warlike ardour to display,
> And show Great Britain's enemies dismay.
> Walk in, St. George.

Times change, and we change with them, says the Latin poet. And the things that we make and do, and enjoy: these change as well.

There were several reasons why the ancient "mystery" should have suffered radical alteration in Britain, just as there are several reasons why it should have survived unaltered to this day (at least until the advent of a Communist government) in Rumania. But nothing disappears in this world: there is only change, and somewhere within the radically altered form there is to be found some surviving element, unchanged, of the original.

The *Stella* of King Alfred's time is still with us: in the form of our pantomime. It may be hard at first glance to see the latter as a derivative of the former; but the history of the pantomime—indeed, to carry the matter further, of the whole modern theatre—shows us that "play-acting," no matter how secular or even farcical, ultimately derives from the simple dramatizations of the Church's services.

No other century in our long history has so far rivalled the eighteenth century as a period of change; change which affected every department, important and trivial, of human activity. We know it, of course, as the age which saw the coming of the Industrial Revolution: but that revolution was matched in many other affairs than purely industrial ones. In any case—as Adam Smith pointed out nearly two centuries ago, and the ordinary man is only now beginning to realize—human activity is not to be neatly compartmented off into the amatory, the feral, the industrial, the political, the artistic, and so on. The bigotry of Madame de Maintenon caused the economic support of Ulster to be the linen-industry. The fashion of powdering hair vanished because Pitt the Younger wished to reduce the National Debt. Lancashire cotton-spinners starved because Abraham Lincoln wished to emancipate some American Negro slaves. The population of Ireland, in the 'forties of the nineteenth century, was reduced by over three millions, because Sir Walter Raleigh had introduced the potato into Ireland three hundred years before.

And all the changes that the eighteenth century saw—the calendar was changed, the language of the law courts was changed, the system of weights and measures was changed, the penal code was changed—all the innumerable changes were to have the effect of changing Christmas.

George I—George Louis, Elector of Hanover—became King of Great Britain and Ireland by virtue of his Stuart blood; but no coronation in Westminster Abbey by the Archbishop of Canterbury could turn him into an Englishman. He never learned to speak English, and he died as he had been born: a German. It is safe to say that the first truly English king to come after George I was

George V; and the fact that, until the accession of Victoria, the British monarchs were also Kings of Hanover, Dukes of Brunswick and Luneburg and Hereditary Arch-treasurers of the Holy Roman Empire, had the effect of introducing into English life more than a trivial element of German taste.

We are here concerned with the German custom of the Christmas-tree, whose introduction into Great Britain has been popularly but erroneously attributed to the Prince Consort, though it is just to say that the immense national interest centred in the Royal Family caused the tree to be adopted in every British home, where, before Victoria's time, it had remained an exotic novelty.

That the tree at Christmas is a custom of great antiquity, there can be no doubt: plants and lights have been associated with the Winter Festival in all countries, from before—long before—Christian times. But the first mention of the Christmas-tree in modern times is, according to Tille, to be found in the notes of an anonymous Strasbourg citizen, under date 1605. "At Christmas, they set up fir trees in the parlours at Strasbourg and hang thereon roses cut out of many-coloured paper, apples, wafers, gold-foil, sweets, etc."

The next reference—not a complimentary one—is in a book called *The Milk of the Catechism,* by the Strasbourg theologian, Dr. Johann Konrad Dannhauer, professor and preacher at the cathedral there. This book, published about the middle of the seventeenth century, mentions "the Christmas- or fir- tree, which people set up in their houses, hang with dolls and sweets, and afterwards shake and deflower. . . . Whence comes the custom," Dr. Dannhauer asks, "I know not. It is child's play. . . . Far better were it to point the children to the spiritual cedar-tree, Jesus Christ."

Miles, who quotes both these references, points out that there is no mention in either of candles; but we know that the association of light with the various feasts of the Winter Festival is an old one. Jumping over bonfires—as they still do in the Shetlands and in the Pyrenees; letting off fireworks—as they still do on that ancient winter festival, Guy Fawkes' Day; burning logs, "The Yule Log," as they still do in Spain, Germany and some parts of Britain: all these customs show the ancient association of light with the festival. And understandably, since the festival commemorates the rebirth of the Sun—the source of light, heat . . . and all life.

One may agree that the candles were not mentioned because the writers took their presence for granted. It is only when we find the Christmas-tree introduced as a novelty into another country that all its features are minutely described.

Thus the first mention of the tree in England is to be found in *Court and Private Life in the Time of Queen Charlotte, being the Journals of Mrs. Papendiek*. The authoress, writing for an English public, says: "This Christmas, Mrs. Papendiek proposed an illuminated tree, according to the German fashion, but the Blagroves being at home for their fortnight, and the party at Mrs. Roach's for the holidays, I objected to it. Our eldest girl, Charlotte, being only six the 30th of this November, I thought our children too young to be amused at so much expense and trouble."

A footnote by A. J. Kempe, in his 1836 edition of the *Losely MSS.*, says: "We remember a German of the household of the late Queen Caroline making what he termed a *Christmas-tree* for a juvenile party at that festive season. The tree was a branch of some evergreen fastened to a board. Its boughs bent under the weight of gilt oranges, almonds, etc., and under it was a neat model of a farm house, surrounded by figures of animals, etc., and all due accompaniments."

Charles Greville, writing of Christmas at Panshanger in 1829, notes: "The Princess Lieven got up a little fête such as is customary all over Germany. Three trees in great pots were put upon a long table covered with pink linen; each tree was illuminated with three circular tiers of coloured wax candles—blue, green, red and white. Before each tree was displayed a quantity of toys, gloves, pocket handkerchiefs, work boxes, books, and various articles—presents made to the owner of the tree. It was very pretty. Here it was only for the children; in Germany the custom extends to persons of all ages."

From *Mary Howitt, an Autobiography,* comes the following: "Our practical knowledge of the Christmas-tree was gained in this first winter at Heidelberg. Universal as the custom now is, I believe the earliest knowledge which the English public had of it was through Coleridge in his *Biographia Literaria*. It had, at the time I am writing of—1840—been introduced into Manchester by some of the German merchants established there. Our Queen and Prince Albert likewise celebrated the festival with its beautiful old German customs. Thus the fashion spread, until now even our asylums, schools, and workhouses have it, through friends and benefactors."

There is a legend that it was Martin Luther who instituted the custom of the Christmas-tree—the *Weihnachtsbaum*—but it is unreasonable to suppose that the custom is no older, even though there is the curious fact to take into account that the Christmas-tree does not appear to have become widespread in Germany until about the same time that its popularity was growing in Britain. That the tree was imported from Germany is certain, but that it was, at least in its present form, nationally popular in Germany before the nineteenth century is a matter of some doubt.

It is suggested that the Christmas-tree was a Protestant rather than a Catholic institution (hence its legendary association with Martin Luther) and that it made only slow progress in those parts of Germany which still clung to the older faith. This explanation seems inadequate to explain the slow growth of the custom's popularity.

The customs of decking the house with evergreens is one of immense antiquity. Polydore Vergil says: "Trymming of the temples with hangynges, floures, boughes, and garlondes, was taken of the heathen people, which decked their idols and houses with such array." And Stow, in his famous *Survey,* tells us of a Christmas decoration which sounds remarkably like a veritable Christmas-tree:

"Against the feast of Christmas, every man's house, as also their parish churches, were decked with holme, ivy, bayes, and whatsoever the season of the year afforded to be green. The Conduits and Standards in the streets were, likewise, garnished; among the which I read that, in the year 1444, by tempest of thunder and lightning, towards the morning of Candlemas Day, at the Leadenhall in Cornhill, a standard of tree, being set up in the midst of the pavement[1], faste in the ground, nailed full of holme and ivie, for disport of Christmass to the people, was torne up and caste down by the malignant Spirit (as was thought), and the stones of the pavement all about were cast in the streets, and into divers houses, so that the people were sore aghast at the great tempests."

The custom of hanging evergreens in the churches and houses was observed long before the Christmas-tree, in modern form, was

[1] What we should now call "the roadway."

known in Britain. The hangings were kept up until Candlemas Eve, and then burnt—a custom which caused a fire in the hall of Christ Church, Oxford, in 1719.

Lights of all sorts were held, too, to be proper in association with the winter celebrations, but it was apparently the fusion of two old customs—lights with evergreens—which gave us our modern Christmas-tree.

An article in the Christmas number of the *Cornhill Magazine* for 1886 looks for the origin of the lights on the Christmas-tree in an ancient Jewish festival. "In the ninth month of the Jewish year, corresponding nearly to our December, and on the twenty-fifth day, the Jews celebrated the Feast of the Dedication of their Temple. It had been desecrated on that day by Antiochus; it was rededicated by Judas Maccabeus; and then, according to the Jewish legend, sufficient oil was found in the Temple to last for the seven-branched candlestick for seven days, and it would have taken seven days to prepare new oil. Accordingly, the Jews were wont, on the twenty-fifth of Kislev, in every house, to light a candle, on the next day, two, and so on, till on the seventh and last day of the feast, seven candles twinkled in every house. It is not easy to fix the exact date of the Nativity, but it fell, most probably, on the last day of Kislev, when every Jewish house in Bethlehem and Jerusalem was twinkling with lights. It is worthy of notice that the German name of Christmas is *Weihnacht,* the Night of Dedication, as though it were associated with this feast. The Greeks also call Christmas the Feast of Lights; and, indeed, this also was a name given to the Dedication Festival, *Chanukah,* by the Jews."

This is all true enough, but it does not prove a Jewish origin for the Christmas lights. If anything, it proves the antiquity of a custom that both ancient Jews and ancient Aryans had in common.

Sir George Birdwood, indeed, recognizes the long descent of the Christmas-tree. "It is, probably, a survival of some observances connected with the pagan *Saturnalia* of the winter solstice, to supersede which the Church, about the fifth century of our era, instituted Christmas Day." Then Sir George goes on to find Egyptian and Hindu practices corresponding to our reverence for the Christmas-tree.

But there should be nothing astonishing in this: at the Winter Festival, which is a feast at once of asking and thanksgiving;

of praying that the Sun will not die, and of rejoicing that he has not died; what more likely than that the two most popular symbols should be the flame and the evergreen—the light which had conquered the darkness, and the plant which has defied the withering which overtakes all other green things?

In old Bavaria the Christmas-tree was still unknown in the country districts as late as 1855, and—according to Tille—the south of Germany had not acquired the custom completely even by the end of the nineteenth century.

Princess Hélène of Mecklenburg brought the tree to Paris in 1840, and its popularity grew rapidly in France—though never to the same extent as in England, where a desire to please the sovereign helped to popularize the custom. 1840 is roughly the date from which its use commences in England: it was in that year that Victoria and Albert had a Christmas-tree, and the rest of Europe, at varying paces, followed the example rather of England than of Germany, from which the modern Christmas-tree came.

German, Swedish, Austrian and Finnish emigrants took it across the Atlantic to the United States, but it was not until those immigrants, by earning enough to take them out of the near-pauper class, had earned social consideration for their imported customs, that the custom of the Christmas-tree received social recognition. A description of a Christmas passed by President Harrison at the White House in 1891 specifically mentions "an old-fashioned Christmas-tree for the grandchildren," and it seems that by that time the Christmas-tree, certainly in New York, was thoroughly naturalized as an American Christmas custom. Today, of course, no nation celebrates its Christmas with more elaborate splendour than the American—not even the German. And, as we should suppose, the American Christmas festival, like the American people, is an amalgam of many distinct national elements.

I have said that the eighteenth century altered the calendar, among many things. This change came about in 1752, when the error which had crept into the British chronology was corrected by Act of Parliament, and the lag of eleven days behind the true date was made up; 2 September, 1752, being thus followed immediately by 14 September, Christmas, 1752, fell, according to the ideas of a number of conservative folk, *eleven days too soon,* and for many years there were die-hards who preferred to ignore the revised calendar and to celebrate Christmas—Old Christmas they called it—eleven days late, as the Greek Orthodox Church still does.

The correction of the Julian Calendar had been made by Pope Gregory in 1582, and there was a religious reason why the English preferred not to accept the astronomical correctness of the Vatican! But the reasons seeming insufficient one hundred and sixty years later, the British Government, in spite of some really alarming mob-violence, made the change which brought the calendar into line with that of all European states but those whose religion was Greek Orthodox.

The same Act of Parliament made the official new year begin on 1 January, instead of on 25 March, the ancient Jewish new year. Thus official usage and popular usage were brought into accord, for the people had unofficially begun their year on 1 January for centuries past. The Treasury, however, being of a conservative nature, did not apply the corrections to its own department. It continued to calculate by the superseded calendar, thereby making its dates eleven days behind the dates of all the rest of Britain—save, of course, those fanatical die-hards who celebrated Old Christmas in defiance of New Christmas.

And, of course, in repudiating the calendar-corrections, the die-hards of the Treasury hung on to the 25 March New Year's Day, which fell, naturally, on 5 April in the corrected calendar.

Indeed, the British Treasury never has accepted the corrections, either of Pope Gregory in 1582 or of the British Government in 1752. It still reckons time by the corrected calendar published by authority of Julius Caesar in 54 B.C., and it still begins its new year on 25 March. So that—eleven days late by our corrected calendar—the income-tax forms go out each year . . . on 5 April!

Three important foreign influences combined in the eighteenth century, not so much to change, as to amplify and—how shall I say it?—to internationalize the English Christmas. And somehow "internationalize" is not the right word, either: nor do I know quite what that word may be. What I need is a phrase to describe the process by which the English Christmas, having something added to it which strengthened rather than weakened its essential quality of Englishness, was freed from a certain parochial quality which had hitherto kept it for internal use alone. Freed from the quality of insularity, the English Christmas, made acceptable to the world by taking on qualities from foreign Christmasses, was to be exported as the ideal Christmas of all. Persons who had hardly heard of Christ, as well as those in whose system of theology He could hold no place, were to celebrate His birth in the ritual of the English Christmas. It is a curious fact that before the world was to achieve a universal currency, a universal law, a universal government, language or system of weights and measures, it was to achieve a universal Christmas.

The three foreign influences which combined to affect the British people, and so the British way-of-life and—inevitably—the British Christmas, were the German, the Jewish and the French.

The first came to Britain through the accident of a German king and a German court; the second was a product of the first, since the German princes invariably used the well-known business skill of the Jews to finance their wars and balance their shaky budgets.

Cromwell had permitted the Jews once more to settle in England. He had refused to let them buy St. Paul's Cathedral and the Bodleian Library (for presentation to the nation) at a price of half a million pounds, but he had a private understanding not unconnected with a cash payment.

The coming of the Hanoverians accelerated the immigration-rate of the Jews into England.

The third foreign influence was the French, who came with the Revolution of 1789.

To these influences may be added a subtler, less obvious influence, which was neither altogether religious, nor altogether political; neither altogether foreign, nor altogether British. This influence was that of the Roman Catholic Church.

Roman Catholicism had not been entirely wiped away in Britain at the Reformation. The mass of the Irish had clung to their ancient faith, and even in England and Scotland there were many who suffered the grievous burdens imposed upon Catholics rather than apostatize. But the steadfast adherence to the faith of some of the leading members of the old aristocracy, together with the fact that the chapels of envoys from Catholic countries provided centres of Catholic worship legally immune from interference, tended to make an eventual lightening of Catholic burdens an inevitability. Governments may only follow public opinion; they are unwise to force it;

and so public opinion had to sanction toleration towards Nonconformists before the Government might legally grant that toleration; but it must be borne in mind that the Government always grants legally only a fraction of what public opinion has already decided to grant far more fully.

The anti-Popish riots of Lord George Gordon did nothing to arrest the move towards complete Catholic emancipation: the nature of Lord George's supporters—the scum of London's gutters—helped, rather than hindered, the Catholic cause; and when the French refugees arrived, an excuse was provided for the open celebration of Catholic church services that the more tolerant British Protestant was most willing to use.

The result of all these influences was seen in the fact that, by 1800, our modern Christmas was evolved. The English genius for compromise had used strangely differing—almost incongruous—elements in that fine synthesis we call the English Christmas.

Then, with the products of her factories, Great Britain exported her ideas to the whole world. Her soldiers and her sailors, her administrators and her merchants, built up a vast empire which was so soundly built that it still remains British even where it has secured "independence." And along with English law and language went, too, the English Christmas.

CHAPTER TWELVE

# COMING OF THE CHRISTMAS-CARD

IN 1814 the London *Times* newspaper was first printed by steam, and there were other improvements besides the cylinder press designed to make printing cheaper and cheaper, and so to put printed matter in vast quantities into the hands of all but the very poorest—or rather, all but the least literate, since even literate paupers may borrow a book or newspaper.

With the steam press came the discovery of stereotyping, of lithography, and of cheap mechanical methods of stitching and binding the printed pages. And do not forget that the old-fashioned presses of the time were not all destroyed when they were ousted by the more up-to-date machines. They went back into the second-hand market, to find operators and so swell the ranks of the journeymen printers.

Chapbooks, games books, children's books, gift books, cheap editions of the classics and expensive editions of insipid modern verse: all this poured from the presses, to be used as presents at Christmas . . . even a present for the buyer.

The interest in chemistry and its application to industry had affected the printing trade. Men were constantly on the look out for improved methods of printing and of reproducing drawings and paintings, and the names of Le Blond and Baxter will come to mind here for their methods of printing in oil-colour. But these two inventors were rivalled by a hundred others with different patents—some better and some not so good. But year by year the standard of book production rose, and the standard of cost dropped, on a sharply descending curve. Sweated labour, too, helped to cut costs down to fantastic levels. A famous manufacturer of soap was giving bound classics away at the end of the century, in return for so many labels from his soap packets. But the books might be bought—if one could not save up sufficient labels. I read Mrs. Henry Wood, Alexandre Dumas and Grace D'Aguilar in this edition, and the volumes have lasted well, in their maroon-cloth-covered boards, lettered with silver. The price per volume was twopence farthing, retail!

It was in this age of cheap printing that the Christmas-card came into being and extensive use; and since one may not now imagine a Christmas without a card, here is the proper place to trace the history of these ephemeral but incredibly important oblongs of tinted and tinselled paper.

It is just over a century ago—in 1846, it is said—that the first Christmas-card known was printed, about a thousand copies being sold at Christmas, 1846. The card, though it was a true novelty, had yet, like all novelties, a history behind it. As our modern Christmas-card first appeared, the custom of the "Christmas piece" was dying out. This was a specimen of handwriting, done by the boy at school —the girls seem to have been excused the duty—so that he might take it home with him on his Christmas holidays as some proof of the progress that he had made in the then highly esteemed art of calligraphy. These "pieces" were always written—at least after the Napoleonic Wars had ended—on specially prepared sheets, with engraved or printed, and sometimes coloured, headings and borders —often of highly artistic workmanship.

"Sometimes," says Ashton, "these sheets were surrounded with elaborate flourishings of birds, pens, scrolls, etc., such as the writing master of the last century delighted in. . . . Here are a few of the subjects: Ruth and Boaz, Measuring the Temple (Ezekiel), Philip Baptizing the Eunuch, The Good Samaritan, Joshua's Command, John the Baptist Preaching in the Wilderness, The Seven Wonders of the World, King William III, and St. Paul's Shipwreck."

A writer in *Notes and Queries* (4 series, vi, 462, 1871)[1] records that "as a youngster, some thirty years ago, in my father's establishment, the sale of 'school pieces' or 'Christmas pieces,' as they were called, was very large. My father published some thirty different subjects (a new one every year, one of the old ones being allowed to go out of print). There were also three other publishers of them. The order to print used to average about five hundred of each kind, but double of the Life of our Saviour. Most of the subjects were those of the Old Testament. I only recollect four subjects not sacred. Printing at home, we generally commenced the printing in August from the copper-plates, as they had to be coloured by hand. They

[1] Quoted by Ashton.

sold, by retail, at sixpence each, and we used to supply them to the trade at thirty shillings per gross, and to schools at three shillings and sixpence per dozen, or two dozen for six shillings and sixpence. Charity boys were large purchasers of these pieces, and at Christmas time used to take them round their parish to show, and, at the same time, solicit a trifle. The sale never began before October in the country, and December in London; and early in January the stock left used to be put by until the following season. It is over fifteen years since any were printed by my firm, and the last new one I find was done in lithography."

This would make the final disappearance of the "Christmas piece" coincide almost exactly with the Crimean War—about ten years after the introduction of the modern Christmas-card. Like the postage stamp, which, in it present form, originated in England, the first Christmas-card was no shoddy commercial affair, but a piece of work of high artistic value. The interesting fact concerning this inseparable adjunct of the modern Christmas is that the man responsible for making the sketch from which the first postage stamp was engraved—Sir Henry Cole, K.C.B.—is apparently the man who suggested the idea of the card to the artist, J. C. Horsley, R.A., who had also been connected with the first issue of stamps.

There is thus something quasi-official about the issue of the first Christmas-card, for not only were the men who sponsored it both eminent, but they had been intimately associated with the introduction of penny postage—one of the most world-shaking of modern inventions.

The history of the first Christmas-card seems—when all contradictions have been reconciled—to be as follows. It was designed by J. C. Horsley, R.A., following a suggestion made by Mr. (afterwards Sir) Henry Cole. It was produced in outline, by the lithographic process, and coloured by hand by a professional colourer named Mason. The lithographer was a Mr. Jobbins, of Warwick Court, Holborn, London; and the card—it was of "the usual size of a lady's visiting-card"—was published by Joseph Cundall, and sold from the offices of *Felix Summerly's Home Treasury,* one of the numerous gift books of the time. The offices were situated at No. 12 Old Bond Street, Westminster. About a thousand of the cards were sold. This well-produced effort seems, however, to have been a little in advance of its time, and it was not until 1862 that Messrs. Goodall began to produce some less elaborate types.

A writer in *The Publisher's Circular* for 31 December, 1883, mentions that Goodalls produced the first cards in 1862, "the first attempts being the size of the ordinary gentleman's address card, on which were simply put 'A Merry Christmas' and 'A Happy New Year'; after that there came to be added robins and holly branches, embossed figures and landscapes . . . they were produced by Goodall and Son. Seeing a growing want, and the great sale obtained abroad, this house produced (1868) a 'Little Red Riding Hood,' a 'Hermit and his Cell,' and many other subjects in which snow and the robin played a part."

The first card cost round about a shilling; methods of mechanical reproduction had so improved by the time that Messrs De la Rue, the well-known London printers, published a facsimile, in 1881, that they were able to sell it for *twopence*!

So much for the commonly accepted origin of the Christmas-card. But there are some apparent incongruities which must be recorded . . . and accounted for.

For instance, though the "official" date of the Horsley and Cole Christmas-card is given—and was given in 1883—as 1846, the author has seen two of the cards, one sent out by J. C. Horsley himself, clearly dated *1843*.

What seems to be the incorrect dating of 1846 appears to be due to a lapse of memory on the part of the artist—though the letter from Cundall, the printer, that I have quoted also gives 1846 as the date of publication.

John Calcott Horsley, R.A.—victim of Whistler's famous and malicious witticism, "Horsley soit qui mal y pense!"—gave this account of the Christmas-card's genesis in a letter written to Jonathan King, the greatest collector of Christmas-cards that the world has known:

"Mr. Henry Cole (afterwards Sir Henry Cole) of the South Kensington Department conceived the idea of an illustrated *Birthday* (not Xmas especially) card which in 1845 or '46 I designed and carried out for him and which I believe . . . was reprinted a few years since[1]. There is no question that this was the first illustrated card issued. The idea was Cole's, the execution of the trifle mine."

There seems to be no doubt, however, that Horsley's memory—

[1] Here he refers to the De La Rue reprint of 1881.

he was then an old man—was at fault, and that the card was designed and printed as early as 1843 (and not 1846, as he claims), unless the card was not made available for general use until 1846. That may be the explanation of the apparent incongruity of dates, since it is certain that the card was being used in 1843.

Horsley's claim that his was the first illustrated card is one which cannot pass without some protest, and there are at least three rival claimants to the honour of being the first to produce the Christmas-card.

A strong claim to have "invented" the card came from W. A. Dobson, a person of much industry and of small artistic merit, who ended his career as Queen Victoria's favourite painter. In 1844, when Dobson was head of the School of Design, Birmingham, he conceived, as he tells, the pleasant notion of sending out hand-painted greeting-cards to his friends at Christmas, instead of the usual letters.

This claim to priority of invention only holds if it can be proved that Horsley issued *his* card in 1846, and not—as the evidence seems to prove—in 1843. And the same objection must lie against the claim made on behalf of the Reverend Edward Bradley, a Newcastle vicar, who wrote best-selling Victorian novels under the pseudonym "Cuthbert Bede." Mr. Bradley went further than Mr. Dobson, and even had his cards—intended "for circulation among his friends" —lithographed. That was in 1844.

But Mr. A. M. Hind, Head of the Department of Prints and Drawings, British Museum, has called attention to a card which—provided that the date on it may be read correctly—would seem to establish a sure priority of invention for a sixteen-year-old artist named William Maw Egley (1826-1916), son of William Egley (1798-1879), the miniature-painter.

Egley junior was, in the words of Mr. James Laver, "a precocious talent, with something of the qualities of Dicky Doyle, his senior by two years." Egley is known as a painter of little pictures of indifferent artistic merit, and he illustrated Dickens, Molière and Shakespeare for popular publishers.

Egley's claim to be the first to issue a Christmas-card depends on whether the date appended to his signature on the card is to be read *1842* or *1849*.

The card, which bears a singular general likeness to that of Horsley—especially in the division of the pictures among three arcaded panels—shows Sir Roger de Coverley, a Christmas dinner, a Punch and Judy, distribution of soup at a house-door, skating and waits, and the blank spaces left in the design show that it was intended for a fairly general distribution.

At the bottom of the card—it is etched on copper—is written:

*W. M. Egley, Junr., Des[igned] and Etch[ed] 1842.*

Except that the "2" may just be a fancifully written "9."

But, apart from the fact that the figure looks most plainly a "2" to me, Mr. James Laver, of the Victoria and Albert Museum, sees verification of the "2" in the fact that the costumes of the ladies are much more in the mode of 1842 than of 1849. Mr. Laver has earned for himself an unrivalled reputation as an authority on the dress of all ages, and his opinion is not lightly to be set aside.

He inclines to the view that the date shown on the Egley card is, indeed, 1842, and that Egley must remain—until a stronger claim to be the inventor of the Christmas-card is put in—the accepted originator of the immortal trifle.

The Egley card was discovered by Mr. A. M. Hind among the remarkable collection of prints and drawings, all illustrating the history of skating, which were presented to the British Museum by Miss F. L. Cannan in 1931. It is possible that some information will be forthcoming to decide which of the two dates—1842 or 1849—must be given to Egley's effort. But until the matter is finally decided the credit for the invention of the Christmas-card, as we know it, must still belong to Sir Henry Cole and Mr. J. C. Horsley.

The Rev. W. F. Dawson's comments on the development of the Christmas-card make interesting reading:

"Christmas and New Year Cards became very popular in the decade 1870-80. But then, however, simple cards alone did not suffice. Like many other things, they felt the influence of the latter-day *renaissance* of art and by a sort of revolutionary process developed cards monochrome and coloured, 'Christmas Bell' cards, palettes, scrolls, circular and oval panels, stars, fans, crescents, and other shaped novelties; embossed cards, the iridescent series, the rustic and frosted cards, the folding series, the jewel cards, the crayons, and private cards on which the sender's name and sentiments are printed in gold, silver or colours; hand-painted cards with landscapes, seascapes and floral decorations; paintings on porcelain;

satin cards, fringed silk, plush, Broche, and other artistically made-up novelties; 'art-gem' panels; elaborate booklets, and other elegant souvenirs of the festive season. Many of the Christmas booklets are beautifully illustrated editions of popular poems and carols."

The fifty years which have passed since the above was written have not outdated it as an adequate description of the rare fancy and immense variety which characterize the production of Christmas-cards. If anything, it understates the case. Technical methods of production have advanced since Mr. Dawson's day, and now offset, rotogravure and other methods of colour printing not invented in the world of half a century ago have been pressed into the task of making the Christmas-card a thing of beauty, even if not—by its nature—a joy for ever.

The crib, introduced into Britain from Catholic countries, and especially from France at the time of the Revolution, has not been one of those foreign Christmas customs as fully assimilated as, say, the Christmas-tree or some of Luther's carols. The crib is certainly a Catholic custom, but not more so than others which have taken root in non-Catholic countries; and certainly the crib dates from long before the Reformation, from a time when Europe shared its beliefs and its religious observances. Its invention is attributed to St. Francis of Assisi, who celebrated Christmas of 1224 at Greccio, with what appears to be an acted representation of the Nativity, including the use of a live ox and ass.

According to St. Bonaventure, St. Francis, when he had decided to seek to kindle devotion to the Holy Child by a celebration of His birth, set about the celebration in a manner which showed his humble submission to his superiors.

"That this (celebration) might not seem an innovation, he sought and obtained licence from the Sovereign Pontiff, and then made ready a manger, and bade that hay, together with an ox and an ass, be brought unto the place. The Brethren were called together, the folk assembled, the wood echoed with their voices, and that August night was made radiant and solemn with many bright lights, and with tuneful and sonorous praises. The man of God, filled with tender love, stood before the manger, bathed in tears, and overflowing with joy. Solemn masses were celebrated over the manger; Francis, the Levite of Christ, chanting the Holy Gospel.

"Then he preached unto the folk standing around of the birth of the King in poverty; calling Him, when he wished to name Him, the Child of Bethlehem, by reason of his tender love for Him. A certain knight, valorous and true, Messer John of Greccio, who, for the love of Christ, had left the secular army and was bound by closest friendship unto the man of God, declared that he beheld a little Child right fair to see sleeping in that manger, who seemed to be awakened from sleep when the blessed Father Francis embraced Him in both arms."

This is over-romanticized and over-simplified explanation. St. Francis, through his deep devotion to the Holy Child, did more than any other man to popularize the feast of Christmas; but he merely popularized, as part of the cult of Christmas, the custom of the crib (*presepe* in Italian; from the Latin, *præsepio*), he did not invent the crib, which had already been many centuries in existence when Francis was born.

Pope Gregory III (731-41) placed a "golden image of the Mother of God embracing God our Saviour, in various gems," in the then already ancient church of St. Mary Major, in Rome. And such a statue was by no means the first. But Francis of Assisi did popularize the crib, for, as I have pointed out, the crib is the drama of the Nativity frozen still at the supreme moment of its plot: the crib presents, as it were, the highlight and the essence of the Christmas drama, and all to whom the legend of the Nativity made an appeal came inevitably under the spell of the crib.

In England the Reformation banished it, but there are still distinct traces of the crib in certain of our country customs. The "kissing bunch" of Derbyshire combines elements of the Christmas-tree and of the crib; for it is a frame of two hoops, covered with evergreen and ribbons and paper flowers, while within the frame are three small dolls, elaborately dressed, which represent Jesus, Mary and Joseph. The dolls hang within the frame of the "kissing bunch" by strings, and are surrounded by apples, oranges and various ornaments also hanging by strings. Sometimes, even, the dolls are arranged in the "bunch" to represent the Nativity scene.

Indeed, the ancient Christmas customs still linger on in our country districts, hardly altered by that "practicalizing" influence which, in the cities, reduces all to a common level of utilitarian dullness.

At the end of the eighteenth century thousands left the countryside to seek work in the towns and cities; and they brought with them their rustic ways of spending Christmas. The cheap methods of printing gave these customs a permanence in their new setting, and revived the celebration of the feast, by imparting a new life to it. Books of Christmas games, Christmas carols, Christmas superstitions, and so forth, all helped to save Christmas from the fate which has overtaken such a festival as, say, Guy Fawkes' Day, which was once celebrated with considerable national excitement.

What happened, historically considered, was this: Christmas, in the cities, was in gradual process of dying through that anaemia which attacks customs in cities. A sudden influx of country-bred thousands into the cities, together with developments in the art of printing, pumped new blood into dying Christmas, while the increase of wealth, following the vast increase of population, gave big commercial firms a vested interest in seeing that the revived Christmas would not again die. That this is a correct analysis of the situation is clearly seen when we consider that some of those Christmas customs revived at round about 1800 by the work-seeking immigrants from the countryside did not survive. And these customs—such as the waits—were those which did not lend themselves to commercial exploitation.

Christmas customs, new or old, which could show a profit for investment, were sure to be carefully cultivated: Christmas cards, the pantomime, "bon-bon" crackers, Christmas-trees and their glittering ornaments, and so on.

The waits are still with us, as is the muffin-man with his napkin-covered tray and his bell which chimes so pleasantly at half an hour before tea-time on a misty October afternoon. But both the muffin-man and the wait have lost their old glory, and there is something not quite natural about the carol singers who now collect about our doorsteps at Christmas-tide. Two urchins were standing on a doorstep one Christmas. After some preliminary sniggering, accompanied by some nudging and what is called "horse-play," the lads —with something of an "after you, George!" hesitancy—piped up:

" 'Ark, the 'Arold angels sing!
Glory to the new-born King!"

"Well," said the prospective patron, "go on! Sing the rest of it!"

But they couldn't.

"Don't know it, Guv!"

Their only regret—it was obvious—that they did not know more of the carol derived from the fear that they might not earn the sixpence that they hoped for. They got their sixpence, and went scampering off into the foggy night. They were laughing as they ran . . . the sadly degenerate descendants of a body which was once one of the established sights and pleasures and dignities of London. This was the body of the bellmen: persons whose office combined the functions of night-watchmen, clocks and the B.B.C. weather-forecast.

In the policeless days of our ancestors the watch used to patrol the streets, but it was the bellman who lit the ways with his horn-lantern, calling out the hours of the night, and telling folk at the crack of each dawn what (in his opinion) the weather would be during the coming day. Machyn mentions him in Mary Tudor's time in a diary entry:

"[the xij day of January 1556-7, in Alderman Draper's ward called] chordwenerstrett[1] ward, a belle man went about with a belle at evere lane, and at the ward [end to] gyff warnyng of ffyre and candyll lyght, [and to help the] poure, and pray for the ded."

The cry of the bellman was "Take care of your fire and candle, be charitable to the poor, and pray for the dead!" They were not police, nor even watchmen. They were rather "company" for sleeping folk; and their voices must have warmed many a fearful heart in the silence of the night.

Shakespeare says:

> It was the owl that shriek'd, the fatal bell man,
> Which gives the stern'st good night.

And Milton, liking the institution, recalls

> . . . the bellman's drowsy charm,
> To bless the doors from nightly harm.

While Herrick's delightful allusion to the bellman is well-known:

> From noise of Scare-fires rest ye free,
> From Murders *Benedicite.*
> From all mischances that may fright
> Your pleasing slumbers in the night;

[1] Cordwainer Street (!), originally the quarter of the dealers in "Cordovan" leather.

Mercie secure ye all, and keep
The Goblin from ye, while ye sleep.
Past one o'clock and almost two,
My Masters all, *Good day to you.*

Our ancestors were fascinated by the bellman: an odd fact, since the ordinary is too often taken for granted. There are not only many allusions to him in past literature, but much praise of him too.

In *Villanies Discover'd by Lanthorne and Candle Light,* published in 1620, the following poetical cry is credited to the bellman:

Men and children, Maides and Wives,
Tis not too late to mend your lives:
When you hear this ringing Bell,
Think it is your latest knell:
When I cry, Maide in your Smocke,
Doe not take it for a mocke:
Well I meane, if well 'tis taken,
I would have you still awaken:
Foure a Clocke, the Cock is crowing,
I must to my home be going:
When all other men doe rise,
Then I must shut up mine eyes.

Sang Vincent Bourne, in 1716, in reference to the custom of the bellman to leave a copy of "Christmas verses" at the houses on his beat:

Should you and your dog ever call at my door,
You'll be welcome, I promise you, nobody more.
May you call at a thousand each year that you live,
A shilling, at least, may each householder give;
May the "Merry Old Christmas" you wish us, befal,
And your self, and your dog, be the merriest of all!

Our ancestors distinguished between bellmen and waits; but these functionaries were differentiated not so much by function as by noise, since the bellman "cried" the watches of the night, while the waits merely called them in a more harmonious manner—usually on a hautboy or flageolet.

A test of flute-playing skill was imposed upon each aspirant to the post of wait, and it is possible that the bellmen were only those men who had failed to pass the musical test for waits.

An entry in *The Black Book of the King's Household* (Edward IV) has this: "A Wayte, that nightely from Mychelmas to Shreve Thorsdaye *pipe the watch* within this courte fowere tymes; in the Somere nightes three tymes, and maketh *bon gayte* at every chambre doare and offyce, as well for fear of pyckeres and pillers (pickers and stealers)."

From acting as nocturnal time-keepers and watchmen, the waits and bellmen gradually assumed an altogether ornamental function, banding themselves together and offering their services for hire as songsters at various public functions and private festivities, such as weddings, and so on.

Every city and borough corporation had its own band of waits, and the City of London's Corporation Waits used to play before the Lord Mayor at his inaugural procession, and always at the City banquets. Their uniform was a blue gown with red sleeves, a red cap, and a silver chain hung about the neck. Ned Ward, in his *London Spy,* has the following lively description of these entertainers:

"At last bolted out from the corner of a street, with an *ignis fatuus* dancing before them, a parcel of strange hobgoblins, covered with long frieze rugs and blankets, hopped round with leather girdles from their cruppers to their shoulders, and their noddles buttoned up into caps of martial figure, like a Knight Errant at tilt and tournament, with his wooden head locked up in an iron helmet; one, armed as I thought with a lusty faggot-bat, and the rest with strange wooden weapons in their hands, in the shape of clyster pipes, but as long almost as speaking trumpets. Of a sudden they clapped them to their mouths, and made such a frightful yelling that I thought *he* would have been dissolving, and the terrible sound of the last trumpet to be within an inch of my ears. . . . 'Why, what,' says he, 'don't you love musick? These are the topping tooters of the town, and have gowns, silver chains and salaries for playing *Lilli-borlero* to my Lord Mayor's horse through the City.' "

On the other hand, an earlier authority, Morley, who composed his *Consort Lessons* in 1599, speaks highly of the skill of the City Waits, and as the "consort lessons" are arranged for treble and bass viol, flute, cithern and a pandora—a wire-strung lute—we must regard Ned Ward's description as somewhat exaggerated.

John Cleland published his *Essay on the Musical Waits at*

Two claimants to the title of "the first Christmas card." *Above:* The card designed and etched by W. M. Egley, Junr. *Below:* That designed by Sir Henry Cole and drawn by J. C. Horsley, R.A. It was published at (Felix) Summerly's Home Treasury Office, 12 Old Bond Street, London, and though the date of its publication has been officially given as 1846, the example shown is clearly dated 1843 in Horsley's own handwriting.

*Above:* Boxing Day in Upper Regent Street, London, over a century ago. The spire of All Souls, Langham Place, can be seen in the distance. Various tradesmen, along with the beadle, have called for their "Christmas-box." One coalman is denouncing another as an imposter. *Below:* The Norwich coach approaching London laden with fat turkeys from the Norfolk farms. At that time, just over a century ago, as in the illustration below, the finest turkeys in Britain came from Norfolk, as they do yet.

*Christmas* in 1766, and asks: "But where is there any [propriety or object] in such a solemn piece of banter as that of music going the rounds and disturbing people in vain? For, surely, any meditation to be thereby excited on the holiness of the ensuing day could hardly be of great avail, in a bed, between sleeping and waking. But such is the power of custom to perpetuate absurdities."

One smells the deadening hand of the reformer here. The nature, too, of Mr. Cleland's best-known work makes us rather suspect his defence of Christmas's holy associations. Like most other reformers, Cleland hated something sanctified by custom, simply because it *was* sanctified by custom.

Cleland, by the way, derives the word "waits" from "wakes"; and thus equates it with "revels" (from "reveil"), Spanish *medianoche*, French *reveillons*, and Latin *pervigilium*—and this theory may be correct. Neither philology nor commonsense utterly condemns it.

Jones, in his *Welsh Bards*, 1794, indicates how the status of waits had dropped by the close of the eighteenth century. "Waits," he says, "are musicians of the lower order, who commonly perform on wind instruments, and they play in most towns under the windows of the chief inhabitants, at midnight, a short time before Christmas; for which they collect a Christmas box, from house to house. They are said to derive their name of *waits* from being always in waiting to celebrate weddings and other joyous events happening within their district. There is a building at Newcastle called Waits' Tower which was, formerly, the meeting-house of the town band of musicians."

The waits survive in Westminster to this day—I live in that ancient city, so that I can testify to the fact!—but their official status was preserved there until a very recent date. The Court of Burgesses of the City and Liberty of Westminster used to issue licences to the waits, granting them permission to sing or to play some musical instrument, and to solicit alms, euphemistically called "asking for a Christmas-box."

The official waits were duly sworn before the Court of Burgesses, provided with a warrant, and given permission to wear a silver badge (but paid for by themselves). Their rights were sufficiently regarded that Mr. Munroe, the Official Wait (appointed in 1820), sued some "blackleg" musicians—one of whom was his old indentured pupil, Mr. Clapp—for having, without a warrant, performed music and solicited Christmas-boxes.

In 1822, at the request of the Official Wait, Mr. O. Bond, the Constable, arrested Charles Clapp, Benjamin Jackson, Denis Jelks and Robert Prinset. They were charged at Bow Street Office with having performed on several musical instruments in St. Martin's Lane, at half-past twelve in the morning. Mr. Munroe, who had them charged, declared himself the authorized principal wait, appointed by the Court of Burgesses for the City and Liberty of Westminster, and further declared himself alone entitled, by his appointment, to apply for Christmas-boxes.

"He also urged that the prisoners, acting as Minstrels, came under the meaning of the Vagrant Act, alluded to in the 17th Geo. II; however, on reference to the last Vagrant Act of the present king, the word 'minstrels' is omitted; consequently, they are no longer cognizable under that Act of Parliament. . . . The prisoners were discharged, after receiving an admonition from Mr. Halls, the sitting magistrate, not to collect Christmas-boxes."

There is a pleasantly antique flavour about that last sentence. In other words: You are not guilty, but please do not imagine for one moment that you are therefore innocent! There is evidence that the granting of "warrants" to the authorized waits was in use in Westminster as late as the year 1871. When the custom fell into disuse I cannot trace, nor can the Westminster archives tell me.

Since one of the principal duties of the "authorized waits" was to collect their Christmas-boxes, it is the place here to examine the origin and development of this old custom of soliciting alms at the feast of the Nativity. In the first place, the custom ante-dates Christianity. In the "Cronia" of Lucian that I have already quoted, the dialogue between Cronus (or Saturn) and his priest considers, among other matters, the sending of gifts at the time of *Saturnalia,* and the type of gift proper to each class of recipient. Of what sort, for instance, shall be the clothing, utensils or money presents sent by rich men to poor, and of what sort shall be the gifts in return? "If the poor man have learning, his return gift is to be an ancient book, but of good omen and festive humour, or a writing of his own after his ability. . . . For the unlearned, let him send a garland or grains of frankincense."

Libanus, the Greek sophist of the fourth century, says, in talking of the Kalends—the period at the beginning of the year which was marked by Saturnalian revelry: "The festival of the Kalends is celebrated everywhere, as far as the limits of the Roman Empire extend. . . . The impulse to spend seizes everyone. He who the whole year through has taken pleasure in saving and piling up his pence, become suddenly extravagant. . . . People are not only generous towards themselves, but generous towards their fellow-men. A stream of presents pours itself out on all sides. . . . The Kalends festival banishes all that is connected with toil, and allows men to give themselves up to undisturbed enjoyment. From the minds of young people it removes two kinds of dread: the dread of the schoolmaster and the dread of the stern pedagogue[1]. . . . Another great quality of the festival is that it teaches men not to hold too fast to their money, but to part with it and let it pass into other hands."

What truer description could there be of the spirit of Christmas than the above passage? How clearly it shows how ancient is that spirit, and how little altered the winter feast has been as Europe had passed from paganism to Christianity!

Note particularly the emphasis on gift-making in the old—as in the newer—days of rejoicing. On New Year's Day, the Kalends of January, gifts were exchanged among all classes of the population, and the modern French word for such gifts—*étrennes*—is only the very slightly altered Latin *strenae*. It is recorded how the Emperor Caligula, taking the custom of giving a little too seriously, published an edict, making gifts to himself compulsory, and even stood in the porch of his palace to receive them!

"Christmas-boxes" have been traditionally given on the day after Christmas, St. Stephen's Day, which is why we now call it Boxing Day. After gifts to the family and to friends comes the Christmas-box to tradesmen, postmen, policemen, and all those useful persons who, though not of the family circle, have come to acquire an intimacy with us through the accident of constant daily familiarity.

The custom survived the many changes of rule and social behaviour in Britain; so that, in the accounts of the great monastery at Syon, in Middlesex, we find Dame Agnes Merett, the Cellaress, entering, among the "foreigne paymentes": "Reward to the ser-

[1] Thus we see that modern opinion has come around to the Roman idea that the schoolmaster and the pedagogue are not necessarily identifiable.

vauntes at Crystemas. with their aprons xxs. Reward to the Clerk of the Kechyn, xiijs. iiijd. Reward to the Baily of the Husbandry, vis. viijd. Reward to the Keeper of the Covent Garden, vis. viijd." And Beaumont and Fletcher, in their *Wit Without Money*, say: "A widow is a Christmas-box that sweeps all."

Writing to Stella on 26 December, 1710, Swift complains: "By the Lord Harry, I shall be undone here with Christmas-boxes. The rogues at the Coffee-house have raised their tax, every one giving a crown, and I gave mine for shame, besides a great many half-crowns to great men's porters."

And again, on 24 December, a year later: "I gave Patrick half a crown for his Christmas-box, on condition he would be good; and he came home drunk at midnight." If any quotation from other days more clearly marks the difference between then and now, I cannot recall it. Where today could an Irish servant get drunk on Christmas Eve on half a crown? Note that the expression "for his Christmas-box" was an exact one. There was an actual box for the receipt of gifts—the Christmas Box—and when it was filled, the box (usually made of fired clay) had to be broken to get at the contents.

In Mason's *Handful of Essaies*, 1621, there is the aphorism: "Like a swine, he never doth good till his death; as an apprentice's box of earth, apt he is to take all, but to restore none till hee be broken."

Aubrey, in his *Wiltshire Collections* (about 1670), records the finding of a hoard of Roman coins. "Among the rest was an earthen pott of the colour of a Crucible, and of the shape of a prentice's Christmas Box, with a slit in it, containing about a quart, which was near full of money. This pot I gave to the Repository of the Royal Society of Gresham College."

It is not often that the custom of taking survives less than the custom of giving, but fewer callers for their Christmas-box ring the door-bell these days. The postman, even, sometimes forgets to remind the householder, and of all his once numerous companions hardly three are left—and their calls are sporadic where once they would have come with the unfailing regularity of Christmas itself.

On St. Stephen's Day it used to be the custom to blood all the cart-horses.

Let Christmas be passed, let horsse be let blood,
For manie a purpose it dooth him much good;
The day of S. Steeven old fathers did use;
If that do mislike thee, some other day chuse.

In some parts of Wales they had the singular custom, on this day, of blooding humans instead of horses, by whipping each other's legs with holly, until the blood ran: possibly in symbolical representation of St. Stephen's death by stoning. This day was sometimes celebrated with great festivity, even though it was but one day after the Nativity. Southey, the Poet Laureate whom Byron so heartily detested, records in his *Common Place Book* that the Vicar of Bampton, Oxfordshire, used to serve out beef and beer on St. Stephen's morning to any who cared to partake of the refreshment. This was called "St. Stephen's breakfast."

An alderman of Leicester, writing to his brother in Wood Street, Cheapside, London, on 2 January, 1614, says: "Yow wryte how yow reacayved my lettar on St. Steven's day, and that, I thanke yow, yow esteemede yt as welcoom as the 18 trumpytors: w^t in so doing, I must and will esteme yowres, God willing, more wellcoom then trumpets and all the musicke we have had since Christmas, and yet we have had prety store bothe of owre owne and othar, evar since Christmas. And the same day we were busy w^t hollding up hands and spoones to yow, out of porredge and pyes, in the remembraunce of yowre greate lyberality of frute and spice, which God send yow long lyffe to contynew, for of that day we have not myssed anny St. Steven this 47 yeare to have as many gas [guests] as my howse will holld, I thank God for yt."

We used to observe a curious Christmas custom in my native Kent, to which the name of "hodening" was given; and the character of which custom tempts one to see in it old memories of the first Jutish invaders, whose totem-animal was the horse.

"When I was a lad," wrote a contributor to the *Church Times* of 23 January, 1891, "about forty-five years since, it was always the custom, on Christmas Eve, with the male farm servants from every farm in our parish of Hoath (Borough of Reculver) and neighbouring parishes of Herne and Chislet, to go round in the evening from house to house with the hoodining horse, which consisted of the imitation of a horse's head made of wood, life size, fixed on a stick about the length of a broom handle, the lower jaw of the head was made to open with hinges, a hole was made through the roof of the mouth, then another through the forehead, coming out by the throat; through this was passed a cord attached to the lower jaw, which, when pulled by the cord at the throat, caused it to close and open; on the lower jaw large-headed hobnails were driven in to form the teeth. The strongest of the lads was selected for the horse; he stooped and made as long a back as he could, supporting himself by the stick carrying the head; then he was covered with a horse-cloth, and one of his companions mounted his back. The horse had a bridle and reins. Then commenced the kicking, rearing, jumping, etc., and the banging together of the teeth. As soon as the doors were opened the 'horse' would pull his string incessantly, and the noise made can be better imagined than described. I confess that, in my very young days, I was horrified at the approach of the hoodining horse, but, as I grew older, I used to go round with them. I was at Hoath on Thursday last, and asked if the custom was still kept up. It appears it is now three or four years since it has taken place. I never heard of it in the Isle of Thanet. There was no singing going on with the hoodining horse, and the party was strictly confined to the young men who went with the horses on the farms. I have seen some of the wooden heads carved out quite hollow in the throat part, and two holes bored through the forehead to form the eyes. The lad who played the horse would hold a lighted candle in the hollow, and you can imagine how horrible it was to anyone who opened the door to see such a thing close to his eyes. Carollers in those days were called hoodiners in the parishes I have named." The last sentence seems rather to contradict an earlier one, in which the writer says: "there was no singing going on."

But in other parts of Kent—where the horse was called a "hoden," and not a "hoodin"—songs and bell-ringing accompanied the noise of the clacking jaws. Both at Ramsgate and at Walmer, hodening was the annual custom.

Whether or not the "hoden" is a relic of our Jutish ancestors, whose totem was, as I said, the horse, we cannot say; but that "hodening" is a custom of immense antiquity is certain. At least as far back as the seventh century of our era, we find a similar custom condemned in the *Penitential* of Archbishop Theodore of Canterbury (died A.D. 690). His Grace lays down penalties for those who "on the Kalends of January, clothe themselves with the skins of cattle and carry heads of animals." It may be noted here that the Ramsgate "hodeners" carried a real horse's skull, and not a wooden imitation.

The Archbishop's condemnation makes it evident that the custom was of pagan origin—or so considered; and as it was the custom of our Teutonic ancestors to offer up sacrifices of horses to Odin, to secure victory to the tribe, the name of the Teutonic All-father—Odin, Woden or Wotan—may be perpetuated, hardly altered, in the name of the Thanet Christmas "hoden."

Another ancient custom of which traces still survive in the country parts is that of "wassailing the trees." The custom combines two of the main elements in primitive fertility magic—fire and noise; and though shotguns are sometimes used, they are obviously only an innovation replacing earlier means of producing similar results.

In the *Gentleman's Magazine* for 1791 there is a clear description of this ceremony, which, in Devonshire, took place on Twelfth Night.

"On the Eve of the Epiphany, the farmer, attended by his workmen, with a large pitcher of cyder, goes to the orchard, and there, encircling one of the best-bearing trees, they drink the following toast three several times:

Here's to thee, old apple tree,
Whence thou may'st bud, and whence thou may'st blow!
And whence thou may'st bear apples enow!
Hats full!—Caps full!
Bushel—bushel—sacks full!
And my pockets full, too! Huzza!

"This done, they return to the house, the doors of which they are sure to find bolted by the females, who, be the weather what it may, are inexorable to all entreaties to open them, till some one has guessed at what is on the spit, which is generally some nice little thing difficult to be hit on, and is the reward of him who first names it. The doors are then thrown open, and the lucky clodpole receives the tit-bit as his recompense. Some are so superstitious as to believe that, if they neglect this custom, the trees will bear no apples that year."

In this Devonshire custom the sacred, the ritual fire is represented only by the fire on which the roast "tit-bit" is cooking; but the fire is very much more in evidence in the Herefordshire "wassailing" whereon to the beliefs of ancient paganism had been grafted the newer concepts of Christianity.

"A farmer's wife," says Cuthbert Bede in *Notes and Queries* (2 ser., viii, 488), "told me that where she had lived in Hertfordshire, twenty years ago, they were wont, on Twelfth Night Eve, to light in a wheat field twelve small fires and one large one. . . . She told me that they were designed to represent the blessed Saviour and his twelve Apostles. The fire representing Judas Iscariot, after being allowed to burn for a brief time, was kicked about and put out . . . the same person also told me that the ceremony of placing the twelfth cake on the horn of the ox was observed in all the particulars . . . It was twenty years since she had left the farm, and she had forgotten all the words of the toast used on that occasion: she could only remember one verse out of three or four:

> "Fill your cups, my merry men all!
> For here's the best ox in the stall!
> Oh, he's the best ox, of that there's no mistake,
> And so let us crown him with the Twelfth Cake."

The "Twelfth Cake," of course, was the rich cake—usually plentifully daubed with almond-paste—which was cooked especially for eating on Twelfth Night. Ceremonial cookery has always been a part of primitive religion. In Spain, they thread thin, sweet biscuits, delicately coloured, on string, to be given away at the church doors at Christmas. These biscuits are called "the Baptism of Jesus"—or perhaps it is more correct to say that the giving and the eating of the biscuits is so called.

The ceremony is certainly pre-Christian. The Punic Astarte and the Alexandrian "Kore the Maiden" were both "worshipped with small cakes."

According to an article which appeared in the *Illustrated London News* of 11 January, 1851, some of the tree-wassailing in Devonshire was done with shot-guns, the noise and fire demanded by the necessities of the ritual being supplied together in the discharge of the weapons into the apple-trees' bare branches. Then followed the song "Here's to thee, etc.," the ritual cider-drinking, and the return to the house with barred doors.

Herrick knew the custom of "wassailing the fruit-trees" well;

and in some parts of the country it was on Christmas Eve and not on Twelfth Night Eve that the wassailing was done. Twelfth Night being more intimately associated with the Ritual Fire (though the Yule Log and our modern Christmas crackers show that fire was associated with Christmas Day as well), the wassailing done on Christmas Eve was usually—though not always—confined to serenading the trees and pouring out libations to the Spirit of the Tree. In Devonshire this old fertility-rite was sometimes carried out by the farmer and his party dipping cakes into cider and eating them; then proceeding with more hot cider and a cake to the principal apple tree, where the cake was solemnly dipped in the cider, and laid in the fork of the tree, the cider being thrown over it.

In the New Forest, the sung charm was:

Apples and pears, with right good corn,
Come in plenty to every one;
Eat and drink good cake and hot ale,
Give earth to drink, and she'll not fail.

Says Herrick:

Wassaile the Trees that they may beare
You many a Plum and many a Peare;
For more or lesse fruits they will bring,
As you do give them Wassailing.

In West Sussex the wassailing was called "worsling," and much —indeed, a vital—importance was attached to its proper observance. In West Sussex the singers were called "howlers," and they were accompanied by a trumpeter, who carried a cow's horn "on which he makes sweet music." A party of young men—mostly farm-labourers and the like—would call on a farmer with the inquiry: "Please, sir, do you want your trees worsled?"

Proceeding to the orchard, the party then chant some doggerel to the trees in a low voice, then finish up with a shouted chorus; the trumpeter giving a brave blast on his cow's horn. The party then beat the trees with sticks, as they do to this day in the Pyrenees. This act is to ensure the trees' fertility.

Not until all the trees have been wassailed do the party enter the kitchen of the farmer, and join in the Christmas feast.

One of the Sussex wassail rhymes goes:

Stand fast, root; bear well, top;
Pray the God send us a good howling crop.
Every twig, apples big;
Every bough, apples enow.
Hats full, caps full,
Full quarters, sacks full.
Holloa, boys, holloa! Hurrah!

Another runs:

Here's to thee, old apple tree;
May'st thou bud, may'st thou blow, etc.

This is almost identical with one of the Devonshire wassailing toasts, and shows how widespread—and therefore, presumably, how ancient—the custom is.

"Midnight mass" is regarded as so very particularly a Roman Catholic institution that it may interest many readers to know that a similar ceremony used formerly to be held in Wales. This was the service of *Plygain*, and was more properly a dawn, rather than a midnight service. The custom survived well into the last part of the last century, but—possibly as a reaction to the revival of Welsh episcopalianism—nonconformity in Wales grew more "strict" as the century came to an end; so that a custom seeming to smack of Romanism or episcopalianism was dropped. There was an attempt to revive it, but a custom which has been discontinued can rarely be revived; and *Plygain* belongs to the past.

Since the Winter Festival was originally a feast to celebrate the re-birth of the sun after the apparent decay of that luminary, fires were always associated with the celebrations of the festival. I have mentioned that Guy Fawkes' Day is a part of the old "Christmas" festival, and it is proper that fireworks should be let off on that day. But ritual fires (or lights of any other kind) are found associated with all the other days of the Winter Festival, particularly on the day now called the Feast of the Epiphany, or Twelfth Day.

The cracker, as I mentioned, is the vestigial remains of a ritual fire—accompanied by noise (to simulate a storm of thunder and lightning)—and the modern cracker is less true to its nature because of the paper which has come to surround it. The cracker that John

Leech's timid young ladies shudder as they pull was a real cracker: designed only to make a loud bang and to give a bright flash. A true Christmas cracker.

But it was the custom to hold real fire-ceremonies, and I see in the columns of the newspapers that the custom appears to be taking a fresh hold upon the popular fancy, just as the public Christmas-tree is doing.

A notice of 1830 has this to say of Herefordshire customs at Christmas: "On the eve of Old Christmas Day[1] there are thirteen fires lighted in the cornfields of many of the farms, twelve of them in a circle, and one round a pole, much longer and higher than the rest, in the centre. These fires are dignified by the names of the Virgin Mary and the Twelve Apostles, the lady being in the middle; and while they are burning, the labourers retire into some shed or outhouse, where they can behold the brightness of the Apostolic flame. Into this shed they lead a cow, on whose horn a large plum cake has been stuck, and having assembled round the animal, the oldest labourer takes a pail of cider, and addresses the following lines to the cow with great solemnity; after which the verse is chaunted in chorus by all present:

"Here's to thy pretty face and thy white horn,
God send thy master a good crop of corn,
Both wheat, rye, and barley, and all sorts of grain,
And next year, if we live, we'll drink to thee again.

"He then dashes the cider in the cow's face, when, by a violent toss of her head, she throws the plum cake on the ground; and if it falls forward, it is an omen that the next harvest will be good; if backward, that it will be unfavourable. This is the ceremony at the commencement of the rural feast, which is generally prolonged to the following morning."

Not all of these old customs have disappeared, and, like the lighting of Christmas bonfires, some which appeared to be obsolete or obsolescent have acquired a new life. The Scots custom of the "first-footing" is still widely observed, and not only in Scotland, nor even exclusively among persons of Scottish descent or affiliations. *Chambers's Book of Days*, in an edition of near a hundred years ago,

[1] See page 178. "Old Christmas," falling eleven days after "New Christmas," would thus coincide with Twelfth Night.

stated that the custom was then dying out, but if it was dying out it has since acquired an astonishing vitality. "To such an extent did this custom prevail in Edinburgh, in the recollection of persons still living, that, according to their account, the principal streets were more thronged between twelve and one in the morning than they usually were at midday. Much innocent mirth prevailed, and mutual good-feelings were largely promoted."

This description might apply, without the alteration of a single word, to the streets of London on any New Year's morning in these times. But—fortunately!—the rest of the description of old Edinburgh's New Year's morning is not so applicable to the present day.

"An unlucky circumstance, which took place on the 1st January of 1812, proved the means of nearly extinguishing the custom. A small party of reckless boys formed the design of turning the innocent festivities of first-footing to account, for the purposes of plunder. They kept their counsel well. No sooner had the people come abroad on the principal thoroughfares of the Old Town, than these youths sallied out in small bands, and commenced the business which they had undertaken. Their previous agreement was—to *look out for the white neck-cloths,* such being the best mark by which they could distinguish, in the dark, individuals likely to carry any property worthy of being taken. A great number of gentlemen were thus spoiled of their watches and other valuables. The least resistance was resented by the most brutal maltreatment. A policeman and a young man of the rank of a clerk in Leith died of the injuries they had received. An affair so singular, so uncharacteristic of the people among whom it happened, produced a widespread and lasting feeling of surprise. The outrage was expiated by the execution of three of the youthful rioters on the chief scene of their wickedness; but from that time it was observed that the old custom of going about with the *hot pint*—the ancient wassail—fell off."

But whether or not the "Lord Mayor of Pennyless Cove," a fisherman of Tenby dressed up in a coat of evergreens, and wearing a mask, still makes the rounds, collecting at the houses, I do not know. The "Lord Mayor" used to be carried in a chair, by fellow fishermen, with two violinists playing before him—as the Corporation Waits played before the Lord Mayor of London. The escort used to knock at the Tenby doors, and the "Lord Mayor" used to wish the householder a Merry Christmas and Happy New Year! To respond to the "Lord Mayor's" good wishes with something a little more material brought cheers both from the "Lord Mayor" and from his escort. It was also the pleasant custom of the young men of Tenby at four o'clock on Christmas morning to light their vicar with torches from his residence to the church.

Nor do I suppose that the inhabitants of the Lancashire town of Walton-le-Dale still sit up on Christmas Eve, with the doors of all the houses open, so that St. Luke, who they know is passing through the town, will be able to pass through each house.

But Christmas is a living thing. The methods of observing the Nativity may tend towards uniformity and a lack of variety, as national newspapers and the radio break down the distinctions between town and country custom. But Christmas will always be celebrated in some fashion—and if rationing has the effect of further lightening the once too-heavily laden tables of Christmas, be sure that there will be found means to distinguish the season from all the other days of the year.

"To think," said Queen Victoria, in her *Journal*, "that we have two children now, and one who enjoys the sight already, is like a dream!" And the Prince Consort, in writing to his father, echoes the same sentiment: "This is the dear Christmas Eve, on which I have so often listened with impatience for your step, which was to usher us into the present-room. Today I have two children of my own to give presents to, who, they know not why, are full of happy wonder at the German Christmas-tree and its radiant candles.

"The coming year was danced into in good old English fashion."[1] In the middle of the dance, as the clock finished striking twelve, a flourish of trumpets was blown, in accordance with a German custom. This, the Queen's *Journal* records, "had a fine solemn effect, and quite affected dear Albert, who turned pale, and had tears in his eyes, and pressed my hand very warmly. It touched me, too, for I felt that he must think of his dear native country, which he has left for me."

That is the universal and timeless magic of Christmas: that it binds the Prince, listening to the trumpets at Windsor, and "the oldest labourer" on the Herefordshire farm, dashing a pail of cider in the cow's face, and wishing for good crops in the ensuing year.

[1] *Life of the Prince Consort,* Sir Theodore Martin.

CHAPTER THIRTEEN

# COMMERCIALIZING FATHER CHRISTMAS

In the "want ad." column of an evening paper shortly before Christmas I recently noticed the following:

> Big West End store requires FATHER CHRISTMAS.
> Good wages. Staff canteen. Apply Box——.

Every year similar advertisements appear in newspapers all over the country—all over the world, for that matter; and that there are successful applicants for the job we see by the fact that, cloaked and hooded in scarlet, benignly bearded and tenderly cheerful of mien, Father Christmas is to be seen each year "upstairs in the Toys," shaking hands with hundreds of children as he hands them their presents.

It might be a profitable investigation for the novelist—even for the sociologist—to discover what all these Father Christmasses are when, during the other forty-eight weeks of the year, they are not being Father Christmas. But it is no part of my duty here to go off on *that* chase!

I mentioned the advertisement, and the fact that it implies, because a modern Christmas without Father Christmas—Santa Claus, if you prefer; though that name is American-Dutch and not English—would be unthinkable.

For Father Christmas *is* Christmas . . . literally. He is not, in his present guise, very old: hardly more than a hundred; but he has come to be, in that century, at once a person and a symbol. He is at once the Spirit of Christmas and a real person: yes, even though we may be aware that he does not exist.

Christmas Eve used to be known, in the very oldest Church

calendars, as "Adam and Eve Day," the idea underlying the selection of this day for the commemoration of our First Parents being that Christ wiped out, by His sacrifice, the burden that Adam and Eve's sin had laid upon the whole human race.

There is an ancient legend that, when Adam, driven out by the angel with the flaming sword, left Eden, he took with him—as a souvenir of lost happiness—a twig from that apple-tree which had caused all the trouble. Somewhere in the hard world outside the gates of Eden this twig was planted and eventually grew into a tree. And, eventually, by a singular accident, which yet may have had more of design in it than men saw, the wood of that apple-tree provided the timber for the Cross.

Father Christmas is commonly equated with St. Nicholas—hence the nickname "Santa Claus"; and St. Nicholas, Bishop of Myra in Asia Minor in the fourth century, is the patron saint of children, as well as, in southern Italy and Greece, of sailors.

But our modern Father Christmas has something much more universal in him than any one historical personage could exhibit. For Father Christmas—Santa Claus—is the personification of paternity. He is a sort of universal father, and not just some kindly guardian of children's rights and pleasures. In the opinion of this writer at least, the likeness of Father Christmas to Adam, the Universal Father, is much more evident than his likeness to St. Nicholas, Bishop of Myra.

St. Nicholas's Day is celebrated on 6 December; and this date has a non-Christian significance. It seems that, though there were certain pre-Christian festivals—such as the Kalends of January and the *Saturnalia*—which coincided with our present Christmas-tide (so that we may not unreasonably infer that the Church merely adapted old festivals to newer uses) not all the peoples whose various customs have been welded together to form our own had their great yearly festivals at the same time.

The Celts, for instance, had a great annual feast that they called *Samhain*, which appears to mean either "summer's end" or "gathering." MacCulloch, in his *Religion of the Ancient Celts*, says that it is probable that it had its origin in a "pastoral and agricultural festival, which in time came to be looked upon as affording assistance to the powers of growth in their conflict with the powers of blight."

This feast coincided with—and, indeed, was dependent upon—

the great annual slaughter which followed immediately upon the coming of winter: the first snowfall probably being the fact formally recognized as marking the end of the summer.

Poor methods of agriculture in ancient days prevented the storage of hay and root-crops for cattle-feed, and most of the beasts had to be killed off on the approach of winter, their meat being salted down for food, and their hides providing the necessary replacements of clothing for the tribe.

Killing-time, then, marked the end of the year among some primitive peoples, and modern research has tended to show that the realization of astronomical phenomena came late in the history of the Aryan-speakers. First came the feast made possible by unavoidable killing of the cattle; then came the feast to celebrate the solstices and equinoxes—or, rather, the original practical origin of the annual winter feast was forgotten as the advancement of learning brought knowledge of the movements of the heavenly bodies, and of the realization that the seasons bore some intimate relation to those movements.

One point must be borne clearly in mind in talking of the great festivals of our remote ancestors: that the calendar is a very recent invention except among the most civilized peoples.

Nor does a calendar come into being save until after a people has settled down in one place for a long period. Both our Celtic and our Teutonic ancestors were nomads until only a few hundred years ago, and the seasons for them terminated at different dates in different regions of the world. The end-of-the-year among the Celts of Galatia in Asia Minor (to whose Church St. Paul wrote one of his most famous epistles) would naturally fall on a different date from the end-of-the-year kept by the Celts of the Danube Basin; and when the Celts of the Danube moved farther west—to Gaul, to Britain, to Ireland and Wales—their end-of-the-year would tend to become later, as the milder climate made the cattle-killing keep to a later date.

Dr. Tille, the eminent German writer on the origins of Yule and Christmas, points out that, while the annual killing of beasts took place originally in mid-November, the progress of agriculture tended to destroy the mid-November celebrations. He further points out that in the Carolingian period an improvement took place in the cultivation of meadows, "and the increased quantity of hay made it

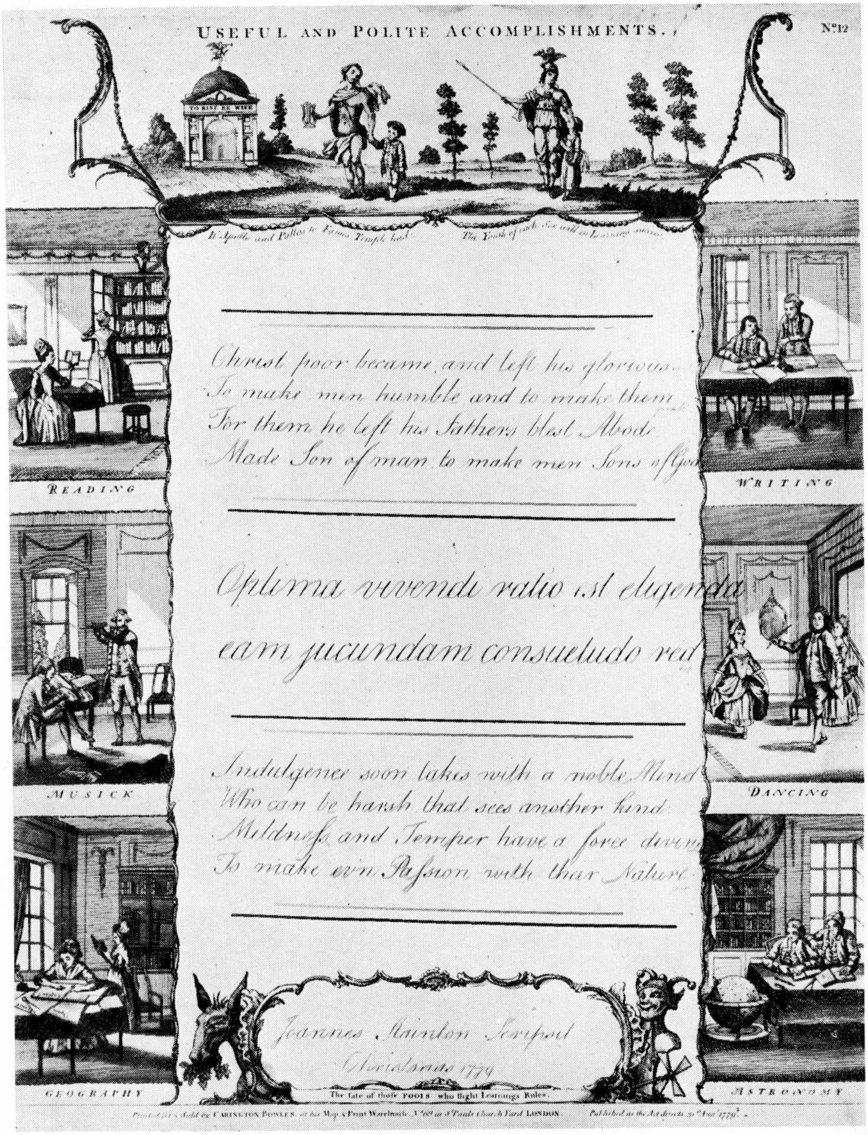
USEFUL AND POLITE ACCOMPLISHMENTS.
No. 12
Christ poor became, and left his glorious
To make men humble and to make them
For them he left his Fathers blest Abode
Made Son of man to make men Sons of God
Optima vivendi ratio est eligenda
eam jucundam consuetudo red
Indulgence soon takes with a noble Mind
Who can be harsh that sees another kind
Mildness and Temper have a force divine
To make ev'n Passion with their Nature
READING
WRITING
MUSICK
DANCING
GEOGRAPHY
ASTRONOMY
Joannes Stainton Scripsit
Christmas 1779
The fate of those FOOLS who slight Learnings Rules.

A "Christmas Piece." "Useful and Polite Accomplishments"—*If Apollo and Pallas to Fame's Temple lead, the Youth of each Sex will in Learning succeed.* These sheets with decorated borders—the example is dated 31 August, 1779—were sold to schools, and were taken home at the Christmas holidays complete with samples of the children's handwriting. John Stainton, who signed himself "Joannes Stainton," was only seven when he wrote this beautiful "piece" at Christmas, 1779.

The itinerant ballad-monger of the not-so-good-old-days. A sprig of holly in his hat, watched by a charity boy, he offers a broadsheet of Christmas carols, while he and his family sing the airs to the words that he hopes to sell.

*Above:* Christmas customs in Serbia, then a province of Turkey-in-Europe, now part of the Republic of Yugoslavia. The illustration, from an old wood-cut, shows oxen dragging the *Badujak*, or Yule-log, home; burning of the Log by the head of the household; and the arrival of the *Polaznik*, or messenger of Luck—a custom comparable with the Scots "first-footing." *Below:* Breton peasants playing Christmas music on their bagpipes.

A "Lazarus"—blind beggar—visits a Russian household of the last century with his illuminated crib. The Epiphany-star is to the Russian Christmas what holly and mistletoe are to the British, and on Epiphany Eve the maidens went into the fields to pray to the "Stars, stars, dear little stars" to find them husbands.

possible to keep the animals fattening in stall, instead of slaughtering them as soon as the pastures were closed. Thus the killing-time, with its festivities, became later and later. St. Andrew's Day (30 November) and St. Nicholas's (6 December) may mark stages in its progress into the winter. In St. Nicholas's Day, indeed, we find a feast that closely resembles Martinmas, and seems to be the same folk-festival transferred to a later date. Again, as regards England, we must remember the difference between its climate and that of Central Europe. Mid-November would here not be a date beyond which pasturing was impossible, and thus the slaughter and feast held then by Angles and Saxons in their old German home would tend to be delayed."

England is notorious for its conservatism; but what a hint of immense antiquity there is in the fact that the Lord Mayor of London begins his new year on 9 November! And if we like to think of Guy Fawkes' Day as another New Year's Day, we have an even earlier chronology represented in a still-honoured festival.

St. Nicholas's Day, then, marks a period in the gradual deferment of the end-of-the-year until the date at which we now celebrate it, and which has been fixed by the calendar now universally used; just as the introduction of printing standardized our spelling —putting an end to all but the most trivial change.

But though the year's end became progressively later, until the use of the calendar prevented all further postponement, the older years'-ends were not altogether forgotten. They remained as a sort of subsidiary years'-ends; and though not any longer the year's most important festival, each continued to be held in regard as very important festivals, being "Christianized" as the feast-day of some saint, though their original significance was never allowed to be quite forgotten.

St. Nicholas's Day, then, is an old year's-end—or year's-beginning—which has been sanctified by the patronage of a Christian saint. How that saint became the peculiar friend of children and sailors (the same thing, in the opinion of some!) it is not easy to say. Certainly the miraculous legend of St. Nicholas's life pays some attention to his early piety, learning and power to restore children to life; but this is not at all unusual in saints.

I should hate to cast doubts on the actuality of this good man merely on the strength of his name; but it is a fact—I believe hitherto unnoticed—that his name *could* be derived from two Greek words, and could mean "darkness lifted": a significant sort of name for a "saint" whose day was an old New Year!

In an earlier chapter I talked about the Boy Bishops. It was on St. Nicholas's Day that they were enthroned, and their reign lasted from that day until Holy Innocents' Day. Boy Bishops and, indeed, the celebration of St. Nicholas's Day, went out of fashion in England and Scotland with the Reformation; but in the Catholic countries of Europe his feast-day is still one of the most important in the calendar. In Germany, Switzerland and Austria adults dress up as St. Nicholas, as in Britain they impersonate Father Christmas; and in Holland and Belgium, where the shops on St. Nicholas's Day are full of gilt gingerbread images of the saint, the children hang up their stockings for presents; and in these countries, too, fathers and uncles and elder brothers dress up as St. Nicholas, in robes and mitre and carrying an episcopal crozier, to visit the children, and to question them on their behaviour: a rebuke for the bad ones, and the promise of a present for those who have been good. When the children hang up their stockings for the promised gift, they do not forget to put a carrot or a wisp of hay in the stockings for the saint's white horse.

The fact that Santa Claus seems to have a reverse identity in Old Nick seems to be something more than a coincidence when we see that in the Tyrol, when St. Nicholas "in all the splendour of a church-image; a reverend grey-haired figure with flowing beard, gold-broidered cape and pastoral staff," comes to visit the children, he brings with him the terrifying Klaubauf (note the similarity to, and difference from, the name of the saint). This monster is covered with a shaggy hide, wears horns, has a black face, fiery eyes, long red tongue, and clanks in chains.

Children are asked by St. Nicholas to say their Catechism, and for those who know the responses there are good things out of the basket that the saint carries. To those who fail to give the correct answer, St. Nicholas points out the hideous Klaubauf—who is, of course, the Saint's double, his Doppelgänger—or worse self. Indeed, St. Nicholas, abroad, is very much of a double character; a mixture of good and evil; as are we all.

All through the Germanic countries he goes attended by this sinister Other Self, which bears the name of Krampus (or Grampus) in Lower Austria, Bartel in Styria. And sometimes the saint is somehow amalgamated with this other self, so that the composite is neither as good as Nicholas nor as grim as Klaubauf: an ordinary sort of out-of-the-ordinariness, in fact, like Pelzmärte, with his bell, or Aschenklas with his sack of ashes.

Often we find St. Nicholas accompanied, not by a worse, but by a better self. At Warnsdorf, near Rumburg, he comes to visit the children attended by the famous "Knight Rupprecht" (an ancient Aryan personification of the splendour of aristocracy), St. Peter, an angel, or even the Saviour Himself.

At Warnsdorf a little play is given, in which children play the parts. St. Nicholas, St. Peter and Knecht Rupprecht wrangle over the punishment to be awarded to the naughty children, until Der Heiliger Christus comes in and intercedes for all.

In the Tyrol, St. Nicholas's Day is the occasion for the performance of plays, of a robust and sometimes coarse humour. Sometimes, the demon attendant upon St. Nicholas takes a female form—Budelfrau in Lower Austria, Berchtel in Swabia, Buzebergt in Augsburg—and sometimes even the female demon appears alone, to dispense rewards and punishments in the manner of St. Nicholas.

St. Nicholas, as Santa Klaus, was taken to America in the seventeenth century from Holland, readily adopted by the English settlers who, beginning as neighbours, eventually became the conquerors of the Dutch. From English America, Santa Claus was exported to the Old Country, where he found as warm a welcome as had been given to him by the colonists that the Old Country sent out three hundred years ago.

The derivation of Santa Claus's trappings and accessories is obscure; but they are as established by custom as are Uncle Sam's strapped trousers, goatee and American-Flag-coloured hat, or John Bull's low-crowned topper, buff-topped hessians and Union-Jack waistcoat. It is easy enough to account for the scarlet hooded cloak: this must have been a common enough garment among the early Dutch settlers of Manhattan and Haarlem and Poughkeepsie—as common, indeed, in its day, as Uncle Sam's strapped pantaloons were in theirs. And since legend represented the saint as coming from the north (but there is a historical query: *why* the north?) he would be given reindeers as his beasts of burden. As for his preference for chimneys, this can be explained easily and convincingly by an association of St. Nicholas with the Celtic old New Year and thus with the ritual fires which are still so intimately associated with the great popular festivals.

Remember that the chimney itself is a comparatively modern invention. At Penshurst, in Kent, the great hall of the Sidneys' ancestral home has its hearth in the middle of the room, and the smoke escapes through louvres in the roof. Surely the original Santa Claus was rather connected with the hearth—the great open hearth that the Romans called "focus" and so gave us our idea of "a central point"—than with the chimney?

There is a Slavonic custom which bears out this theory; for the Slav equivalent of St. Nicholas in his "Aschenklas" identity is the *polaznik*, who visits the Crivoscian farms on Christmas Day, and takes up handfuls of ash from the Yule Log, dashing them against the cauldron-hook above, so that the sparks fly.

In any case, that aspect of St. Nicholas called "Aschenklas," who wears bells and carries a long pole with a bag of ashes at the end, has two of the characteristics of Santa Claus: the "jingle-bells," "sleigh bells," and the affinity with ashes and soot.

But there is another Santa Claus in America: a far more shadowy personage who, so far, has escaped materialization at the pens and brushes of American artists. His name is Krishkringle, which is certainly derived from "Christ(us)-kindlein"—"Christ-child." In American nurseries he is credited with the same kindly intentions and powers as those which make Santa Claus so great a favourite with the children. For so vague a personage, Krishkringle has a most easily traceable pedigree in his native Germany—for he is German, where Santa Claus is Dutch.

I mentioned above that, in the Warnsdorf St. Nicholas plays, the Saint is accompanied by, among others, Christ. The tendency in some parts of Germany has been to transfer the attributes of St. Nicholas to Christ Himself, as the year's-end which once fell upon St. Nicholas's Day has been transferred to the day most intimately associated with the Saviour.

But the curious aspect of the transfer of attributes is this: that in acquiring St. Nicholas's love of chimneys and his habit of putting gifts into stockings and of threatening bad little boys and girls with punishment, Christ has lost, not only His divinity but, we would say, His human identity as well. As "Christkind," he becomes a mere shadow, an effigy, a puppet, an abstraction: indeed, what Krishkringle is in present-day America.

Perhaps the reason for this is to be found in the origins of "Christ-kind." He is not, like St. Nicholas, an entirely spontaneous product of centuries of custom and observance; rather is he an artificial attempt to substitute the worship of the Godhead for that of His creatures; of Christ for that of His saints. "Christ-kind" is a Protestant conception; a deliberate attempt to remove a Catholic element from a traditional folk-custom. It would have pleased strict Protestantism better to have removed the conception of a mythical gift-bringer altogether; but as this was seen to be impossible, it was decided to substitute Christ for St. Nicholas. It was essentially a compromise, and, like most compromises, it failed. St. Nicholas is alive; "Christ-kind" is an anaemic fabrication.

Indeed, so little resemblance does "Christ-kind" bear, either to episcopal Nicholas or to divine Christ, that "Christ-kind" often appears as a tall young girl, with long flaxen hair, dressed in white! "He hovers, indeed," says Miles, "between the character of the Divine Infant and that of an angel, and is regarded more as a kind of good fairy than as anything else."

The difference between the orderliness of the German mind and the happy-go-lucky tolerance of the English is well shown in the German insistence upon the punishers of the bad children being as important characters in the Nicholas Myth as the rewarders of the good. The Alsatian girl who impersonates the "Christ-kind" always has with her the "terrible Hans Trapp, dressed in a bearskin, with blackened face, long beard, and threatening rod." He menaces the naughty children, who are saved from his claws only by the merciful intervention of the "Christ-kind." In England, of course, there is only the Rewarder in the Christmas fable: the bad, if they are punished, are punished in a negative, typically English way, by the mere absence of reward; not by any positive penalty. English Father Christmas never has a Hans Trapp or a Klaubauf with him; German St. Nicholas is never without something of the sort.

*Note:* In the Basque country and in the Dauphiné they look to St. Nicholas for more important gifts. In those primitive parts this saint has become—or, as anthropologists would prefer to say, still remains—a fertility god. Rocks of a certain shape are called by the saint's name—the Rocher de St. Nicholas, in Béarn, is an example—and girls go to the stones for husbands, and married women for children. *See* Van Gennep: *Le Folklore de Dauphiné*.

CHAPTER FOURTEEN

# ST. FRANCIS OF ASSISI

In the beginning of the thirteenth century the Church was moved by a mighty change: a change which was far more fundamentally important than ever the Reformation was later to prove; for the Reformation was a change mainly of political nature, while the great change at the beginning of the thirteenth century was a change of heart.

With this earlier change the name of St. Francis is most intimately connected, but he was rather the agent than the initiator of change. He canalized a surge of emotion which was sweeping the world, and, by his own personal response to that universal emotion, gave it form and permanence, and then brought its force to the service of the Church—which in those days meant the service of the one source of culture and civilization.

And yet the change involved none of the apparent elements either of culture or of civilization: there was a renascence of the heart, rather than of the mind. And to observers of the change—contemporary observers—it might have seemed that, intellectually considered, the change was a retrograde one.

Today we would classify the change of which Francis made himself the exponent and principal agent as a revivalistic impulse; save that "revivalism" infers the existence of previous standards from which, by laxity, the body of the Church has fallen away; and, in the days when Francis preached, it was a new and not a revived sentiment which was being preached.

In essence, the change consisted in taking the running of the Church out of the exclusive handling of the professionals, and admitting the laity to a share of the control. It was, in brief, a change in the direction of ecclesiastical democracy.

How Francis achieved this may be read in another place. What concerns us here is that he placed great reliance, in his efforts to "humanize" the Church, upon the avoidance of a coldly intellectual presentation of theological facts; preferring that the people should learn and understand those facts in terms of common life and happening. Seeing the Nativity as the cardinal fact of Christianity, Francis and his disciples hammered home the importance of that fact rather in terms of human sentiment than in terms of theological paradox. He wished the masses to love the Child and sympathize with the Parents, even though, for a moment, they forgot the majesty of God in seeing, with understanding human hearts, His condescension and humility.

The two men responsible for this revolution in sentiment were well fitted by birth, as well as by character, for Francis was the son of a rich, self-made silk-merchant, and Jacopone da Todi was an aristocrat who had voluntarily adopted the status of a working man, a peasant, and had emotionally identified himself with the common people. An hereditary instinct for the management of affairs gave a practical force to Francis's dreams, while Jacopone da Todi's aristocratic birth, together with his study of the mentality of the masses, enabled him to act as liaison-officer between the "progressives" and the "reactionaries": to persuade the "reactionaries" that the new change, though revolutionary, was not destructive; to persuade the masses by speaking to them with the strength of Authority's accustomed voice.

St. Francis instituted the special devotion to the Nativity: that is to say, he held up Christ's humanity rather than His more abstract qualities for the understanding adoration of the people. The most "human" thing in life is birth—for we are all born in the same way, though we may die in a hundred different ways—and so Francis instituted the cult of the Divine Birth, and gave the people the *presepe*—the Crib—to teach their minds by means of their eyes.

To Jacopone da Todi was left the task of "demotizing" the Church ritual: of presenting theological facts in the vernacular—vernacular ways of thought as well as vernacular speech. What helped to popularize the songs of Jacopone da Todi was the sincere emotions that he was able to command in their composition. For instance, what could be more touching or—compared with the chill theological disputatiousness which had before marked the Church's dogmatic utterances—newer than the following song of the Nativity by Jacopone?

It is the deservedly famous *Veggiamo il suo Bambino*, which is given here in J. A. Symonds's translation:

Come and look upon Her child
Nestling in the hay!
See his fair arms opened wide,
On her lap to play!
And she tucks him by her side,
Cloaks him as she may!
Gives her paps into his mouth,
Where his lips are laid.

She with left hand cradling,
Rocked and hushed her boy.
And with holy lullabies
Quieted her toy. . . .
Little angels all around
Danced, and carols flung;
Making verselets sweet and true,
Still of love they sung.

The translation fails to convey all the unaffected simplicity of the original; for Jacopone's simplicity was spontaneous, where Symonds's had, as it were, to be acquired. Miss Anne Macdonnell's translation of another of Jacopone's songs comes much nearer in spirit to the original:

Sweep hearth and floor;
Be all your vessel's store
Shining and clean.
Then bring the little guest
And give Him of your best
Of meat and drink. Yet more
Ye owe than meat.
One gift at your King's feet
Lay now. I mean
A heart full to the brim
Of love, and all for Him,
And from all envy clean.

To Jacopone is attributed the famous *Stabat Mater*, to which Rossini set music that legend tells us he stole from an ancient MS. in a monastery; music that I once heard—I trust without intent!—"swung" in a B.B.C. programme.

"There have been," says Miles, "few more rapturous poets than Jacopone; men deemed him mad; but 'if he is mad,' says a modern Italian writer, 'he is mad as the lark is mad'—*Nessun poeta canta a tutta gola come questo frate minore. S'e pazzo, e pazzo come l'allodola.*"

In the following century Germany experienced a spiritual reawakening, such as had come to Italy at the beginning of the thirteenth century; the difference being that Italy owed her "revival" to a Franciscan—to *the* Franciscan—where Germany owed hers to a Dominican, Eckhardt of Strassburg. The means of revival, though, being similar, the results in Germany did not materially differ from those in Italy, save perhaps that the two revivals differed as the difference between the intellectuality of Francis (which was not high) and that of Eckhardt (which was).

The songs—there is a significance in the word "hymn" which makes it unsuitable here—the songs that Eckhardt wrote are as simple and sincere as any that Jacopone da Todi wrote; and to one of Eckhardt's disciples, Johann Tauler, is credited the well-known:

A ship comes sailing onwards
With a precious freight on board;
It bears the only Son of God,
It bears the Eternal Word.

—one of the earliest of Christmas carols.

Like a later revivalist, General Booth, Eckhardt and his followers agreed with the sentiment that it is wrong to let the Devil have all the good tunes. The song quoted above is an adaptation of a secular song; and just as members of the Salvation Army, five hundred years later, were to put sacred words to popular songs, so did the followers of Eckhardt set the good folk of Germany to singing holy parodies of the songs that they knew and loved.

From this time of deep spiritual activity comes the charming carol which is still popular in Germany, both with Catholics and Protestants:

*Es ist ein Ros entsprungen*
*Aus einer Wurzel zart,*
*Als uns die Alten sungen,*
*Von Jesse kam die Art,*

*Und hat ein Blümlein bracht,*
*Mitten im kalten Winter,*
*Wohl zu der halben Nacht.*

*Das Röslein, das ich meine,*
*Davon Jesajas sagt,*
*Hat uns gebracht alleine*
*Marie, die reine Magd.*
*Aus Gottes ew'gem Rat*
*Hat sie ein Kind geboren*
*Wohl zu der halben Nacht.*

Of which the first stanza, in Winkworth's translation, runs as follows:

A spotless Rose is blowing,
Sprung from a tender root,
Of ancient seers' foreshowing,
Of Jesse promised fruit;
Its fairest bud unfolds to light
Amid the cold, cold winter,
And in the dark midnight.

The fourteenth century was the period of freedom for the lower orders: the period when they emerged from villeinage into something like a state of control over their own lives and labour. It was the period which saw the end of the feudal system in England, and an actual though not official end of it in continental Europe. For the Black Death had come, to take one man in two, and to prove to society that even the worthless clods who were bought and sold with the manors, like the sheep in their pens and the cows in their byres, acquired a formidable value when plague diminished their number by no less than fifty per cent. Short of workmen—for we do not imagine that the plague was mathematically precise in its ravages, and took exactly fifty per cent everywhere, so that all populations were reduced in the same proportion—the employers broke the feudal laws designed for their own advantage in different social conditions. They bid for workmen's services; bid against each other; bid in defiance of the feudal laws that they themselves had evolved. The workman, with employers bidding for his labour, rose rapidly in social condition. And though attempts were made, when the population had recovered somewhat from the depredations of the Black Death, to restore the former conditions of labour, all the attempts failed.

The Church, then—through the activities of such men as Francis of Assisi, Jacopone da Todi, Eckhardt and Johann Trauler—was brought to the people, just as the people were rising to be something more than draft-oxen.

They had always sung, of course; but their songs were now given the admission into polite usage which was to be given later to the rigadoon and the gavotte—both originally peasant dances before they were enjoyed at the courts of kings. Before the "demotization" of religion, the hierarchy and the people had been separated for centuries—as the conquering Norman-French and the conquered Anglo-Saxons were separated in England. The hierarchy used their own language—Latin—and the body of the Church spoke as many tongues as they did in Babel. Around A.D. 1300 the people came to share in the life of the Church, and the Church was the gainer.

Theology might have suffered, of course; it did. For the religion of the doctors and the religion of Jacques Bonhomme were different things: one a chill web of intellectual subtleties, the other a warm tangle of primitive superstitions. The Christ of the great Dominican, Eckhardt, was something essentially more refined than the Christ of the people to whom Eckhardt led his Christ.

The Christ of the people was like something (and I say this in all reverence) out of a modern children's comic. A loving little chap, as astonished as any peasant boy would be to find that He could perform miracles. This Christ-child uses, as we may understand, His magic for simple pleasures—even for childish revenges. But just because He is so simple, so peasant, so earthy, the Christ of the medieval clod lives. He—the Lord of the bumpkin—working the sort of conjuring tricks that Loblolly had gaped at in the country fairs—He lives and breathes and smiles and sulks and loves and forgives. Francis offered Him to the people, and the people, in one blinding flash of intuition, recognized Him as one of themselves, and took Him—bib and nappy and all—into their homes and their hearts, and for His praise they told His story in verses as rude and simple and innocent as themselves: verses which, like their Divine subject, will live for ever.

Here, for instance, is the splendid Scots translation—in *Godlie and Spirituall Songs*, of 1567—of a fourteenth-century German macaronic carol: that is, one in which the lines are given both in Latin and in the vernacular tongue:

*In dulci Jubilo,* Now lat us sing with myrth and jo
Our hartis consolatioun lyis *in praesepio,*
And schynis as the Sone, *Matris in gremio,*
*Alpha es et O, Alpha es et O.*
*O Jesu parvule!* I thrist sore efter the,
Confort my hart and mynde, *O puer optime,*
God of all grace sa kynde, *et princeps gloriae*
*Trahe me post te, Trahe me post te.*
*Ubi sunt gaudia,* in ony place bot thair,
Quhair that the Angellis sing *Nova cantica,*
Bot and the bellis ring *in regis curia,*
God gif I war thair, God gif I war thair!

England produced some carols which deserve to rank among the finest ever written, and some of those finest were written—or collected—for us by a blind parson of the fifteenth century, John Awdlay, of Haghmon, in the county of Shropshire.

At the end of a long and dreary piece of moralizing doggerel, Awdlay writes in red letters:

I pray you, sirus, boothe moore and lase,
Sing these caroles in Cristemas.

Thus proving that our use of the word "carol" for a religious song—especially one sung about or at Christmas—is of very ancient date. Originally the word meant any song; even an amorous ditty of far from religious sentiment. But that the word was adopted early to the meaning it now bears is proved by Awdlay's use of the word in its modern sense.

The tradition that Awdlay's collection represents is a hardy one. All through the Reformation the named and the nameless were penning their simple hymns of praise, and the tradition is not dead today.

What, for instance, could be more charming—aye, and more moving!—than this lullaby of 1530?

In a dream late as I lay,
Methought I heard a maiden say
    And speak these words so mild:

"My little son, with thee I play,
And come," she sang, "by, lullaby."
Thus rocked she her child.

*By-by, by-by, by-by, lullaby,*
*Rocked I my child.*
*By-by, by-by, by-by, lullaby,*
*Rocked I my child.*

And yet, simple as this is, there is a subtle polish somewhere which places it as the product of a more sophisticated age than that which produced, for instance:

What Wat to Bedlem cum was,
He swet, he had gone faster than a pace;
He found Jesu in a simpell place,
Betwen an ox and an asse.
Ut hoy!
For in his pipe he made so much joy.

"Jesu, I offer to thee here my pipe,
My skirt, my tar-box, and my scripe;
Home to my felowes now will I skipe,
And also look into my shepe."
Ut hoy!
For in his pipe he made much joy.

The Catholic and the High Church poets of the seventeenth century wonderfully sustained a tradition that one might have thought to see sadly weakened, if not altogether abolished, in an age of great intellectual activity.

Herrick, Cowley, Crashaw, Withers, Marvell and Milton all produced carols or Christmas poems, and here is a delightful example of seventeenth-century Christmas poetry. The poem is from the pen of the divine, Herrick:

Greene Rushes then, and sweetest Bents,
With cooler Oken boughs;
Come in for comely ornaments,
To readorn the house.
Thus times do shift; each thing his turn do's hold;
*New things succeed, as former things grow old.*

*New things succeed*. . . . Yes: but the old things still retain their charm and their magic for us. The new poems do not replace or displace the older. The anonymous *In Bedlem, that fayer cyte, Was born a chyld that was so fre*, still holds its own with the Christmas poems of Blake, Coleridge, Swinburne, Christina Rossetti, R. L. Stevenson, Andrew Lang, Francis Thompson, James Elroy Flecker and Thomas Hardy; though these do not suffer, indeed, in comparison with, for instance, the splendid fifteenth-century *I sing of a Maiden that is makeles*.

The tradition is immortal. As Miss Viola Gerard Garvin says, in her Christmas poem, *Holy Thorn*:

The bells ring out for Christmas day
With "Gloria" and "Gloria,"
And on the eastern horizon,
Flowers a rose-enfolding sun,
Fulfilling life.

The hawthorn tree,
Waking from what epiphany,
Ponders what winter, what high spring,
Met in that heavenly blossoming.

## CHAPTER FIFTEEN

# MODERN TENDENCIES

THERE is an universalizing influence at work in today's world. This might not be so bad a thing if the confounded influence were not always working in the direction of universal drabness, rather than of universal colour.

Mustafa Kemal Atatürk, "re-creating" the Turkish nation, abolishes the fez and orders, under the sternest penalties, that his emancipated subjects wear that grimmest of all headgear (especially when worn by a non-Anglo-Saxon): the bowler hat. Shawls and clogs vanish from Yorkshire, and baggy breeches and peaked caps from the Frisian Islands.

"Now," says Violet Alford, in her *Pyrenean Festivals*, "the damsels who don valley dress to dance at Ax or Luchon must be dosed with aspirin by the regionalist chemist, such headaches do their mothers' caps inspire."

Photographs of "popular rallies" from those countries the farther side of the Iron Curtain show that the people have abandoned their picturesque national costumes, and now wear a drab uniform which is as hopelessly dull as the regime which has enslaved them. It is not quite so bad the hither side of that sinister Curtain, but the tendency to sameness, to a preference for the drab in clothing and living, against what is colourful and romantic, goes on. Day by day an old custom passes, failing to stand up against the horrible test of the utilitarian and the practical.

Christmas has not escaped; and the lopping off of its "trimmings" has been going on for some time now. It was in 1821 that the annual bull-baiting at Wokingham on St. Thomas's Day was abolished. Under the will of George Staverton, who died in 1661, £4—later increased to £6 on the death of his wife and her daughter—was left to the poor of Wokingham parish, to be laid out in the purchase of a bull, whose flesh was to be divided up after the beast had been baited.

The mob took the abolition of their baiting very hard. As late as 1835, they broke into the place where the bull was being kept, prior to its being slaughtered, and baited it themselves. They used to throw bread and cheese from Paddington steeple, on the Sunday before Christmas, according to the will of two maiden ladies, who were "relieved there with bread and cheese when they were almost starved; and Providence afterwards favouring them, they left an estate in that parish to continue the custom for ever on that day."

Alas, the "for ever" ended on the Sunday before Christmas, 1834, when three or four dozen penny rolls and an equal number of pieces of cheese were thrown down for the last time from the belfry of St. Mary's Church, by Mr. William Hogg, the parish clerk.

*Plygain* is no longer celebrated at St. Asaph, Carewys, at dawn on Christmas morning, and no longer, I believe, do "a number of persons" assemble on Christmas Eve—or *Oiel Verry* (Mary's Eve)—in the Isle of Man, to "shout carols or *Carvals*."

The fact is that the highly utilitarian English Christmas, in which the simple elements are Father Christmas (Father in his stocking-feet, not to wake the children), a tree, a Christmas pudding and some crackers, does so very well for a world daily growing more to love the utilitarian in all things. The English Christmas, just because it is utilitarian, has been exported to all parts of the world.

Of course, at the Swedish Christmas, St. Lucia—a pretty girl with a crown of lighted candles—is still seen, and in France, where the Latin influence is still strong, the old Roman custom of *strenae* (*étrennes* in modern French) is still observed. In Paris, the bachelors give boxes of sweets to those of their friends who have entertained them during the past year; and on Twelfth Night, in France, there is a cake, called *Gâteau des Rois* (i.e., the Three Wise Men) in which a china figure of a king and another of a queen are waiting to be found by the two who will draw them in their piece of cake, and be the "king" and "queen" for Twelfth Night. This custom was observed in England up till about 1800.

In Sweden, the parlours are still strewn with rye-straw, and in Germany, in the Protestant parts, it is the Haus-Christ who brings the children their presents with His own hands. German children still, I hear, receive their apples with a coin inside; and in France, Father Christmas of the American–Anglo-Saxon pattern

At this party, in 1859, "Father Christmas" is attended by a motley group under the direction of the Lord of Misrule.

Bringing in the Boar's Head at Queen's College, Oxford, on Christmas Day, 1873, to the singing of the carol *Caput apici differs, redens laudes Domino*. Tradition says that the ceremony commemorates a student who, while reading Aristotle in Shotover Forest, was attacked by a wild boar and escaped by thrusting the book of philosophy down the animal's throat.

has not usurped the function of the *petit Jésus* Who brings the presents to the good children.

In Arles, that ancient town of Roman Provence, they sing still, as they go cadging pence in the streets:

*Caritat, Senyora, caritat si os plau!*
*Que venim de Roma*
*I portem Corona*
*De Sant Nicolau!*

Charity, Lady; Charity, if you please!
For us who come from Rome,
Bearing the crown
Of good St. Nicholas!

And in all the Catalan lands they still beat the Yule Log, until the cloth covering it is removed to show the chocolates and other gifts hidden under the cloth.

They employ an odd method of giving their Christmas presents in Sweden, Mecklenburg, Pomerania and other parts which were formerly more or less Swedish territory. They wrap up the gift in innumerable coverings—it has then become the *Julklapp*—and then throw it into the room of the person for whom it is intended.

The great secret of giving a *Julklapp* properly is to open the door rapidly, throw the *Julklapp* into the room, and to close the door and escape without betraying one's identity.

Another custom in Sweden, found in the "better-class" households, is for the gifts to be given by two masked figures: an old man and woman. The man rings a bell, and the woman delivers the gifts from a basket.

Shrines and cribs are still splendid in Italy at Christmas, and in Italy, as in Spain, they eat a special sort of nougat (*torrone* in Italy, *turrón* in Spain) at Christmas. In Little Russia they may even still sit down to *koutia*—honey and porridge—on Christmas Eve. "They cherish the custom as something which distinguishes them from Great and White Russians. Each dish is said to represent the Holy Crib. First porridge is put in, which is like putting straw in the manger; then each person helps himself to honey and fruit, and that symbolizes the Babe. A place is made in the porridge, and then the honey and fruit are poured in; the fruit stands for the body, the honey for the spirit or the blood.[1]

[1] Stephen Graham: *A Vagabond in the Caucasus.*

And so on. . . . The Tyrolese peasants eat *zelten*, "a kind of pie filled with dried pear-slices, nuts, figs, raisins and the like. It is baked on the Eve of St. Thomas . . . (and) the sign of the Cross is made upon it and it is sprinkled with holy water and put in the oven."

They *say* that the strange custom of hunting the wren is still practised in Ireland. Why this innocent little fowl should have been singled out as an ill-omen I cannot gather; but the lads, on Christmas morning, after the bells have rung out midnight, go hunting the wren. They kill it, fasten the poor little body to a board, and carry it from house to house, chanting this ditty:

> We hunted the Wren for Robin the Bobbin,
> We hunted the Wren for Jack of the Can,
> We hunted the Wren for Robbin the Bobbin,
> We hunted the Wren for every one!

A queer business altogether!

Blackbird pie may still be eaten in Cornish villages, for all I know, but the old customs are dying . . . fast. There is a standard Christmas on its way, as there is to be a standard speech and a standard dress and a standard wage and a standard goodness-knows-what else.

I feel very sad when I consider this inevitability.

And yet, to paraphrase Chesterton, the astonishing thing about the inevitable is that it so rarely happens. There are signs that I hardly dare hope that I see, that the standard Christmas it not altogether the certain thing that I have feared it to be.

Accidents happen, and they are not always disastrous. That Norway should wish to express its gratitude to Britain by sending a Christmas-tree for public erection in Trafalgar Square is just one of those happy accidents, but the accident has created a new custom, and has diverted the path of Christmas from that ultimate standardization that we feared.

Who would have thought that London's Trafalgar Square would ever have seen a vast illuminated Christmas-tree, as New York's Times Square has seen its own tree these many years past?

There's hope for an unstandardized Christmas yet.

But how much hope. . . ?

I consider, and I think that I see hope in the fact that there is a small but sure revolt against that trend which emptied the countryside into the towns and cities. The trek back has begun, as men realize that, in a world of natural and artificially contrived scarcity, the nearer that one gets to the earth, the better chance one has of feeding.

And the countryside is the place for traditions; the place where traditions are made and preserved. Only in ritual do the towns preserve traditions; the countryside preserves them in its daily habits.

The class of person who is returning to the countryside will make fresh contact with old customs—customs that the town has forgotten. The highly artificial revival of the morris dancing has had some surprisingly permanent success, and it may be that our new class of gentlemen-farmers may revive a more picturesque Christmas for the towns for which they must still have some allegiance.

Again, the last war caused an immense migration of peoples; and not all those refugees were rich or even well-to-do. Hundreds of thousands of peasants and labourers are represented in the mass of refugees who have sought shelter in Britain, America, Canada and Australia; refugees from lands in which a colourful domestic tradition was one of the happiest features of the social life. Their customs they will have taken with them to their new homes, and those customs they will keep in their new lives. The neighbours cannot go altogether unaffected.

Polish *opłatki*—small packages of wafers, blessed by the priest, with figures stamped upon them, and sent by Poles as we send Christmas-cards—may yet be adopted by Australians; and *zelten* may yet be baked in every British oven on St. Thomas's Day.

Christmas has survived because of its immense adaptability; to standardize it would be to kill it. But it has lasted so long that only the most profound pessimism would debit it with the power of self-destruction.

## CHAPTER SIXTEEN

# CHRISTMAS IN AUSTRALIA

ONE of the most irrepressible of all human instincts is that which establishes a tradition. The human animal is an ambivalent—at times almost a paradoxical—creature, and he is always torn, it seems, between contrary, diametrically opposed, ideas. He loves change and he fears it; he has opened up the whole of the planet on which he lives; has delved a league into the earth, and has mounted to the stars on wings.

And, at the same time, he has wished to remain within one tiny plot of earth—has fought, indeed, bitterly to remain there. He is a wanderer and a home lover—all at once. He wishes time to stand still—which is what makes him wish to repeat today what he did yesterday—and he wishes eagerly for the morrow—which makes him the greatest innovator among created beings.

But, as though an inner voice has warned him, from the days of his arboreal existence, that too much innovation would one day lead him to innovate himself out of existence—say with an H-bomb!—he has found the urge to traditionalize, to fossilize behaviour, to have customs which last, to inhibit the desire for change, at least as strong as the desire to begin each day with a new idea and with a different set of behaviour-patterns.

The Pilgrim Fathers took away with them a decided contempt—if not a decided hatred—for the "wanton" customs of the land that they had left. It was not long before they had manufactured some feast-days of their own. Thanksgiving Day, which is now celebrated all over the world even by Americans whose ancestors came across the Atlantic elsewhere than in the *Mayflower*, is the principal of these feasts.

Australia is the latest of the continents to be colonized by emigrants from Europe, and, as a nation, Australia is among the newest. She inherited her traditions ready-made. The principal elements of her Caucasian population were recruited from the

British Isles, and so we find that the ordinary basis of British custom —English, Irish, Scots and Welsh—is the ordinary basis of Australian custom, save that the Scot is predominant in Western Australia, and the London English in New South Wales.

But the settlers came up against a tremendous difficulty in the matter of transporting a way of life half-way around the world: that it was exactly half-way, and that all the feast-days of the Old Country fell just about six months too late (or too early, if you prefer that).

It is a fact that the Australians have shown a fine British doggedness, well worthy of the land of their origin, in keeping up the traditions of a northern winter festival in a land where December falls in summer weather—or what is summer weather to us.

As the late Douglas Sladen rather doggerelly sang, sixty and more years ago:

The port was old, the champagne dry,
And every kind of luxury
Which Melbourne could supply was there.
They had the staple Christmas fare,
Roast beef and turkey (this was wild),
Mince-pies, plum-pudding, rich and mild. . . .

. . . yet in a way
It did not seem like Christmas day,
With no gigantic beech yule-logs
Blazing between the brass fire-dogs,
And with 100 deg. in the shade
On the thermometer displayed.

Only the carols seemed familiar things in that topsy-turvy weather:

When dinner ended, nearly all
Stole off to lounges in the hall . . .
All save the two old folks and Lil,
Who made their hearts expand and thrill
By playing snatches, slow and clear,
Of carols they'd been used to hear
Some half a century ago
At High Wick Manor, when the two
Were bashful maidens: they talked on
Of England and what they had done
On bygone Christmas nights at home,
Of friends beyond the northern foam,

And friends beyond that other sea,
Yet further—whither ceaselessly
Travellers follow the old track,
But whence no messenger comes back.

In the sixty years which have passed since those lines were written, the memories of the Old Country have changed from first-hand to third-, fourth- and even fifth-hand. The memories of Britain are now the tales of a grandfather, of a great-grandfather, and, though the spiritual ties which bind the Commonwealth to the Motherland are even stronger than they were fifty or a hundred years back, they are ties of a different sort, and they no longer depend upon personal recollection for their existence.

As the date of the founding of Australia has receded into the past, there has come an awareness of the fact that Australia is no mere annexe of Britain, but a nation in her own right, and it was an act of rare political sagacity on the part of the British Government to realize the arrival of Australia's nationhood almost before that realization was shared by the mass of Australians.

Very well, then: Australia is now a nation—a sovereign independent state, owing suzerainty or allegiance to none, and linked to Britain only in that she shares, with Britain, the same king. She has her own distinctive fauna and flora, and she has her own Christmas weather. Now it seems as though she is developing the power to create her own traditions.

It was perhaps inevitable that this power of tradition-making was first expressed in respect of Christmas—since it is that feast which is the truly universal festival of the Christian world. "And, on earth, peace to men of good-will. . . ."

The curious aspect of this piece of Australian custom-making is that the innovation, within a space of fifteen years, has taken on all the stability of ancient tradition, and has achieved a fame which has gone far beyond the limits of the Australian continent.

It was on the evening of 24 December, 1937, that an Australian commercial-radio announcer, Norman Banks, was sitting in the window of his Melbourne flat. Across the street a window was open. Through it, clear to Banks's ears, came the sound of a wireless, playing a Christmas carol. He glanced at the window and saw that an old lady, with an expression of rapt attention on her face, was listening to the song. She held a candle in her hand as she listened—and it was this fact which caught Banks's attention, caught it, held it, and set his imagination leaping ahead of time and place.

"Carols by Candle-light!" he whispered—and, in that moment, perhaps the most modern of all traditions was born.

Banks, looking at the old lady—his neighbour—as, candle in hand, she listened to the carol, thought of the life which, in her case, was drawing gracefully to a close. And he thought, too, of some other lives, only just beginning, but in the prospect of the darkest overshadowing. Lives not to be lived out as the old lady's had, evidently, been lived out.

He thought, on this Christmas Eve of 1937, of a child that he had seen that afternoon: a victim of the infantile paralysis which was claiming its prey all over the world. The child lay stricken, immobile, in its cot in one of Melbourne's public hospitals, and the management of the hospital in which the child lay had asked Banks to broadcast a special message to its patients. In Banks's mind, the thought of the stricken child and the sight of the rapt old lady began to fuse, to make food for an idea which, by the following Christmas Eve, had taken shape, and found achievement as the now world-famous ceremony of "Carols by Candle-light."

Banks arranged that there should be carol-singing on Christmas Eve in the lovely Alexandra Gardens, which lie beside the river, and are entered at Princes Bridge, the gateway to the city of Melbourne. Until the commencement of "Carols by Candle-light," the section used by the Festival was a rubble-heap, but with the development of the tradition there has been a corresponding increase in the extent of the area and in the improvement of the lawns, surrounding trees and shrubs.

Banks had hopes of a small initial band of carol-singers: he was hardly prepared for the fact that no fewer than ten thousand people turned up. When Christmas Day dawned, a new and immensely important custom had been introduced into the social life of a great continent.

Today, more than two hundred and seventy thousand people—a full quarter of the city's population—turn out, with a lighted candle, to sing carols in the crowd which throngs the lawns of Alexandra Gardens and stretches across St. Kilda Road, and along both banks of the river.

The crowd, a mile in diameter, centres about a large dais which is erected, each year, in the garden-theatre, and only in the square of St. Peter's, in Rome, is there a sight comparable to that of Melbourne's quarter of a million, holding candles, singing the ancient carols of Christmastide.

The wireless gathers up the immense volume of sound, and carries it to the many thousands of homes throughout the Commonwealth which have tuned-in to "Carols by Candle-light," but, since the first ceremony arranged by Norman Banks in Alexandra Gardens, the custom has been widely copied, so that today "Carols by Candle-light" are sung in every capital of the Commonwealth and in innumerable provincial towns and villages.

Since 1947 Radio Australia has been broadcasting sections of the Festival, so that the ceremony has reached an audience extended far beyond the limits of Australia, and in 1950, in response to requests from Australian servicemen stationed in Japan, the Australian wives of returned American soldiers and Allied ex-servicemen who remembered pleasant leaves, some part of which were spent in Alexandra Gardens, Radio Australia decided to broadcast the "Carols by Candle-light" to the world.

Already, in its short existence, the tradition has acquired its accretion of tales, and during the Second World War Allied servicemen and women were conspicuous among the crowd.

Some roughs decided one year to break up the carol-singing. Well organized, they shouldered their way through the crowd, seizing programmes and candles, and making themselves generally noisome. But the singing began, and it was the roughs who sang the loudest; singing, indeed, with such fervour that they formed an unofficial choir-leading group.

The ceremony is non-sectarian—as all Christmas services should be. Persons of all religions come to the service, and join in the singing, and the carols which are sung derive from Catholic and Protestant sources, from English and French, from German and Russian, the majority of the choristers being from public schools, from Anglican and Roman Catholic schools and from colleges conducted by various churches.

At midnight, the vast crowd joins hands, and all sing *Auld Lang Syne,* as the bells of Australia ring in the day of Christ's birth.

The tradition is new, but it was not born complete. Each year sees something added to it—but always an addition, and never an alteration. In 1942, "guests" of the service spoke from overseas to the organizers and principal singers of "Carols by Candle-light." In that year these "guests" included the Mayor of New York and the Lord Mayor of London.

The founder of this service—and I like to think that he should take his place in history with Jacopone da Todi and Eckhardt—had, in the meanwhile, written a "Melbourne Carol." Of it, we may say that there have been better carols, but never an earlier Antipodean one. It deserves social recognition for this fact alone. Honour to the pioneer!

On Christmas Eve, 1943, the carol, with words and music by Norman Banks, was sung for the first time in Alexandra Gardens:

> Yule-tide in Melbourne means mass jubilation,
> And carols by candle-light on Christmas Eve:
> Thousands assemble in glad dedication
> To hail Him with joy, and the vow—"I believe!"

The "Melbourne Carol" has been recorded by several leading choirs, but the Columbia recording of St. Patrick's Cathedral Choir, directed by Dr. Percy Jones, is sold for the benefit of juvenile victims of infantile paralysis and blind babies and children.

We have seen in an earlier chapter that Lord Mayor's Day—9 November—almost certainly represents an ancient Teutonic end-of-the-year festival. Christmas Eve in Melbourne is attracting to it those elements of folk-festival—as distinct from purely religious celebration—which have attached, over the passing of centuries, to Lord Mayor's Day. For instance, in 1945, the carol-singing was accompanied by a "peace pageant" and grand tableau, and in 1946, not only was there a procession of barges, each carrying a freight of candle-bearing choristers, along the river, but Miss Florence Austral, the well-known singer, broke her voluntary retirement in order to assist at "Carols by Candle-light."

"Celebrity artists" who are in Melbourne over the Christmas period are anxious to sing at the Festival. Joan Hammond told Norman Banks in 1949 that when she next returned to Australia it would be for the express purpose of appearing at "Carols by Candle-light." "New Australian" artists, people who have settled in the Commonwealth since the war, are beginning to add lustre to the tradition, not only with their splendid voices, but also by their singing of ancient carols that have not before been heard outside Europe.

Now, the annual ceremony is always held around a vast Christmas-tree, upon which the public hang gifts for the sick children of Australia's hospitals.

It is a pleasant thought that the child, stricken by infantile paralysis, whose plight inspired Banks to inaugurate the carol-singing festival, is now completely recovered of her illness; grown up to womanhood; and herself brings her own small daughter to the ceremony which has helped, financially as well as spiritually, so many who were in her own perilous state.

For, in 1947, work began on the building of a magnificent annexe to the Children's Block, within the Austin Public Hospital complex. This new block has been built and equipped entirely out of the £250,000 subscribed by Melbourne's million people in response to Christmas appeals over Broadcasting Station 3 KZ, and brings the number of beds in "the first radio hospital in the world" up to one hundred and sixty-five.

It is a far cry from the Manger at Bethlehem to a white-enamelled cot in the Austin Hospital at Melbourne, but a quarter of a million persons gathered to hail Christ the King in Melbourne's—and all the other cities'—public places are distant only in space and time from that night on the hillside when "there were shepherds abiding in the field, and keeping watch by night over their flock. And an angel of the Lord stood by them; and the glory of the Lord shone round about them."

"If any feature of 'Carols by Candle-light' in Melbourne transcends all others, it is the genuine democratic coming-together of people from all social strata; witness the manner in which men and women wearing evening dress join hands with shabbily-clad folk in the lusty performances of *Auld Lang Syne*. Even more important, though not so obvious, except to people on the dais, is the visible effect of 'Carols by Candle-light' on every individual in the vast concourse of people. Their eyes shine as though brightened by some inner light; their faces are softened by the gentle glow of candles."

CHAPTER SEVENTEEN

# CHRISTMAS IN AUSTRIA, GERMANY AND SCANDINAVIA

No matter what Alfred Rosenberg and the late Adolf Hitler claimed, philological science upholds the view that German is the modern descendant of an ancient Aryan tongue spoken by a people not themselves originally Aryan. That this tongue was imposed on a non-Aryan race, either by the needs of commerce or by the force of conquest, is not to be denied. Exactly the same sort of thing, in fact, which happened in Wales, where an Aryan tongue was imposed upon a population of non-Aryan origins and of non-Aryan speech.

In the view of some early Fathers of the Church, the Germans were not to be considered quite human, the opinion of these learned men being that the Teutonic tribes were the offspring of unwary travellers and those female demons who were known to frequent the vast Hercynian forest which then stretched unbroken from the east bank of the Rhine to the Steppes of Russia.

This opinion may not have been founded in precise observation, but the Germans, historically considered, have always been the Odd Men Out of Europe. Non-Aryans, who have preached the gospel of Arya with fire and sword; reformers of the Christian Church against whom a paganism-exterminating expedition was undertaken by the French king, Charles IX, a contemporary of our Queen Elizabeth; "purifiers" of the Aryan speech that they got at second hand, and spoken originally as a Hottentot speaks English . . . no wonder that they puzzled and annoyed those races who first came into contact with them!

Their name for themselves (an Aryan name) is simply "The People," while the name of their country—rendered *Alemania* in Latin—is plain Arabic: *Al-Yaman*, "(on) the left-hand"; the same, in fact, as the name for that part of southern Arabia we call "The Yemen." If we could know when the name was first applied to the country occupied by The People, we should be able to state what the geographical position of that country was, which lay "on the left hand" of the Arabian searchers for—Baltic amber?—Cornish tin?—Whitby jet?

We do not know; but that the land of the Teutons should have been known throughout the ancient world by a non-German name would seem to imply that its topographical limits were hardly fixed —or, if fixed, then unknown to all but the dwellers within the Teuton pale.

There is the same vagueness about the name, "On The Left Hand," as there is about such names as "The North," "The West" or even "World's End."

The Germanic peoples, at the very beginning of our era, bit into the fringes of the Roman Empire, and were converted to the culture that they had attacked. The Germanic tribes which invaded Gaul became, in time, as Latin in sentiment as the Gauls themselves had become. Wherever the German came into contact with the Latin or with Latin-educated peoples, he absorbed the superior culture.

But there remained a hard core of Teutonism on the Baltic shores; on the windy marshes where the blood chilled in the icy blasts from the Steppes and the Pole—where, between the blue-eyed demon-worshippers, gathering meerschaum and amber to trade for bronze, and the civilizations of the warm South, was interposed a vast and trackless forest, through which ran, as the only highways, the weed- and leaf- and branch-choked tributaries of the Danube.

These Asiatic marsh-dwellers, these Mongol settlers by the flat Baltic shores and on the bleak plains of Poland, were not altogether cut off from those ancient sources of culture which centre in Asia Minor and about the eastern end of the Mediterranean. The amber-seekers from North Africa passed Gibraltar and came up the western coast of Spain and France, to the Scillies and Britain and the Hebrides. They pushed across the North Sea, that some think was dotted with sandy islands in the century before the beginning of the Christian era, when important migration-movements were setting Scandinavia and the Baltic shores in some ferment.

There is an ancient Norse tradition that Denmark and Norway were invaded by "new people" from Britain at the very dawn of our era, and these "new people" brought culture as well as bronze, to trade for the amber which was so highly prized in the Levant. They had an alphabet—or, rather, an alphabetical system of writing —these Teutons, which was surely not their own unaided invention. But even today scholars cannot state with absolute certainty whence the system of writing came, such curious features does it display. There is some evidence that it was derived from the Greek, for—to this writer at least—the sign for the sound "ng" is obviously composed of two gammas, the two gammas (g) in association, making, in Greek, the sound "ng."

Then, again, there is a sign like an angular P, which stood for the sound of English W, and is so used on the coins of William the Conqueror, minted in London, where the legend reads, *PILLELMVS REX ANGLIE*. This sign could have been derived from the Greek *digamma*, which looked like an F, and represented a sort of breathed W.

But there are other indications which seem to point to a Latin origin, and other indications of an origin so far unplaced. For this writing-system, though it has much in common with the Phoenician-derived Greek, and the Phoenician-Etruscan derived Latin, has the unique feature that it begins, not with a, b, c, etc., or a, b, g, etc., but with f, u, th, a, r, k.

It is fairly certain that, at some time in the past, the proto-Latin alphabet[1] began, not with a, b, c, but with l, m, n—which is why the Latin word *elementa* means "basic things." But no "alphabet," other than the ancient Teutonic, is known to have begun with f, u, th, a, r, k.

Another thing: as though it were not enough that the Baltic-shore-dwellers had twisted the traditional order of the alphabet to suit some obscure impulse of their own,[2] they scorned the wonderful power of writing to record the deepest thoughts of man; to perpetuate an idea into eternity, and to make the humblest the potential sharer of wisdom with the wisest.

They had only one, to us, practical use for writing: they wrote their names—mostly on the things that, to them, were the most

[1] It is technically incorrect to refer to any writing system as an "alphabet" whose letter sequence does not follow that of the proto-Semitic alphabet as found, for instance, on such ancient monuments as the Moabite Stone.

[2] The impulse shared with the "Druids" who used—see later—the Ogham system of lettering.

valuable things in the world: drinking-cups and swords—and they wrote curses. Indeed, incredible though it may seem, one may hardly avoid the conclusion, in studying the ancient Teutonic script, that those who introduced it consciously adopted it only in order to use it for magical purposes. That this is almost certainly the fact seems to be borne out by the coincidence between the old Teutonic word for an (alphabetical) letter and that for a secret—in both cases, *rune*. Again, the division of the Runic "alphabet" or "futhark" into three groups of *aettir* or "families" is oddly paralleled in a similar division of the letters of the Ogham—ancient British Celtic—"alphabet"; itself a system of writing used for purely magical purposes.

Runic inscriptions, though they cover a period of considerably more than a thousand years, are rare, because their essentially magical quality made their chief use that on scraps of parchment or wood, which—spells, of course, to ensure victory in war or love, or to encompass the ruin of an enemy—were burnt as part of the magical ritual.

It is to be admitted that these Teutons must have received all the other elements of our common civilization in a similar curiously left-handed fashion (it is a point not without significance that, when the nation came later to adopt the ancient mystical symbol of the swastika as a national emblem, it should have been depicted *reversed*). Christianity was acquired very late by the Germans who had remained in Germany—and it was a Christianity which did not come from Rome, but from Britain and Ireland, and it was a Christianity which was frowned upon by Rome as something heretical.

South Germany—"Austria" only means "the Southern (Province)"—was, naturally, much more under the influence of Latin civilization than the North, whose independence, both of political influences and of cultural forces, was preserved by the sad lack of communications.

In the South, too, that grand fiction, the Holy Roman Empire, had splendidly succeeded the splendid fact that it had been on the Christmas morning, in the year A.D. 800, when Pope Leo III had crowned Charlemagne Emperor of the Romans. "Neither holy, nor Roman, nor an empire"—to use Gibbon's immortal phrase—the romantic fiction lasted for a thousand years, until it was abolished by that plebiscite Emperor, Napoleon the First.

But the "Holy Roman Empire" served to bring the southern parts of Germany, together with what we now call Hungary, Czechoslovakia and Yugoslavia, into cultural contact with Rome. The Emperor exerted a power not dependent primarily upon the use of force, though, during the long history of the Empire, he would sometimes endeavour to give his hegemony the sanction of martial authority. The Emperor, though, exercised a power derived from spiritual roots: he ruled the hundreds of German princes by virtue of that crowning on Christmas morning, in the year 800. His power extended most over the rulers of the South—his power over the lordlings of the North, over the rulers of wind-swept marsh and impenetrable forest, was nominal, and when the power of the Empire was overthrown it was the never truly Christianized north—Prussia—which overthrew it.

Napoleon objected to the phrasing of Austrian pretensions: it was Bismarck and Kaiser William I who made it impossible for Austria to survive as a great power.

In short, then, Christianity came very late to the northern peoples, and its influence was never more than superficial, a fact that we may probably attribute to the weak influence possessed by the ruling class in the "peripheral" districts of Europe, especially in those parts speaking Slavonic and Old High German.

We may go further and admit, in all seriousness, that German Christianity did not so much overlay the ancient pagan basis as tag along behind it. We may disagree with Baring-Gould's theory that St. Ursula is nothing more than the old Germanic goddess, Hörsel, but paganism never put up so vigorous a defence against Christianity as in northern Europe. We shall see that, even where the Germans and other northern peoples introduced Christian elements into their traditional winter festival, those elements were always those whose "Christianity" was the most suspect; which were those most obviously to be matched by pagan customs.

The first point: even the German name for Christmas has nothing distinctively Christian about it, and, indeed, as we have seen in another chapter, a well-known German scholar has even claimed a Jewish descent for the German *Weihnacht*. But there is no evidence that the name is connected with Christian beliefs even as nearly as that. It seems to the writer that we need assume nothing more complicated than that the modern German name for the winter-festival is one of the very oldest names, preserved by that obstinate peasant traditionalism which has always been so marked a characteristic of the northern European.

The Tree—since, wherever they originated, the ancestors of the Teutonic peoples came to a long halt in the impenetrable forests which stretched between the Rhine and the Volga—was one of the principal religious symbols of the ancient Woden-worshipping Teuton. The Tree is still the principal religious symbol of Christmas-keeping Germans today. It is, indeed, the German's Christmas symbol *par excellence,* and they have, through the agency of their own loyalty and a foreigner's love of the exotic, disseminated its worship throughout the world.

The influence, indeed, of stubborn, of mulish, attachment to primitive racial beliefs is seen in the desire, manifest in a number of hymns and other religious writings, to identify the Cross with ancient Teutonic symbols, by calling the Cross "The Tree," and thus seeking to gloss over its essential Christian significance in favour of an appeal to deep-rooted Germanic pagan sentiments.

Historical record confirms what one might have suspected: that intense nationalism has always been—one need not say the ruling fault, but certainly—the most marked characteristic of the Teuton. Two thousand years ago, the Scandinavian sea-rover even had his own style of hair-cut—called *nørre harskur*—and he had a regrettable tendency to give all his customs the high sanction that his racial integrity depended upon his strict observance of tribal conventions. He hated foreigners as much as—and for the same reasons that—he admired his own tribesmen. There were, in his own estimation, no other races in the world fit to be compared with "The People"—he had no other name for his own race. That self-sufficient designation seemed to him not only perfectly adequate, but, indeed, the only possible name.

It is well to point out here that psychology cannot remain indifferent to the conclusion that such self-conceit is to be encountered only in connexion with deep feelings of self-mistrust—the classic, so-called "inferiority-complex."

*Freiheit*—which means something more than mere "freedom": it means, rather, a state of being left alone by every other man and (especially) by every other opinion—is the dream of the German

Christmas Day in New South Wales over seventy years ago. Australia in those days was distant six weeks' journey by steamship from England, and our fathers in Britain found the thought of a midsummer Christmas almost incredible. This wood-cut startled those who first saw it in *The Illustrated London News*.

"Carols by Candlelight," the Melbourne ceremony which is modern Australia's notable and almost certainly permanent contribution to Christmas ritual. Started less than twenty years ago to raise money for charity, the annual carol-singing ceremony has taken a deep hold on the imagination of the Commonwealth, and has established itself firmly as an integral feature of Australian custom.

A rich burgher of old Nuremberg and his wife visit the Christmas market, while their servant bears a Christmas tree behind them.

"Frau Berchta," accompanied by the terrible "Hans Tripp," comes to an Alsatian household, she to reward the good children with presents, while her companion punishes the bad. Under various names—sometimes she appears as the "Christ-child," accompanied by Knight Rupprecht as well as by the hobgoblin—she takes the part in Germany that "Father Christmas" takes in Anglo-Saxon countries.

people. And for years they *were* free—free of contact with the fuller life of the South. "They flourished free from the restrictions of their fellows, but cowered in an appalling slavery to the dismal phantasms of their own minds. Divorced from the enlightenment of civilization, the strength of these Puritans turned into singular channels; and in their isolation, their morbid self-repression, and struggle for life with relentless Nature, there came to them dark furtive traits from the prehistoric depths of their cold northern heritage.

"By necessity practical, and by philosophy stern, these folk were not beautiful in their sins. Erring as all mortals must, they were forced to seek concealment above all else."[1]

In short, our Teutons are the permanently "displaced persons" of our western Christian civilization. And they are the foundling children, too, whose origins cannot even be guessed. It is a pity that they were not adopted early in our history, but wishful thinking never altered historical fact, and we must accept the Teutons as they are: children, with a child's joy in colour and noise, and a child's power to people the world with demons and to trace a lurking terror in the folds of a tumbled sheet. And their folk festivals truly reflect the diverse and often conflicting elements of their essentially childish temperament.

The days are long past when it was possible to say, of Germany, what Tacitus had to say, in his *Germania*: "They have but one kind of public show: in every gathering it is the same. Naked youths, who profess this sport, fling themselves in dance among swords and levelled lances."

Curiously enough, it is among the inhabitants of the Pyrenean districts, who preserve the memory of Visigothic forebears, that the sword-dance is today found in its most uncorrupted form—with the Germans of Germany, the one ancient "show" has been modified, as it has shared its popularity with so many other shows.

But with the Teutons of farther north, of the lands that we collectively call "Scandinavia," the ancient customs still hold their ancient sway. In Sweden, for instance, there is a Christmas game which seems obviously related to the ancient sword-dance of which Tacitus tells. This game is played by several youths; faces blackened, and in disguise. One plays the victim, one his executioner—

[1] *The Picture in the House*—Howard Phillips Lovecraft.

this latter dressed up as an old woman, in rags and with the face grotesquely, hideously painted. First the victim is put to death by the old woman, with her knife, and then, the corpse revived, the victim dances with his executioner, the dance being performed with the coarse gestures always found in primitive fertility-rites.

This dance, sequence for sequence, gesture for gesture, may be matched in northern Spain. In Gothland, the victim wears an animal's skin, and holds in his mouth a straw cut sharp at each end. This straw, which is held straight out, is supposed to represent a swine's bristle, so that the "victim" symbolizes a hog sacrificed to Freya, the ancient man-goddess of the Teutons.

Sacrificial customs are still practised in Teutonic lands in earnest—though human sacrifice, in normal times, has been discontinued. On Christmas morning, in the provinces of Lauterburg and Mecklenburg—un-Romanized parts of Germania—a dog is thrown into the water that the cattle are to be given to drink, so that the cattle may not suffer from the mange. In this case, the dog may take his chance of life; and in the Uckermark, where the same custom employs a cat instead of a dog, the cat may swim to safety—if it can. But the sacrifice is real and complete in Bohemia, where they catch a black cat, boil it, and bury it at night, under a tree, so that the fields may be kept free of "the business that walketh about in the dark."

The fairy-tales of Hans Andersen and the Brothers Grimm, with Ibsen's play *Peer Gynt,* have brought back the trolls to the attention of the town-dwellers—non-human, but material creatures whose existence is taken very much for granted by country-folk, all over the world.

In Sweden, the trolls are said to celebrate Christmas Eve in riotous fashion, and it is held to be dangerous to walk abroad between cock-crow and daybreak on Christmas morning, such power have the trolls over mortals at this time.

In this belief, the essentially non-Christian basis of Teutonic superstition becomes most apparent. In Ireland, the leprechaun—Irish counterpart of the troll—not only has no Christian belief, since he has no soul, but would rather die than celebrate a festival of the Church. In Sweden, of course, he celebrates Christmas *because that feast is commonly accepted to be not Christian at all.* The belief that the trolls have power over human beings in the dawn of Christmas morning is another proof that Teutonic opinion is, at heart, fundamentally non-Christian. For Shakespeare, in summing up Christian opinion, says of Christmas morning:

> And then . . . no spirit dares stir abroad;
> The nights are wholesome; then no planets strike,
> No fairy takes, nor witch hath power to charm,
> So hallowed and so gracious is the time.

Thorpe, in his *Northern Mythology*, which was published a century ago, has this to say of Swedish belief: "On the heaths, witches and little trolls ride, one on a wolf, another on a broom or a shovel, to their assemblies, where they dance under their stones. In the mount are then to be heard mirth and music, dancing and drinking."

The ancient belief, held by the Romans, that the dead return to their homes at the year's end, is still held by the modern northern peoples, but the slight hold that Christianity has had upon racial opinion is well shown by the fact that the customary preparations for entertaining the dead—the fire lit, the cloth spread, the chairs wiped with a clean towel, the jug of Yule ale set out, even, in some parts, the bath prepared—are made sometimes "for the dead," sometimes "for the trolls," and sometimes "for Christ and His angels." The equation of the returning dead with either the trolls or the Saviour and His angels sheds a most illuminating light on the essential qualities of northern folk-belief!

In the chapter on Spain, we shall see that belief is divided on the opinion concerning the harmlessness of the returned: some holding the dead to be harmless, others holding them to be capable of much malignancy. It seems to the writer that these two possible aspects of the same visitation reflect an original belief in two entirely different classes of returners or visitants, and that this very ancient belief is reflected in the present northern confusion regarding the actual identity of the visitants on Christmas Eve, for whom, in some places, the living even vacate their own beds.

In the Tyrol, the most Christianized part of Germany, it is expressely stated that it is for Christ and His Mother that milk is left out when the household go off to Midnight Mass, as it is for the Virgin that food is left out in Brittany. (But the ancient, and thus essentially pagan, nature of these food gifts is demonstrated by the "explanation" that two old maiden ladies, living in Poole,

Dorset, gave to the author of their habit of putting out a saucer of milk on Christmas Eve. They used to say: "It's for the hedgehog!")

However much the present rulers of Russia wish to emphasize, for subtle political reasons, the "Asiatic" affiliations of their empire, their culture is not Oriental at all, but Teutonic, overlaid with Byzantine. The Princes of Novgorod established their Russian dominions as Swedish lords, and our own king, Harold, who was killed at Hastings, married a princess of the house of Dolgoruki, he regarding the lady as no more different in culture than would a present-day Frenchman consider a Belgian lady to be different in her cultural background.

The customs, then, of all those lands which fringe the Baltic Sea are seen to share a common origin—and that origin is certainly not Christian. Even when SS. Cyril and Methodius introduced Christianity to the Slavs, and brought the "Cyrillic" adaptation of the Greek alphabet to Slavonic use with them, the Slavs at once twisted the letters of the new "Roman" alphabet to resemble as much as possible the old, "magical" runic letters.[1]

It was a belief of the early Church that the coming of Christ had not proved the gods of pagan Greece and Rome sheer myths, but had simply deprived of power what were still felt to be real beings. This belief died very slowly, especially as it was linked with another belief which held that, deprived of their power, the Old Gods and Goddesses continued their existence as a sort of demons.

In the northern countries, these linked beliefs have never really died, and this fact is possibly to be explained in observing how the ancient Teutonic gods were closely identified with natural phenomena: the man-shaping impulses were never strongly applied to gods in the northern lands. Odin was the aurora borealis and the biting north wind, Thor the growling thunder behind the mountains, Freya the chill golden glitter on the icy peaks, and Loki the sly quills of light on the wind-brushed surface of a fiord. And as these things remain, so the gods with whom these things were identified may never completely pass out of men's consciousness.

It used to be believed in Norway that, at intervals, the Old Gods would rouse themselves to make war upon the Christians, who had

[1] The convention is still observed in Slavonic ecclesiastical usage.

betrayed the ancient faith. The Old Gods always chose Christmas Eve to sally forth. They came down from the mountains in a howl of wind, shouting to drown the screaming blast, and carrying off a Christian unlucky enough to be out of doors. As late as the beginning of the present century, the belief in these raiding, punitive expeditions of the Old Gods continued.

In a book published as recently as 1896, it tells how, as a village was preparing to celebrate Christmas, the warning sounds were heard coming from the direction of the mountains: "In a second, the air became black, peals of thunder echoed among the hills, lightning danced about the buildings, and the inhabitants in the darkened rooms heard the clatter of hoofs and the weird shrieks of the hosts of the gods."

The Cross was a mystical symbol among the northern peoples long before Christianity, as it was among the peoples of the South. It is a symbol of incalculable antiquity and of an origin not to be determined. It is even found in the religious art of pre-Columbian America. So that, though the sign of the Cross is often used in Protestant Scandinavia and Germany as "a protection against uncanny visitors," and though it is marked with chalk or tar on gates and doors, made of straw to be hung in stables and byres, and even smeared with the wax of the Yule-candle on the udders of the cattle, it would be a hardy man who would dare affirm that the sign is of Christ's Cross and not that of Miolnir, the Hammer of Thor.

The chief purpose of the runes—the letters of the ancient Teutonic script—seems to have been in casting spells or making predictions, and though the runes themselves have gone, divinatory practices have lasted as a popular amusement in the northern countries, as they used to be popular amusements among the people of Britain.

German girls, especially of the peasant-class, spend much ingenuity in applying traditional methods of divination to the important business of divining the name of their future husbands. The methods are too numerous to mention, but they include the pouring of molten lead or egg-white into water (the first into cold, the second into hot water), the casting of a slipper over a girl's shoulder, the casting into the air of slips of wood—so that one may see the pattern that they make as they fall—the floating of nutshells, and the rest.

In the Slav countries on the south-eastern border of Germany, the girls lay the table on Christmas Eve, put out plate, knife, fork, spoon and white loaf. At midnight, the future husband will appear and cast the knife at her. If the knife falls without hurting her, she will wed and be happy; if the knife injure her, she will die early. Do the girls believe these things? Or, if they do, may we say that the figure of the future husband is altogether a shadowy abstraction? Perhaps he is an ambitious young man, very much of flesh and blood!

For the young men who wish to know what their future wives will look like there is a different divinatory ritual. The young men must wait at home on Christmas Eve while the others go to church, and there, naked and alone, and in total darkness, sieve ashes through a sieve. "His future bride will then appear, pull him thrice by the nose, and go away." But if the darkness is total, how does he see her? Folk-lore is full of these paradoxes; but a paradox never yet killed a piece of folk-lore.

Sweden has a day of its own, even though St. Lucia's Day is celebrated in the neighbouring countries and even in Sicily, which was once a fief of the Normans. But St. Lucia's Day is always felt to be peculiarly Swedish, since Sweden has made that day peculiarly its own. The day used to be called "little Yule," and was once the year's shortest day—when the Old Style calendar was in force.

In Swedish households, the sleepers used to be awakened at cock-crow by the prettiest girl there, herself dressed in a white robe, with a red sash, and wearing a wire crown covered with whortleberry twigs, and having nine lighted candles set in it. The girl used to hand around a sweet drink or some coffee, sing a special song, and be greeted by the title of *Lussi* or *Lussibruden* (Lucy Bride).

*Lussi* is not "St. Lucia," any more than "Holy Cat" (*Sant Gato*) is "St. Agatha," for in some parts of Gothland *Lussi* can be a cow with a crown of lighted candles on her head. *Lussi*, indeed, seems to be the personification of Light (the Indo-European root, *lugh*, light, seems to be at the back of the name *Lussi*) and the pretty girls, light-crowned, seem rather to represent a force of Nature than any saint of the Christian calendar.

In Denmark, it is a belief that the future is revealed to the girls on St. Lucia's Day. By custom, before retiring, they pray: "Sweet St. Lucia, let me know whose cloth I shall lay; whose bed I shall make; whose child I shall bear; whose darling I shall be; whose arms I shall sleep in."

We saw in an earlier chapter that migrations of the Aryan peoples have produced many "ends of the year," and that among these former year-endings, St. Thomas's Day was still one of the most revered. It is the true Winter Solstice—the shortest day of the year; and in Denmark it used to be celebrated as the children's feast; the day on which schools broke up for Christmas.

The children used to bring presents to their teachers, and in return, they were invited to a feast. There was a topsy-turvydom about St. Thomas's Day which recalls something of the spirit of the Roman *Saturnalia* and the medieval English customs of Boy Bishops. At school feasts in Denmark, the children used to acquire exalted, even if only temporary, rank, and testimonials to their industry and diligence, made out by the schoolmasters, were taken by the children and made the vehicle by which presents were collected. These testimonials were, by ancient custom, always made out to the child with some fanciful prefix to the name: Emperor, mostly, but King at least.

The masters' rods were burnt without reproof on this day, and generally the Danish children behaved in a manner which recalls the locking-out of schoolmasters which used to take place in Belgium and Antwerp on other days of the year as well as on St. Thomas's.

In the villages of the Sudetenland and Slovakia, St. Thomas's Eve is supposed to be as "uncanny" as Walpurgis Night. St. Thomas himself is believed by the Czech villagers to drive about on his Eve in a chariot of fire. Awaiting him in the churchyard, risen from their graves to wait on him, are all the men named Thomas. They assist him to alight from his chariot, and walk with him to the churchyard cross, which glows crimson with unearthly radiance. Before the cross, St. Thomas kneels and prays; then rises to bless each of his namesakes. Then, as he disappears beneath the cross, each Thomas returns to his grave.

This "St. Thomas" is very different a character from the Apostle of India: he seems to have acquired many of the more flamboyant characteristics of the Demon Coachman. "In the houses, people listen with awe for the sound of his chariot, and when it is heard, make anxious prayer to him for protection from ill."

In Czechoslovakia, they throw salt over the heads of the cattle, saying to each: "St Thomas preserve thee from all sickness!" and in Lower Austria, it is believed that sluggards may cure themselves of their lie-abed habits by saying a special prayer to the Saint. In Westphalia, the child who was last at school was mocked by the name of *Domesesel* (Thomas's Ass). Miles suggests that the fact that St. Thomas's Day is the shortest of the year may account for his connexion with lazy-bones.

It is in eastern and northern Europe that peasant-song is found at its best, and it is because it is only during the last century that a middle class has arisen among the peoples east of the Rhine that the songs of the peasant have not been banished in favour of more "refined" numbers. It is hardly more than a century since a middle class interposed itself between the lord and the serf, and the songs of the soil are still the songs of the manor-house as we go eastward from the Rhine.

The Christmas-time songs are called *Kolyadki* (from the Latin, *Kalendae*) in Russian, and they may be indifferently concerned with Christian or pagan subjects. Sometimes they seem to be pure pagan songs, which have been "re-edited" to make them seem Christian. The actual song-festival is called *Podblyudnuiya,* and it serves for divination. A dish (*blyudo*) filled with water is set on the table, and personal possessions—rings, bracelets, etc.—are dropped into the dish, which is then covered with a cloth. Songs are sung, and, at the end of each song, a guest puts his hand into the dish and draws out the first object to be touched. Divinatory conclusions are drawn from the nature of the object, taken in conjunction with the sex of the person drawing it.

Germany has given the world a treasure of music, both religious and secular, and Luther himself it was who translated into German the ancient *A solis ortus cardine* and the *Veni, redemptor gentium*, besides writing for his little son, Hans, that most charming of all Christmas carols—*Vom Himmel hoch, do komm Ich her*, of which a splendid Scots translation was published in 1567.

The *Vom Himmel hoch* became one of the most popular of German hymns, and it used to be sung from the church-towers of all German towns, though the custom has not altogether passed away, and may yet be revived in all its old fervour.

A newer German carol, which, after initial neglect, has had a curiously wide success among non-German peoples, in the *Silent Night, Holy Night* of Franz Xavier Gruber. Born in 1787, the third son of a poor linen-weaver, Gruber was the schoolmaster and sexton of the village of Hochburg, in Upper Austria, a few miles from the German border.

On Christmas Eve, 1818, the parish-priest, Father Joseph Mohr, was preparing his small church for the Midnight Mass when, to his horror, he found that mice had eaten the cloth of the organ-bellows completely away, and that, in consequence, there could be no organ-music in church that Christmas night. To his friend, the thirty-one-year-old schoolmaster-sexton, Father Mohr turned for help. The priest had written the words of a Christmas carol: could Gruber set it to music in time for the hymn to be sung at the Midnight Mass?

The young schoolmaster accepted the urgent commission. He set to work, and within a few hours had produced a hymn which is now world-famous—and one might add, of promised immortality. There was no organ in the church that night: schoolmaster Gruber's new hymn was sung to the accompaniment of Father Mohr's Italian guitar—a simple setting indeed for the birth of so famous a carol.

It is not always that the enduring qualities of a work of art are immediately recognized, but Gruber's wife, as the pair walked home from Hochburg Church, said to her husband: "I am proud of you! People will sing your carol long after we both are dead!" as the late King Edward VII, at the end of the first performance of *Pomp and Circumstance,* said to Edward Elgar, the composer: "This tune, Mr. Elgar, will go round the world!"

Gruber died in 1863, long before fame had come to his carol; indeed, it had to wait until the popularity of Bing Crosby's singing made popularity certain for any song that he chose to sing. Twenty-five years ago, sheet-music of this carol was unsaleable: in the past few years, the gramophone and the radio have made the carol into a best-seller, and in 1950, the Austrian Government, recognizing how *Silent Night, Holy Night* had earned the love and admiration of the whole world, issued a special postage-stamp, commemorating the carol that Father Mohr and Franz Gruber made together on a Christmas Eve, one hundred and thirty years ago.

In another chapter, we saw how the "mystery" and the carol arose in Germany. The greatest writer of Christmas hymns, after Luther, was Paul Gerhardt, a Berlin pastor who lived in the seventeenth century, and whose hymns have been made familiar to British people through their having been adapted for use by Bach in his wonderful "Christmas Oratorio."

But there is a carol popular in Britain—one of the most popular of English carols, indeed—which has a Germanic setting, but which is not to be classed as a German hymn. This is the famous *Good King Wenceslas,* whose popularity as a subject is hard to explain.

Wenceslas—or Wentzel—lived. He was a real person: a nobleman of Bohemia, who was born in A.D. 908, at a time when Bohemia—or Czechoslovakia—had hardly been converted from the darkest forms of paganism. Wentzel's reputation for sanctity did not have to wait until his death in order to flower: even during his lifetime, he was credited with the power to work miracles, after having been himself converted to Christianity by his paternal grandmother, Ludmilla.

Offered the crown of Bohemia by the Emperor Otto I, Wentzel refused, preferring to remain plain Duke. His ambitions, indeed, were not concerned with worldly affairs, and, at the age of twenty-six, Wenceslas, Duke of Bohemia, was assassinated by his mother, Drahomira, and his brother, Boleslav—persons of an ambitious nature, who were irritated by Wenceslas's lack of "drive."

The hymnologies give the fine old tune to which *Good King Wenceslas* is sung as "traditional," and this writer has not been able to discover the identity of the composer. Nor has he a better reason to advance for the fact that a hymn about a Bohemian saint should have been introduced into Britain and there have become popular, than can be given in suggesting that the introduction of the hymn may be connected with the marriage of King James I's daughter, Elizabeth, to the Elector Palatine, King of Bohemia. Both French and British soldiers were sent out to Bohemia—fighting for different causes. The French soldiers brought back the necktie knotted "in the Croatian manner" or *à la cravate*—hence the modern French *cravate* and the English equivalent, cravat. The English-Scots troops may well have brought back with them a hymn in honour of a saint of their own Princess's adopted land.

"Robin Goodfellow" has vanished altogether in Britain—even

from Christmas tale and legend; but his counterpart in the various northern countries seems possessed of hardier powers of survival.

We have seen how the mysterious figure of "Knecht Rupprecht" comes, in Germany, into the Christmas ritual. In Scandinavia, Tomte Gubbe makes his appearance during the winter festival—he being a sort of house-spirit, equivalent of the "drudging goblin" than Milton refers to in *L'Allegro*. Miles suggests that he may represent the spirit of the founder of the family. Porridge and new milk are set out for him on Christmas Eve (as they are for the spirits of the dead) and sometimes even new clothes, tobacco and strong waters are added, so as to win his help during the forthcoming year.

And all these northern customs have been exported to new Swedens, new Denmarks, new Polands, new Germanies, new Russias and new Bohemias across the Atlantic—even to that lonely little outpost of Denmark, Bouvet Island, which lies un-neighboured amid the wastes of the South Atlantic, but a few hundred miles from the South Pole.

Ancient customs, established in heaven knows what Asiatic homeland, heaven knows how many years before Christ, have been preserved by stubborn traditionalism, and then transplanted in a new world.

And what of the homeland? A strange thing is happening in eastern Germany. From the very centre of Asia, from the old emirates of Turkestan—Trebizond and Samarcand and Tashkent; from Tannu-Tuva and Inner Mongolia; from the hordes which roam the great plains of Inner Asia along the ancient Silk Road; the Russian Government is bringing thousands to re-settle the Baltic plains. Once more, history repeats itself, and the Mongol is settling in Europe. It is no new thing, and it has happened many times before. In the end, Europe has absorbed the new blood.

But what legends they must be bringing with them—new Asiatics to settle on the lands from which the old Asiatics have been expelled! They are the "Locusts" against which Joshua had to fight as he brought the hosts of Israel across the plains of Inner Asia. The Jewish sacred books have the ancient memory of them preserved still. Have the settlers folk-tales of the battle which was fought when the ancient Jews passed through their lands, on their way to a north where the sun stood still in the heavens?

CHAPTER EIGHTEEN

# CHRISTMAS IN FRANCE

THERE is a French nation, but there is nothing which may be called a French race. The elements which have gone to make up the nation are as diverse as those which have gone to the composition of the British people.

There is a little more Celtic blood in the north and north-west of France, a little more Basque and Mongol and Saracen in the south and south-west, while around the port of Marseilles, in that hinterland that the Romans called the Provincia Narbonensis, there are elements derived from every race which ever set out to travel the Mediterranean Sea. But the bulk of the population of France is Celt on a basis of something earlier and something not quite so easy to define: so much the same as is the case with Britain that it is astonishing how widely French customs differ from those of the land now only twenty-two miles distant across the Channel, and, in Caesar's day, just the half of that.

It is even more astonishing when we consider that the English court spoke Norman-French even before Duke William conquered England, and that, for more than three centuries after the Conquest, French or, rather, the French of "Stratford-atte-Bowe"—was the language of polite intercourse, and that, for nearly seven centuries after the Conquest, Norman-French remained the language of the law-courts.

But the reason why the customs of the two near-neighbour countries have remained so diverse is that each derives its culture from a different source: the French from the Greek and Roman, the British from Teutonic, culture.

It is not true to say that the French are a Latin people—they are not—but it is true to say that France is a Latin nation. It is equally true that, despite the fact that only a small proportion of the blood of the British people is of different origin from that of the

French, Britain is a nation which has built its culture up from Teutonic, rather than from Latin, sources.

It is for this reason that the French pay much attention to New Year's Day, *le Jour de l'An*, where the English tend to neglect that feast in favour of Christmas Day: the French, conversely, having taken to celebrating Christmas with Anglo-Saxon fervour only during the past few decades—and then only under the influence of a fashionable Anglophile craze. Yet even today, the secular Christmas—considered distinct from the religious feast of Christmas, which is still, and has always been, celebrated in France—is only for the children. It is the children's feast, and the adult French reserve their gaiety for the New Year.

The Gauls of France, or what we now call France, fought bitterly against the Romans, and one of their kings, Vercingetorix, enjoyed a romantic renown among the conquerors. The Gauls of Britain did not fight more fiercely than did their cousins across the narrow straits of Dover. But the Romans imposed their culture upon the Gauls of France where they did not impose it upon the Britons: when the legions marched down to Rutupiae and Portus Lemanus and Dubris, in Britannia Prima, and sailed away to Rome, they left behind them a population which was to become part Anglo-Saxon and part Celtic—so far as language, manners and customs were concerned.

Practically nothing more than the ending "chester"—or its variants—to certain town names, and the word "went" in other names—Caerwen, Ventnor, etc.—from the colloquial Latin, *venta,* a market, remained to testify to a Latin influence which had lasted for four centuries[1], but which survived the occupation hardly more than a century—if as long.

It is a curious fact that members of the same Celtic clans were settled on both sides of the Channel, and kept up a constant intercourse—the Menapiae occupied districts both in the south-west of Ireland and at the mouth of the Scheldt; the Parisii were settled both

[1] That, in certain parts of Britain, there were "pockets" in which the Roman culture survived cannot be denied. The above remarks have only a general application. Professor Geoffrey Webb, of the Royal Commission on Historical Monuments, pointed out to the author the most interesting fact that the ruins of the great monastery of Tintagel reveal that, so late as the ninth century—when Anglo-Saxon England was enjoying primitive conditions of domestic comfort—the architects of Tintagel were installing hot-air heating (hypocausts) on the ancient Roman plan.

on the Sequana River, with their chief city of Lutetia there (now Paris, on the Seine), and in the Holland district of Lincolnshire; the Brigantes were in Ireland, Yorkshire and on the Alpine borders of Italy (Brienz in the Austrian Tyrol marks the site of one of their many settlements)—but that, while the Celts of Gaul became almost completely Romanized, the Celts of Britain and Ireland remained obstinately Celtic—resisting both Roman and Teutonic cultural influences.

But when the legions marched away from Gaul, the Gaulish Celts remained Roman. And when the Franks moved in from Germany, the Celts did not adopt a Teutonic tongue—the Franks adopted the Roman speech of the Gauls.[1]

It is most probable that the fact that Gaul retained its Roman culture after the collapse of the Western Empire may be explained by the conversion of Gaul to Christianity, which was effected early and completely, the power of the Druids being broken in a manner which had no counterpart on the other side of the Channel. And again, where the Christianity of Gaul was Roman, the British Christian Church had its origin elsewhere than in Rome—and the Britons identified Roman Christianity with the Roman civil power, resenting both equally.

The links, then, between Gaul and Rome were not broken when the Roman Empire collapsed. Civil power fell away, but religious power remained; and the first Frankish kings were easily converted both to the Roman brand of Christianity practised in Gaul and to those Roman manners that adherence to the Christian faith had perpetuated in Gaul after the Roman viceroys had gone for ever.

But even the fracture of the purely civil link between Rome and Gaul was mended when, at dawn on Christmas Day, A.D. 800, Pope Leo III solemnly crowned Charlemagne Emperor of the Romans; and, if the formal civil link endured only a short while after that truly momentous event, the nominally purely religious link between France and Rome was, in reality, more than half a civil one.

Avignon was a papal city for centuries, until the French revolutionary government incorporated it into metropolitan France, and the Concordat between France and the Vatican, denounced by the Republicans and restored by Napoleon I, endured until 1904.

[1] We must bear in mind, however, that an estimated proportion of over one-third of all French words in common use are of Teutonic origin.

This unbroken association between Rome and France must always be borne in mind in accounting for the classically Roman bias in French manners and thought, and—as a corollary—the Roman element in the French manner of celebrating Christmas and the New Year. But Caesar was especially struck by the Druidic views on the afterlife, and, in general, the Celtic seeming over-preoccupation with death—a preoccupation that the Celts shared with the Egyptians, whose name occurs so often and so significantly in Celtic myth. And there is no doubt that the Celts, when they adopted, first, the pagan beliefs of the Romans, and, later, the Christian ideas emanating from Rome, gave a decided Celtic bias to those ideas and beliefs.

In the ancient, pre-Christian Winter Festival celebrations of the Romans was included that feast of the death-cult which has now been shifted back—at least, in the Church's calendar—a couple of months, but which was in ancient Rome, and still is in modern Pyrenea and the Southern Slav countries, as well as in Finland and Scandinavia, celebrated in connexion with "Christmas."

Thus it was almost to be expected that the first positive historical reference to All Souls' Day is found in French records. That is to say, the first mention of the shifting-back of the feast to 1 November from a previous date on or near Christmas Eve. The mention shows that much importance was attached to the feast—and thus to its date-alteration—and it follows that we may imply that the feast was already celebrated with much solemnity.

This shifting-back, of course, merely gave the feast two different dates instead of a previous one. The new date was honoured, and on the old one the feast of the family-dead continued to be celebrated.

The Latin word for hearth is *focus*, and the other, wider meaning of that word indicates the presence of an ancient Indo-European concept that home-life had its stimulus, origin and support in the family-hearth. So, when the dead return to their homes—as the folk-belief of the Aryan peoples holds—it is to the hearth that they turn their steps. Food is put out for them, and, as we have seen, games—as games were put out for them in ancient Rome and are still in modern Spain, and southern France. And for them the Yule Log is cut with ritual, and drawn with pomp, and lighted with elaborate and unchangeable ceremony.

We shall see, in the chapter on Spain, that the Yule Log is still an honoured custom in northern Spain and southern France. In the other parts of France, too—though now only in the provincial districts—the Yule Log is still honoured.

In northern France, it is called the *souche de Noël* (*souche*—stump of a tree), but the Roman origin of modern French manners, if not of the Yule Log itself—which is decidely older than Rome—is seen in the names that the log has in Dauphiné (*chalendal*) and Provence (*calignaou*), both of which are derived from *Kalendae,* the Kalends (of January), around which time the Roman winter festivals took place.

In Provence it is sometimes called *tréfoir,* and in the district of Orne it is called *tréfouet*, and its collection and burning are a matter for the whole family's common effort. The Provençal family —all of it—goes out on Christmas Eve to collect the log, a carol being sung in accompaniment of this important act: a carol which asks those material blessings that country-folk need—"blessings on the house, that the women may bear children, the nanny-goats kids, and the ewes lambs, that corn and flour may abound, and the cask be full of wine."

Then, in the name of the Trinity, wine is poured on the log by the youngest child present. When the log is burned, the charcoal is carefully collected, to be used throughout the ensuing year as a universal remedy.

Frédéric Mistral, the Provençal poet, has described the ceremony of bringing home the Yule Log—in his district it had to be cut alive from a fruit-tree. In his description there appears a ritual "monstration" of the Log, the family—eldest at the head, youngest bringing up the rear—carrying it three times around the kitchen. But in the ceremony with which Mistral was acquainted it was the father and not the youngest child, who poured the wine-libation over the Log.

Mistral has recorded the doubtless age-hallowed phrases of dedication:

"'Joy, joy! May God shower joy upon us, my dear children. Christmas brings us all good things. God give us grace to see the New Year, and if we do not increase in numbers, may we at all events not decrease!'

"In chorus we responded:

Sprinkling wine on the Souche de Noël—or Yule-log—in Touraine. The log, variously named, is burned in many parts of Europe.

Gathering mistletoe for Christmas in Brittany in the last century. The plant, sacred to the Druids, is still reverenced throughout Europe and North America.

" 'Joy, joy, joy!' and lifted the log on the fire-dogs. Then, as the first flame leapt up, my father would cross himself, saying, 'Burn the log, O fire!' and with that we all sat down to the table."

The ceremony of bringing the Yule Log home in southern France so closely resembles the corresponding ceremony in Serbia and Dalmatia, as described by Sir Arthur Evans, Mannhardt and Mijatovitch, that we must assume an origin for both so ancient, and so deeply rooted in custom, that, either the impact of the Roman culture on that of the Celts of southern Gaul failed to wean them from their old ritual habits, or—which is the correct answer—that the Romans (themselves of similar origin to the Celts) observed similar customs.

The resemblance between Provençal and Serbian custom is most striking when we consider the reverence paid to the ashes of the burnt Log. In Slav countries, it was taboo to disturb the ashes of the Log as they lay on the hearth, or in a stove, lest the disturbing "might cause the ancestors to fall into hell."

In some places in France, they burn the log—the *tréfoir* or *tison de Noël*—every night, during the thirteen nights of Christmastide, and magical powers are credited to the charcoal. Put under the bed, the charcoal protects the house from lightning;[1] its touch will save a human from chilblains, and an animal from a number of ailments, including that known as "the staggers." In Périgord, the unconsumed part of the burnt log is incorporated into a new plough, specially credited with the ability to quicken the earth.

In this custom I seem to detect the not uncommon process of myth- and superstition-building by the semantic shift, due to the similarity of two sounds expressing different ideas.

Charcoal, in French, is *charbon* (*du bois*), from the Latin, *carbo*. But the phrase *char bon* means "good cart" and the syllable *char-*, begins a great many words, all connected with the idea of movement, such as *charroi,* waggon-traffic; *charron,* a cartwright; and —particularly—*charrue,* a plough. The concept behind the superstition which holds that a piece of wood from the Yule Log will make a wonder-working plough would, then, seem to be represented by the following semantic equation:

*charbon* (*du bois*) = *char bon* = *charrue bon.*

[1] In the extreme south of France, and in northern Spain, a similar power is credited to the candles blessed at Candlemas, and to rung church bells.

This suggestion may sound far-fetched to the reader who is unacquainted with the processes behind the development of folk-lore and popular superstition, but we may observe a similar example of myth-building from unintentional punning in English. The holes cut in the bulwarks of a ship are called the "cat-eyes," and many are the legends, told and believed, to account for the presence of "cats" aboard a ship. These legends are given added impressiveness by the fact that it was the custom among the ancient Greeks to paint formalized human eyes each side of the prow; a custom which was adopted by the Romans, and is still observed by the mariners of the Mediterranean.

But the truth is that the "cat-eyes" have nothing at all to do with the domestic pet that Shakespeare calls the "harmless, necessary cat." "Cat-eyes" was once "cat-eyen"—"eyen" being the older plural of "eye"—and "cat-eyen" is simply a corruption of the Latin word, *catena,* a chain. So do myths grow: not the only thing to flourish on ignorance and misunderstanding!

In Brittany, the culture is Celtic and not Latin, for this part of France was colonized by emigrating non-Romanized Celts from Britain, crossing the Channel either to acquire land[1] or to escape the pressure of the invading Anglo-Saxons.

Yet the *tison* is here as much an object of superstitious reverence as in those parts of France owning a Latin culture, which underlines the point earlier made, that the Yule Fire is an Aryan custom dating back to the times when there was no distinct division between Roman and Gaul, when both were units of one relatively small Italic tribe.

The Breton holds—with the people of southern France and parts of northern Spain—that the charcoal of the Yule Log is a specific against lightning, but there is something peculiarly Celtic about the Breton belief that the powdered charcoal from the log keeps well-water sweet throughout the year. The Celts have always had a strange attraction towards wells.

The belief in the miraculous power of the Candlemas candles is held both in Brittany and the Franche-Comté, on the other side of France, as well as in many other parts of the country. They are always lighted in times of storm or sickness.

[1] The density of its population was one of the aspects of Ancient Britain which most impressed the visitors to our islands.

Another belief prevalent in France—it seems impossible to state definitely whether it be Celtic or Latin or something even older—is that, on Christmas Eve, at midnight, all water turns to wine. This belief is especially prevalent in the Channel Islands, and the story is told that a Guernsey woman, once wishing to prove this belief, went to a well at midnight, to let down a bucket. Before she could draw the water, a stern voice came from out the depths of the well:

> "*Toute l'eau se tourne en vin,*
> *Et tu es proche de ta fin!*"
>
> (All water here to wine has turned,
> And by this act, thou death hast earned!)

The legend then tells how the woman was stricken of a mortal sickness, and died within the year. The morality of fables and fairy-tales is always interesting to study; but it is not often so obscure as in this tale. Why so shocking a punishment for a little human inquisitiveness?

In the tiny island of Sark, there is a variant of this legend, promising death to the rash doubter who tries to prove the truth of it; but in the Sark version it is to blood and not to wine that the water changes for a moment or two at midnight. There is a hint here of the transubstantiation—the miraculous change by which, according to Roman Catholic belief, the elements of bread and wine are "transubstantiated" into the body and blood of the Saviour. If, as the Sark legend seems to hint, this change somehow takes place in the wells, then the punishment visited on the person who goes to see or to touch the miraculously changed water is simply the punishment for grievous sacrilege.

Russia and France share a curious belief concerning the genealogy of Christ—or, rather, its public recitation. In this belief it is impossible not to see the influence of Jewish mysticism, even though that influence may not have come directly from Jewish sources. For the belief that certain sounds have a magical power in themselves is one of the most ancient among the Semitic peoples, and is a belief constantly to be found at the bottom of legends in Rabbinical lore, where the *Schem Hamphorasch*—the Ineffable Name—is credited with almost omnipotent powers.

So deep was the belief in the power of the very sound of God's name that the Jewish priests never pronounced it aloud, and when coming to it in the Scriptures, subsituted for it the word, *Adonai,* meaning *Lord*. (In time, the correct pronunciation naturally came to be forgotten—but that is another story!)

The French belief which seems to reflect the ancient Jewish —or, it may be, Arab from Spain, via the south of France—is that, while the genealogy of our Saviour is being recited during the Midnight Mass on Christmas Eve, buried treasure reveals itself—French legend giving us many examples of the manner in which this happy event comes about. Mostly it is because a solitary traveller notices witch-lights or a shimmering blue haze settled about some spot—often one of those barrows which have always interested the country-folk. Sometimes, a worshipper at the Midnight Mass looks up to see a troll peering in the window—for a troll, having no soul, cannot enter a church if he would—and beckoning the worshipper to come out and help himself to the treasure revealed. And here again, in these treasure-tales, the morality seems to be something not quite our own; for the wealth comes either to the traveller who is not at church, or to someone who is sufficiently distracted at Mass to be looking up at the window, and sufficiently careless of the holy occasion to wish to follow the beckoning gnome.

The Breton folk-lorist, Anatole le Braz, has collected the many legends of his land which deal with death. One of the most impressive concerns the sacred character of Christmas Eve, and the danger of ignoring its holy influences. Taking no notice of the sacring-bell, ringing during the Midnight Mass, a Breton blacksmith went on working in his forge. A tall, bent old man came to the smithy, asking the owner to mend a broken scythe.

The smith was willing. The broken blade of the scythe was welded whole. The scythe was returned to the old, bent man as good as new. The old man gravely thanked the smith. In payment, he had this advice to give: "Send for a priest, now. For this work that you have done is the last that you will ever do!"

The old man disappeared, and the blacksmith fell stricken with a mortal illness. At cock-crow, he died. For the scythe that the smith had mended had been that of the *Ankou*—of Death himself.

Remnants of the ancient sacrificial rituals of the Winter Festival become increasingly rare, in France as elsewhere, and it is a century and more since, in the region of the Ardennes, the school-children were given hens by their teachers, so that the children might chop off the hens' heads, but the Hunting of the Wren has not died out in France, in the country districts, especially of the south and west.

The game that we call Blind Man's Buff is a Christmas game, and folk-lorists see in it the degenerate survival of a ritual sacrifice, in which the masked ("blind") officiant carried out the killing. The probability of this explanation is heightened by the fact that the game is called all over Europe by names associated with animals, and always with the word "blind" prefixed, so that it would seem that, originally, the sacrificer wore the mask of, and, for the period of the ritual, assumed the character of the animal sacrificed—as the Bull, in the Pyrenean mumming, is at once "the killer and the slain."

"The degeneration of religious rites into mere play," says Clement Miles, "is, indeed, as we have seen, a process illustrated by the whole history of Christmas."

This truth is well illustrated by the custom of the Epiphany cake, or, as it is called in France, *la galette des Rois*—something that we must add to the almost limitless tally of ritual foods. It is a thin cake, flavoured with lemon and vanilla, baked of flaky pastry, and it used to be sent, as a present, by the baker to his regular customers. It appears now that one pays for it—so has one more small graciousness gone out of the world!

*La galette des Rois* means "The Kings' Cake," and it is the French form of the Epiphany cake that we find baked all over Europe—as it was once baked in England, where it was called Twelfth Cake. The French peasants put a bean, of the kind called *fève* in French, into the cake-mix, the finder of the bean, when the cake is baked and cut, being "King" for the evening, choosing a "Queen" to share his honours.

This custom used to be observed in England, and the "King of the Bean" was a familiar character in the Christmasses of two hundred years ago. In the French towns, a china doll is substituted for the bean (sometimes a silver coin is used, as it formerly was in England) and folk-lorists may ponder the fact that the hair of the china "king" *must* be black.

The custom of choosing the "King of the Bean" is mentioned

in English records of date as early as the reign of Edward II, and the "king" belongs to the family of Boy Bishops, Christmas Fools, Lords of Misrule, and the rest. The sixteenth-century French writer, Etienne Pasquier, describes a somewhat elaborate ritual of election, and in some parts of France, the cutting of the *galettes*—or *gâteaux—des Rois* is accompanied by some singing by children. In Berry, it was the custom to divide the cake up amongst the guests, and to leave one extra portion, which was called *la part du bon Dieu,* and the same custom was observed in Lorraine.

The custom of the Twelfth Cake in France is exceedingly old. In the thirteenth century, the monks of Mont St. Michel chose their Epiphany "king" by means of a cake, and a special throne was provided for him in the monastery chapel, in which he sat during Mattins, High Mass and Vespers.

These Kings of Topsy-Turvy quite often attach themselves to Christmas Day, or to other days in the Christmas festival. At Salers, in central France, a "king" and "queen" were chosen to preside over the Christmas festival. They had a place of honour in the church, and headed the processions. Their reign began on Christmas Day, and they were not elected by vote or chosen by lot. They bought their exalted position at an auction held on the church steps, and "it is said to have been so much coveted that worthy citizens would sell their heritage in order to purchase" the honour.

The belief that evil influences are scared away by noise—especially the noise of certain instruments—is an ancient one. The ancient Egyptians placed great faith in the magical properties of the *sistrum,* a sort of wire rattle, and the Chinese used fireworks to scare off devils long before they thought of putting gunpowder into tubes, in order to scare off more material enemies. "Rough music" is played in many parts of Britain for the same purpose, and on Twelfth Night the inhabitants of Labruguière, in southern France, run through the streets, making "rough music," with a din more devilish than the demons that this noise is intended to disperse.

Hone, in his *Year Book, 1832,* reports that at Rouen, in his day, the "office of the Shepherds" was celebrated on Christmas Eve, and if his description is accurate, the service represents one of the most astonishing survivals in history, for what Hone describes is, word for word, the service of *Quem quaeritis?* which is found in a St. Gall manuscript of the ninth century. In another chapter, we have seen how this simple dramatization of the Gospel narrative gradually developed into the full religious drama, and so led to the foundation of the modern stage. If Hone is to be believed, it would seem that the very earliest form of the religious drama, the *Stella,* was either fossilized at Rouen, or revived at some unknown date, in circumstances of complete obscurity. But almost certainly, the service of the Shepherds is a strange survival; the stranger in that Rouen is no remote country village, but a city which stands at the very gateway of France.

An English writer, talking of Paris in 1823, refers with disarming pity to the French ignorance of the joys of Christmas, adding that the most renowned maker of Christmas puddings in France, Harriet Dunn, is kept in constant activity only by the English residents. "Her fame has even extended to the provinces. For some time previous to Christmas Day, she forwards puddings in cases to all parts of the country, ready cooked and fit for the table, after the necessary warming."

After adding that you would "offend a Frenchman for ever if you compel him to eat plum-pudding," the writer has this to say of the then French king:

"Louis XVIII, either to show his contempt for the prejudices of his countrymen, or to keep up a custom which suits his palate, has always an enormous pudding on Christmas Day, the remains of which, when it leaves the table, he requires to be eaten by the servants, *bon gré, mauvais gré*; but in this instance even the commands of sovereignty are disregarded, except by the numerous English in his service, consisting of several valets, grooms, coachmen, etc., besides a great number of ladies' maids in the service of the duchesses of Angoulême and Berri, who very frequently partake of the dainties of the king's table."

But the Paris correspondent of the *Daily Telegraph,* describing Christmas of 1886, shows how strong a hold the English Christmas customs had taken of the Parisian fancy: "Another custom, that of decorating Christmas trees in the English and German style, has become quite an annual solemnity here since the influx of Alsatians and Lorrainers, while it is considered *chic,* in many quarters, to eat approximate plum-pudding on the 25th of December. Unfortunately, the Parisian 'blom budding,' unless prepared by British hands, is generally a concoction of culinary atrocities, tasting, let us say, like saveloy soup and ginger-bread porridge." Then the correspondent repeats the old tale, that we could have quoted from the English writer of sixty years earlier, that the 'blom budding' is sometimes served by the ignorant Parisians in a tureen.

But he admits that the French would still have their *boudin,* or black-pudding, after the Midnight Mass, "the rich baptizing it in champagne, the *petit bourgeois,* who has not a wine cellar, in a cheap concotion of bottled stuff with a Bordeaux label but a strong Paris flavour."

We have seen elsewhere in this book how Princess Hélène of Mecklenburg introduced the Christmas-tree to Paris in about 1840, and how it became a fashionable Christmas adjunct before the end of the nineteenth century. Yet, even today, with two German occupations of Paris, and two Anglo-American, within the past eighty years, the Parisians still cling as obstinately as before to their preference for the New Year over Christmas. Neither modern German nor Anglo-American tastes have weaned the French away from their classical preferences, any more than they were weaned away by the Germanic conquerors of the fifth century, or the Norse conquerors of the ninth.

This is not to be regretted. Latin habits of logical thought, allied with the imaginativeness and artistry of the Celt, have created the modern French temperament—and the world, as well as France, has been the gainer. The French love novelty, but are never bewitched with it: they combine the most lively curiosity with the most dogged conservatism—and if they sometimes give, to the superficial, an impression of superficiality, let us not forget that the wonderful Christmas hymn, *Adeste Fideles,* is a Latin carol which came out of France when England's art was chilled by the cold precision of Augustan agnosticism. The really typically French aspect of the hymn is that it was written, not in French, but in Latin.

Indeed, the French Church was producing Latin hymns all through the eighteenth century, which was also the century of Diderot and d'Alembert, of Mirabeau and Rousseau, of Voltaire and Beaumarchais, and the fine hymn of Charles Coffin's, *Jam desinant suspiria*, to be found in *Hymns Ancient and Modern*, as *God from on high hath heard* is a product of that period.

The development of the French "mystery" and of the *chanson de Noël*—with which the great names of Lucas le Moigne, Jean

Daniel, Nicholas Denisot ("Comte d'Alsinoys") and Françoise Paschal are associated—has been described in another chapter. It is to be mentioned in this chapter only to point out that, while religious song and drama began in France to develop on "romantic" lines, both came to perfection only after having been taken over by "classical" influences.

England came to, and passed through, her period of "classical" song and drama, but the romantic in England, though sometimes overshadowed, was never suppressed, and, in the end, the romantic conquered the classical, which is only today beginning to show some signs of revival.

The difference between the progress of French and English dramatic art could not be better perceived than in observing that what is played, year in and year out, by the company of the *Théâtre français,* as an honoured French national institution, is played in England, as a joke, by Mr. Tod Slaughter's company, for the connoisseurs of "ham tragedy." This is not to say that *Phèdre* is to be classed with *East Lynne*; we only point out that the impulse to produce the classic drama strengthened in France until it could produce a *Phèdre*—in England it never acquired more strength than was necessary to write an *East Lynne.*

Latin France . . . "But the Virgin says what she has to say in classical French. In the refinement of her diction, her elevation above those with her is expressed. . . ." The quotation refers to a Provençal village procession—a movingly simple dramatic representation of the Flight into Egypt—of the sort which so delighted the German Jewish poet, Heinrich Heine, and caused him to say that he had never seen anything prettier in all his life. He was a man of the world—something of a cynic; a self-indulgent dreamer, that too many found too many good reasons to call a social parasite. And he was a great poet. In the traditional customs of the French people, Heine found something to appeal to every aspect of his curiously diverse nature.

## CHAPTER NINETEEN

# CHRISTMAS IN ITALY

CHRISTIANITY did not originate in Rome, and several flourishing Christian Churches, established independently of Rome—the Church of Britain was one—were in existence when the Bishop of Rome put forth his claim to supremacy—financial, political and doctrinal—over all other Christian Churches. This claim was everywhere strongly resisted, and in several instances was imposed only by the use of physical force, such as in the massacre of the monks of Bangor, a great British Christian monastery, and the spiritual headquarters of a Church which has the renown of having Christianized Switzerland and the better part of Germany.

Rome, then, imposed its own customs—as it imposed its discipline—on the other Churches who might not hold on to their independence, and so in Rome, we should expect to find Christmas celebrated in a more orthodox manner than anywhere else in Christendom; for here in Rome are the fount and origin of those spiritual and ritual manners which, elsewhere, have been corrupted by the survival of older and less worthy canons of behaviour and belief.

But Rome itself had a religion before Christianity became the religion of the Empire—or, rather, many religions, all grafted upon that ancient pastoral faith which was identified, in the public sub-consciousness, with the very greatness of Rome. A Roman citizen might have turned—at that appropriate moment—from Jove to Christ, but he could not forget the fig-tree which grew in the Comitium of the Forum: grown from a slip of the original tree under which the she-wolf had suckled the twin sons of Mars and Rhaea Silvia. Everyone knew about that tree: how it had originally grown on the bank of the Tiber, below the Palatine Hill, where the mouth of the Lupercal grotto showed the promise of shelter to the she-wolf. And how, later, it had been miraculously transferred —in the manner of the translation of the Holy House of Loretto

—to the Forum. Then, how, after having stood eight hundred and forty years, it showed signs, in A.D. 58, of dying, so that a successor was raised from slips of the old tree.

There was not this one reminder of the Rome of Romulus and Remus: there were hundreds, if not thousands; and it was seen, in the introductory chapter of this work, how existing customs in Rome had a profoundly modifying effect upon the practices of early Christianity. It is tempting to connect the reverence later paid to the *Santa Scala*—the Holy Staircase—with the fact that the original tree supposed to have sprung from the javelin of Romulus, the eponymous founder of Rome, was killed by workmen damaging the roots when they were repairing a flight of steps which ran close by. The cornel-tree was one of the most sacred objects of Pagan Rome, and, according to Plutarch, "if a passer-by noticed any sign of fading in its foliage, the fearful news ran like wildfire through the City, bringing the populace with fire-buckets as to a conflagration to revive the wilting talisman and avert impending disaster."

Christian Rome, indeed, had exactly the same problems confronting it as had any other Christian city: the pagan elements proved ineradicable, and conversion, if it were to be total, could never be more than a matter of compromise.

But into Pagan Rome had come travellers and settlers from all over the world, each bringing something to add to that store of exotic custom and belief which had been superimposed on the original customs and beliefs of the pure Roman stock. Nor did the influx of strangers cease with the change of the state religion to Christianity: centuries had to pass after Constantine had accepted the Cross before the time came when Rome fell into such poverty that it could hardly feed its own people, let alone support a vast population of visitors. But in the days when there were twenty-one aqueducts, carried on tall brick pillars across the plains and marshes, bringing water to Rome, custom was being modified with every dazzled stranger who entered through one of the twenty gates.

There is this to be said for strict orthodoxy: it makes heresy very clearly defined, and highly conscious of itself. In Britain and Germany and Spain, pagan elements are generally either christianized or accepted as being of no religion at all. But, as the growing power of the Roman Church first forced the pagan priesthood into a subordinate position, and then forced paganism itself underground, paganism came to take on a secret, parallel existence. Pagan elements in popular belief and custom were assimilated into Church practice, but there were certain elements in paganism—organized, bitterly intractable elements—which were not assimilated in the establishment of Christianity as the state religion of Rome, and have not been assimilated to this day.

The Italians call this paganism *La Vecchia Religione*, the Old Religion, and though it is now no more than rustic Diana-worship; its priestesses "wise-women"—country witches from the hill villages of the Appenines and the stone-hutted hamlets of utterly primitive Eboli; it has had its period of dark greatness, when its poisons ended dynasties, and the whispered counsels of its ministers were heard in the shadow of the Vatican itself.

What, then, will be said about the Christmas customs of Spain may apply more or less exactly to the corresponding festivals and celebrations of Italy: a deep faith in the essential facts of Christianity, allied with an intractable intention to observe the customs of their forefathers, no matter how bitterly the Church denounce those —to their observers, harmless—customs.

In another chapter, I have discussed the origin of the Christmas Crib and of the carols with which the name of Jacopone da Todi's name is associated: the manner, in other words, in which Italy has contributed to the common fund of Christmas celebration. What I intend, in this chapter, is to describe the manner in which Italians celebrate Christmas in ways peculiar to themselves: to show, in other words, how the Italian celebration of Christmas differs from others' celebration of the feast.

First: in the matter of food. Italy is a land in which meat is used to provide little more than a sauce for the vegetables and the wheaten dishes which form a substitute for the flesh eaten in other lands. The writer has lived in Italy, and he knows that the Italian, though he may perform miracles of the culinary art with his farinaceous foods—his *pasta*—is never completely reconciled to the absence of much flesh from his menu. He thinks himself hard done by, in comparison with the eaters of other lands; and it is possibly with this fact in mind that a paternal ecclesiastical government ordained, many years ago, that the Vigil of the Nativity—Christmas Eve, in our own usage—be a fast, no meat being allowed upon that day, save by a special exemption.

Calabrian shepherds playing their bagpipes at Christmas before a Roman street-shrine of the early nineteenth century.—*From Hone.*

This wise provision makes it possible for the Italian not to regret the absence of vast quantities of meat at his great *cenone* or ritual banquet, always held on Christmas Eve. Here, most of the dishes have fish and flour for their basis, and a favourite side-dish is stewed eel. The fish was a sacred emblem in the early days of Christianity, and the prohibition of meat upon the Vigil of the Nativity may have a mystical as well as a practical significance.

The Italians share with the Spaniards a liking for *turròn*—almond rock—the Italian slightly altered form of the name being *torrone,* but the *panettone*, or currant loaf (spiced) is a favourite tasty with Italians at Christmas, and—well in the tradition of the Roman *strenae,* which used to be exchanged on the Kalends of January—is sent to friends, as we send Christmas-cards.

These old customs are kept up more among the peasant and mechanic classes, of course. The tendency among the upper orders is to send Christmas and New Year's cards, in the English manner.

Italy has several times been invaded by the Celts, and the Latins were originally part of a great linguistic group to which both the Greeks and the Celts belonged. Holly was a plant enjoying a mystical reverence among the Celts, and it is used in Italy today, as it is in Britain.

Chestnuts, too, appear at Christmas, roast and "glacé"—crystallized in sugar. For the writer, the memory of standing on the steps of Trinità de' Monti, in Rome, looking across the Piazza di Spagna, where Keats lived, to St. Peter's dome, seen blue-black in the gathering mist of evening, is a memory which always recalls the glow of holly berries in the twilight and the sharp odour of roasting chestnuts.

A *purée*, or mash, of boiled chestnuts, mixed with sifted sugar and brandy or the sweet wine called marsala, is a favourite Christmas dish. Named *zabaglione* or *zabaione,* another dish, made of eggs whipped with wine and sweetened, is a prime favourite, the dish lending itself to an elaboration to match the pocket or the kindly ambitious intentions of the maker.

It is perhaps too much to hope that the Calabrian shepherds—the *pifferari*—still come down from their mountains at Christmas-time, to wander about the streets of Rome in their shaggy sheep-skin jackets, their strong legs cross-gartered, to play their bag-pipes—*zampogne*—before the street-shrines of the Virgin—but if they have gone altogether (swept away by the ruthless flood-tide of "progress") they have gone only in recent years.

The Italians know the Yule Log, but only the Italians of the north, who are of a different racial origin from that of the bulk of the southern Italian population. If the Yule Log is Teutonic in derivation—as it most probably is—it may be that the same race which introduced it into Spain and Britain, introduced it into northern Italy, which was seized and occupied by that Teutonic people called the Lombards: cousins of the Goths who invaded Spain, and rather more distant cousins of some of those elements which invaded Celtic Britain.

The Yule Log is called *ceppo*—just "log"—in northern Italy; but in Tuscany, Christmas Day is named after it—*Festa di Ceppo*. The Piedmontese call it *suc,* but honour it with reverences similar to those given in the Vale of Chiana, where the whole family gathers about the fire on which the *ceppo* is burning, and the blindfolded children of the house beat the burning log as all prepare to sing an *Ave Maria del Ceppo*.

The ancient name for the log, in Tuscany, was *ciocco di Natale;* in Lombardy, *zoppo di Natale,* and, since the first mention of it, in the eleventh century, it is found as a city custom in Italy all through the Middle Ages. Miles refers to a "little book, probably printed in Milan at the end of the fifteenth century," which gives minute particulars of the ritual to be observed in preparing and burning the Log.

From this book we learn that, on Christmas Eve, the father—or the head of the household—would call the family about him, and reverently, and in the name of the Most Blessed Trinity, put the Log on the blazing fire. Juniper was placed beneath, money above—to be given later to the servants. The father then drank wine, reminding us of the ritual draught from the Ballafletcher crystal goblet, the "Fletcher Luck," by the head of the family, at Christmas; the draught being drunk to the "peaceful spirit" of Ballafletcher, the Lhiannan-Shee. All, following the father, drank and wine was then poured three times on the Log.

In northern Italy, as in northern Spain and Brittany, the ashes of the *zocco* were kept as a protection against hail-storms. A modern custom ordains that small pieces of the Log, kept over from the Christmas burning, and fed to the fire which keeps the silk-worms warm, will guard these creatures from harm.

Art, which received a new impetus from Italian patronage in the Middle Ages, has had a thin time of it lately in the land of the Medici, and under the late Duce was almost extinguished quite; but the peasant handicrafts survive astonishingly in an Italy which has feverishly been seeking complete industrialization for close on a century. In the Appenine villages, chairs and tables and mirror-frames are carved up, for sale in the shops of Milan and Bologna, Florence and Naples and Rome; and this peasant handicraft—it stops just short of art—excels in the preparation of those Christmas cribs which, in elaboration of treatment are rivalled only in Spain, and for fidelity to nature are rivalled nowhere on earth.

It has been related elsewhere how St. Francis of Assisi prepared a crib, so that men might learn to worship God in His more human, more tender—and thus more comprehensible—aspects. The crib surely existed long before St. Francis—as it has lived in the warm regard of the Italian ever since.

"Christmas," says Miles, "is for the poorer Italians a summing-up of human birthdays, an occasion for pouring out on the *Bambino* parental and fraternal affection as well as religious worship"; and it was this natural sentiment that St. Francis set out to capture for Christ's service when he instituted the custom of the crib—or *presepe.*

The *presepi* astonish the visitor to Italy in the grandeur of their conception and the lavishness of their execution. The Mother and her Spouse may be bending over a manger under a thatched roof, but the thatched roof is itself protected by the imposing ruins of some imperial palace: vast Corinthian pillars, flowering like winter thorn, uphold an architrave, along whose broken frieze one may trace half a consular title or the defaced inscription to a dead god.

Architecturally correct to the last arris or triglyph, these ruined temples of the Italian *presepi* are but the focus of a vast crowd of worshippers—shepherds, pedlars, Ethiopian kings, Calabrian peasants, hurdy-gurdy men and all the rest—come to worship the Babe. Mostly carved in wood, and finished off in gesso or, better still, in what we call *papier mâché*, and the Italians *carta gesta*, these figures, no mass-produced puppets with featureless faces, but each a living portrait, are dressed with extreme care in clothes which delight a child in that they "take off." There are simpler *presepi,* of course, since there is not an Italian house which has not its *prèsepe,* and even the banks, chain-stores and railway-stations have theirs.

It is for the simpler domestic *presepi* that clay figures of the Holy Family, with their attendants, human and animal, are sold all over Italy—the open-air stalls in the Piazza Navona are the most popular market for these goods in Rome.[1]

Rouse's description of the *presepi* in the Italian churches is excellent: "Thither come the people, bearing humble gifts of chestnuts, apples, tomatoes and the like, which they place as offerings in the hands of the figures. These are very often life-size. Mary is usually robed in blue satin, with crimson scarf and white head-dress. Joseph stands near her dressed in the ordinary working garb. The onlookers are got up like Italian contadini. The Magi are always very prominent in their grand clothes, with satin trains borne by black slaves, jewelled turbans, and satin tunics all over jewels."

Two magnificent Christmas ceremonies, held in Rome each year, are the procession of the *culla*—the planks supposedly from the crib in which Christ was laid—at Santa Maria Maggiore and the exposition of the world-famous *Bambino* of Ara Coeli. The vast basilica of Santa Maria Maggiore is the same, with the outer parts much altered, in which the judges of Constantine gave justice in the fourth century of our era; the church of Ara Coeli (Altar of Heaven) is built from materials taken from a temple of Jupiter which stood on the same site.

Lady Morgan, writing in the early nineteenth century, has left a fine description of the disturbing contrast between the barbaric magnificence of the procession which bears the *culla,* and the squalid misery of the people—beggars, thieves, outcasts, of every sort—who have come to worship the five pieces of ancient wood.

Of the famous Bambino of Ara Coeli, it is said that it was carved by a devout monk of wood from the Mount of Olives, and that its pink and white complexion was painted upon the naked wood by the direct interposition of God.

This Bambino, for which the most wonderful healing powers are claimed by its "clients," is always elaborately swaddled in silk and gold and silver tissue, and fantastically jewelled, being hung

[1] These had their pagan antecedents in the *sigillaria,* clay dolls sold at the *Saturnalia.*

with objects of jewellery that devout maidens and matrons have bestowed upon it. It is incongruous to an English eye—or, at least, to the English eye of the writer—to see a mixed lot of jewellery pinned to the Bambino's robe: such a mixed lot as one sees in the trays of a jeweller's window.

The Bambino, besides an extensive wardrobe, has its own servants and a carriage in which to be taken to visit the sick. There is a legend told about this wonder-working image. It is related that a woman once feigned sickness so that its wardens would leave her alone with the Bambino. She stole the holy image, and left a worthless substitute in its place, taking the true Bambino home with her. But that night, the Franciscan brothers of Ara Coeli were called to the door by a great ringing of bells and hammerings on the oak. There, naked in the blustering storm, was the Bambino, come back to its home! Never since that night has it been allowed out of the care of its guardians.

At Christmas, the Bambino is set up in a shrine behind a small wooden platform, and here come the children of Rome, to stand, quite without self-consciousness, and recite a set piece to the Bambino—it is called "preaching." On the Octave of the Epiphany, a great procession ends with the blessing of the City by the Bambino, which is carried out of the church to the top of the flight of one hundred and twenty-four steps, and held on high by a priest.

It was in Santa Maria Maggiore that the Midnight Mass was first introduced to Rome—to Christendom, indeed—by a Pope of the early fifth century. Here he sang the first Mass—that at midnight—the second was sung at Sant' Anastasia; the third at St. Peter's.

A Christmas Eve service was held at Santa Maria Maggiore, with two recitals of Vespers—the first simple, the second most elaborate in ceremonial. Between the recitals of the Vespers, in the twelfth century, an excellent meal had to be served to the Pope and his household by the Cardinal-archbishop of Albano.

After Midnight Mass and Mattins at Santa Maria Maggiore, the Pope went in procession to Sant' Anastasia for the second Mass—the Mass of the Dawn (called the Mass of the Light in Spain) and Lauds—and then on to St. Peter's, for the third Mass. It was at this third Mass—at cock-crow—that Charlemagne was crowned Emperor of the Romans by Pope Leo III, on Christmas Day, A.D. 800.

Up to the year 1870, the Pope used to perform a curious ceremony at Santa Maria Maggiore, which had taken the place of St. Peter's as the church of the third Mass. On his arrival, he was given a wand with a candle fixed to the end, and with this he set fire to some tow or wadding fixed to the capitals of the church's columns.

Each Christmas Day, in the Vatican, the Pope blesses a hat and sword, and these objects are sent as presents to some ruler. It is said that it was the custom, in medieval times, for some foreign prince to read one of the lessons at Mattins on Christmas Day, and this he did with his sword drawn and laid aside.

It is further said that the present annual custom of the blessing and gift of a hat and sword arises from the older custom. But it is after Christmas, in the week following Twelfth Day, that a ceremony—or, rather, a series of ceremonies—is held, which, more than any other of Rome's many religious services, must fascinate the observer, and remind him, not only of the ancient pedigree, but also of the world-wide dissemination, of the Roman Faith.

Every morning, during the Octave of the Epiphany, at the church of Sant' Andrea, a Mass after the Latin rite is followed by a Mass said according to one of the rites of Eastern Churches in communion with Rome: Greco-Slav, Armenian, Chaldean, Coptic, Greco-Ruthenian, Greco-Melchite and Greek (Catholic). "It is a week of great opportunities for the liturgiologist and the lover of strange ceremonial."

All about the Italian—especially if he be devout—are reminders of the past. For instance, it is recorded in the writings of the fourth-century Eastern Father, Epiphanius, that there was a Gnostic rite held at Alexandria in his day, on the night of the Epiphany—or, rather, on the night, 5-6 January. At cock-crow, worshippers in the temple of Kore, the Maiden, brought up from an underground sanctuary a naked wooden image seated on a litter. This image had the sign of the cross marked upon it in five places—brow, hands and feet.

Paraded seven times around the great hall of the temple, to the accompaniment of music, the image was then taken back to its sanctuary. "In explanation of these strange actions, it was said, 'Today, at this hour, hath Kore (the Maidon) borne the Æon.' "

It is curious to compare this rite with that still practised at Messina, in Sicily, where, at two o'clock on Christmas morning, they carry a naked Bambino from the church of Santa Lucia to the cathedral and back.

But to trace such parallels, even consciously, between pagan and Christian rite is not to impute a false basis to our Faith. The Church has always openly sought to alter where she could not abolish, and to render harmless what she could not render non-existent.

And we must not forget that it was in Italy, by an Italian, that Christianity was subjected to a stern process of democratization in the thirteenth century. There were plenty of reformations in other countries, but it is a fact which is little noticed: that the first and the greatest reformation in the history of the Church came early and from within.

This democratization was deep, and its effect has never worn off. So much so that persons knowing only the ways of other lands are sometimes shocked by the apparently "light" manner in which the Italian treats his Church and his God; the familiarity shocks especially Anglo-Saxon visitors, who tell us that they cannot admire where they cannot respect.

To such visitors to Italy, the spectacle of children blowing their toy trumpets and banging their toy drums in the churches, while their parents gossip of almost anything but religious matters, is insufferable; is "making a mock of religion." The pomp goes on, unchecked and almost unnoticed by the gossiping throng who crowd the church as the market-place; the children, yelling, chase each other around the pillars which received their polish from the mason's pumice before Christ was born.

It is all very strange to visitors to Italy who know only their own more "correct" ways. It is all very natural to the Italian.

## CHAPTER TWENTY

# CHRISTMAS IN SPAIN

SPAIN, like England, has known many invasions by people of widely differing blood and custom—and each culture-wave has left its deep impress upon the Spanish character, and, of course, upon the mode with which that nation celebrates the many feasts of the year.

But since both Britain and Spain were once inhabited by the same aboriginal race—the language of that race surviving in the names of British and Spanish rivers and mountains and lakes—there is a similarity in basic folk-custom to be found uniting Spain and Britain. This is not astonishing—for though languages may change in a country, customs based upon primitive man's consciousness of Nature alter little and never really pass away.

The language that aboriginal Spain and Britain had in common was not Basque, though Basque itself is a very ancient tongue, which preserves in its vocabulary the memory of Stone Age days, just as our English word "book" keeps the memory of the time when our ancestors wrote on the bark of "boc" or beech.

Whence the Basques came, or to what great linguistic family their language is allied, we do not know, but we are able to say, with pretty fair accuracy, the list of the other elements which have gone to make up the race now inhabiting the Iberian Peninsula.

There was, first of all, that race—coming perhaps from Asia Minor along the North African coast—that we call (for lack of a better name) "Celtiberian," of which the small, dark Portuguese, and the "black" Irishman and the "black" Welshman, together with those Hebridean islanders whose Semitic type of features Sir Walter Scott found so fascinating, are the surviving representatives. Then, through North Russia and along the Danube Basin, waves of Celts poured into Europe—the first wave coming probably about 3000 B.C., the last main wave only a few hundred years before our era. These Celts went north-west to Britain and Ireland, south-west to Spain. But they got to a Spain which had already felt the influence of the Carthaginians—that race of commercial pioneers from Asia Minor, who founded their settlements all along the Mediterranean coast, and down Africa as far as Cape Town, and up the west coast of Europe as far as the Orkneys.

Whether or not it was the Carthaginians who built the cyclopean blocks of stone which are found all along the Spanish coast, and which so strangely resemble the walls of ancient Cuzco, the former capital of the Incas, in Peru, we do not know; but Marseilles, Cadiz and Cartagena survive as towns that they founded three thousand years ago.

Rome conquered the Carthaginians, and seized their Spanish colonial settlements. The Spaniards fought bitterly against Rome, and helped Hannibal in his contest with the Romans; but, although preserving that intense nationalistic individualism which still distinguishes the Spanish people, the Spaniard whole-heartedly embraced the Roman culture, as previously he had welcomed the Phoenician culture, and Spain—which gave poets, theologians, generals and emperors to the Roman Empire—preserved Roman civilization in a pure form for a longer period than did any other province of the Empire.

In the first and second centuries of our era, the Goths—themselves pressed on by other impatient peoples—moved west from Crimea and Asia Minor to attack the Adriatic colonies of the Empire, and then on to seize and sack Rome itself. It was to repel these invaders that the legions were recalled from Britain by the Emperor Honorius in A.D. 410.

These Goths—who spoke a Germanic language preserved for us in the great Testament prepared by Bishop Wulfilas, now in the library of Upsala University—soon fell under the sway of that culture against which they had moved in battle. They invaded Italy, the Roman provinces of North Africa and the province of Spain, and in all these places they came quickly and enthusiastically to adopt Roman ways and Roman thought. What concerns us here is that they built, in Toledo, the most splendid capital in Europe—a city of nearly two hundred churches and a library rivalling that of Alexandria in the extent of its scope and the number of its volumes.

For three hundred years, the Visigothic kings ruled Spain from

Toledo, until, in one night, it fell to the Moors—who were not finally to be expelled from Spain until more than seven centuries had passed. So Celtiberian—but Iberian is the better word, I think—Basque, Carthaginian, Celtic, Roman, Visigothic and Moslem elements and traditions combine to make up the character of modern Spain—a country, be it noticed, which stretches from the bitter Pyrenean cold to the bright Andalusian sunshine—where the mistletoe and the holly of the northern Christmas are given at the same time as the south decorates for its own Christmas with spring geraniums and heliotrope: a radical climatic difference which is, naturally, reflected in the character of the national customs.

There is a politico-racial division, too, which matches the climatic division of Spain. When the Visigothic kingdom was overthrown by the Moors, the remnants of the Visigoths retired to the mountainous north and there set up a centre of resistance to Moslem rule. It was into a Romano-Celtic-Greek-Basque country that the "resistance" went—the Visigoths even abandoning their ancient tongue for that bastard Latin spoken in the Provincia Narbonensis. The northern Spaniards, then, came under the influence of a civilization which was predominantly Roman, while the more southern portions of the peninsula came under an influence predominantly Saracen. The north, for centuries, derived its cultural influences from European sources, the south from Asiatic.

Roman Catholicism has acted as the unifying force which has gathered "all the Spains" into one national unit—Catalonia, the "original Spain," still remaining obstinately and self-consciously apart—but even Catholicism has not succeeded in destroying those political differences which are ultimately derived from differences in race and culture—and so custom.

We must bear in mind that, as was pointed out in the introductory chapter of this history, Christmas is the modern form of the ancient festival of winter—of the winter solstice. And the winter solstice is a natural phenomenon which was first noticed by man as he travelled through the more northernly regions. As one comes nearer to the tropics, this phenomenon becomes less apparent, until, as man reaches the regions about the Equator, he is not aware of it.

Universal religions are not found in the ancient world—each people had its own religion, and that religion was inspired by, and intimately connected with, a people's experience of the climate in which they dwelt. This point is well made by comparing the character of the Semitic and Teutonic "hells": "Gehenna" is a place of fire, "Niflheim" a place of ice.

"Christmas," then—or the festival of the winter solstice—is peculiarly a feast of northern peoples, and when found in southern climes is obviously an export from the north—either brought south by peoples originally settled in more northerly climes or in less accountable ways.

Of course, where what were originally no more than feasts to mark some seasonal change have, by receiving the sanction of "religion," become fixed, and so beyond the influence of mere climatic experience, such feasts will be as widespread as the religion, when that comes to be exported beyond its place of origin. The Moslems of Cardiff and Liverpool celebrate the Feast of Ramadan, the Christians of Freetown and Singapore celebrate the Feast of Christmas.

The Moslems who conquered Spain practised a toleration in religious matters which might well have been copied by the Spaniards when, having re-conquered the country, they became the masters. The Christians of southern Spain were permitted to practise their religion, and the church stood beside the mosque throughout Saracen Spain; but seven hundred years of living in subjection to a Moslem authority insensibly affected the Christianity of the Southern Spaniards—as it affected their blood—and because Christianity had selected Christmas to be the principal feast of the calendar, the celebration of that feast inevitably acquired an element of the political, of the anti-Moslem, in addition to its normal religious element. And Christmas, then, tended to be tactfully neglected in that part of Spain subject to Moslem rule.

It was in 1492 that the last Moslem stronghold, Granada, fell to Ferdinand and Isabella, and the last Moslem king, Boabdil, wept to be leaving a place so fair. He and his ancestors had ruled Spain for seven hundred years, but less than five centuries have passed since the Spanish scarlet-and-gold rose over the towers of Granada, and the memory of Islam is still strong in southern Spain.

So, to find the elements in the Spanish Christmas more familiar to us, we must go to the north, beyond even wind-swept Madrid, to the far Spanish north which shelters beneath the ranges of the Pyrenean mountains—an ancient land in which customs live long and which accepts change only with reluctance and, even, downright hostility. In this part of Spain, that Basque and Catalan share, the old, primitive culture is only very thinly overlaid with newer polishes: the essential culture of this part—as indeed it is, in a lesser degree, of the rest of Spain—is that of the aboriginal inhabitants, of the people who built the cyclopean walls of Tartessos and Palos, who worshipped the Sun in ritual dances of mazy intricacy.

Christmas, in the shadow of the Pyrenees, is celebrated in traditional north-Spanish fashion: that is, principally in song-and-dance, and since each of the numerous feasts of the calendar has its own songs and dances, Christmas, of course, has its own.

In a land where tradition has taken so strong a hold upon custom, it is not astonishing that Christmas has not been whittled down—as it has with us—to a mere one day's celebration. It seems that, originally, the Provençals had a preference for Christmas over the New Year, but French influence has rather tended to reverse this preference. Still, all that this has meant is that now Christmas and the New Year receive a pretty equal share of the public interest —and "Christmas" stretches, for the Pyreneans and Provençals, as long as it did for the British of two hundred years ago.

In the long history of the British and Spanish nations, there is a strong Teutonic element to be found, and this may possibly account for the presence of the Yule Log in the Pyrenean as well as in the British Christmas.

Nor is song an expression of joy peculiarly Spanish, though it has tended to die out in Britain since the coming of the Industrial Revolution. In Pyrenean Vallespir, the children run through the streets, shouting:

*Ninou, ninou,*
*L'esquella del bou!*

Little one, little one,
The bell of the ox!

which must have more to do with the bull of ancient Crete than with the ox that tradition has represented as having been present at the Manger.

The Yule Log is dragged through the village streets—as it used to be in England—by the "lads of the village," and is soundly beaten as it is drawn on its way. At the doors where the log-drawers stop, there are chocolates and nuts as presents—the "Christmas box."

In the chapter on the English Waits, it was mentioned that these songsters formerly banded themselves into corporations jealously watchful of their rights and privileges, and the same thing is to be found in Catalonia, though in a form of association peculiar to the district.

In the Catalan villages, the carollers or waits are called *Rosers*—members of a Confraternity of Our Lady of the Rosary—and, like the English Waits of former times, they have contrived to secure for themselves a kind of administrative authority, so that, as Violet Alford points out in her deeply interesting *Pyrenean Festivals,* "no celebration can be arranged without them.

"Not only do they have 'mayors,' but, blending the civic with the ecclesiastic, they elect priors and prioresses (for women are included) who organize balls, lead the dances, attend weddings, baptisms and funerals, and collect money for their Patron Lady and the Church. We shall find their fingers in every pie, more particularly in the musical pie, which when opened gives forth their traditional songs more loudly than four and twenty blackbirds could ever sing. The *Goigs,* or songs of joy, weigh down the Catalonian treasure bag. There are songs for every possible occasion, with verses so apt that one believes them improvised on the spot, as they would be at the Basque end of the mountains."

In some Catalan and Pyrenean villages, they elect *Mayorales* for a year from Christmas Day, and these functionaries go with their traditional Christmas chants from house to house, collecting an egg at each door for their trouble.

Tradition takes an unusually practical form on Holy Innocents' Day—formerly a most notable feast in England, especially among schoolboys. In the Pyrenees, they light bonfires in the town-gateways on this day, and a mock-mayor, who seems to belong to the band of Christmas Princes, Lords of Misrule, Boy Bishops, *Reges Fabarum*, and so on, that we met with in our survey of British Christmas customs, is elected who forces people to sweep up the streets, and collects fines to pay for a celebration.

The Epiphany, Twelfth Night, has not faded away as a feast in Catalonia, as it has in Britain. At Cervera, three boys dress themselves up as The Three Kings, and go forth singing for coppers and other trifling gifts. And on 1 January, the Feast of the Circumcision, Carnival officially begins.

In the valley of the Aude, where once the Moors were close in near-by Narbonne, and the fairy-tale city of Carcasonne is still a sight to outwit belief in one's eyes, the calendar seems to show the influence of the dark invaders. The inhabitants pay small attention to Christmas Day, but have a custom, celebrated on 31 December, which has—or, maybe, had—an exact parallel in Britain and Ireland. On New Year's Eve—from which the Audois "Christmas" season stretches—a "King of the Wren" assembled his company, and, armed with sticks, went out to kill a wren. Found and killed, the wretched bird was fixed to a pole, garlanded with olive, oak leaves and mistletoe, and taken home in triumph. On Twelfth Day, its killer was himself—if he were different from the original "King" who had led the hunt—paraded as "King of the Wren."

Candlemas is still a great feast in northern Spain, for the priest blesses the candles which are bought in the church and these candles are believed to possess magical properties, most useful in guarding cattle and even human beings from misfortune. These candles are always lit during thunderstorms, as was once the practice in England.

The dead are not forgotten in the Pyrenees, where their feast is called *le Jour des Morts,* and where they are not thought of either as souls or as saints, but as dumb nuisances, to be placated with gifts of chestnuts, which are placed on the sleeper's bed, so as to turn the attention of the malign *revenant* away from the sleeper to his placatory gift. It is the ghosts of the dead who return to give a child convulsions, and so, when the little ones have their "fits," you pray even harder for the dead.

"All Hallows" comes, in Britain, almost too early in the year to be regarded as a strictly Christmas feast, but they remember the dead at Christmas in northern Spain and south-western France, where, in Ariège, it is the custom to leave out a loaf, with a knife stuck in it, when you go off to Midnight Mass. This is for the dead. But in the Ariège valleys, Christmas is too snowy—and ways too blocked—to allow for celebration, and so Christmas has to wait until Candlemas, the ancient feast of the Mother Goddess, who takes the curious form, in the Pyrenees, of *Sant Gato* or *The Holy Cat.* The name is said to be a corruption of *Sant Agatha,* whose feast falls three days after Candlemas, but this is to be doubted. Neither spinning nor washing must be done on St. Cat's Day, and there are grim tales of the saint appearing, in the form of a cat, to women who had dared to wash on St. Cat's own feast-day.

To digress for a moment here into the province of philology, the word "cat"—which is the same, not only in all the Indo-European languages, but in Turkish as well[1]—would seem to be a contraction (as "bus" is of "omnibus," "spat" of "spatter-dash," "cab" of "cabriolet") of a word which is found in a near-enough-to-original uncontracted form in the Sanskrit, *mhragatha*—literally, "The Thing Which Washes Itself": a perfectly natural definition of a cat.

The prohibition of washing, then, on St. Cat's Day would rather imply that "Saint Agatha" was derived from "Saint Cat" than the other way about—for we may believe that this custom, like all the other Pyrenean customs, is certainly older than any Christian saint —as such.

In many parts of the Pyrenees, Saint Cat's Day has tended to replace Candlemas Day, on which, so the belief goes, the bears come out of the hibernation into which they entered on 8 December. Folk-lorists may find something to occupy their skill in determining the connexion between the limits of the Pyrenean bears' hibernation and the fact that 8 December is the Feast of the Immaculate Conception of the Virgin, while 2 February is the Feast of the Purification of the Virgin. The writer admits that he can suggest no plausible connexion—if, indeed, there be one at all.

In Genos, in the High Pyrenees—technically in France, but actually in what we may call the Pyrenean Land—they make a cross of beeswax, and, on Candlemas Day, stick it on the church door, but the feast itself they have taken forward three days, owing to the Cat Saint's known power over thunderstorms.

In ancient Rome, at the *Bacchanalia,* it was supposed that the dead returned to their homes. Tables were spread for them, and dice put out, that the dead might play. This superstition is still potent to command belief in the Pyrenees, though what, in ancient Rome, were the Family Dead, have now become, in Pyrenea,

[1] Latin, *catus* gives Fr. *chat*; Spanish, *gato*; Russian, *kot,* etc. The Turkish form is *kedi.*

*Hados*—or fairies—or *Hennos des Dieous*—"wives of the gods."

"They come," says Alford, "on the last night of the old year, bringing good luck in the right hand, ill luck in the left. Doors are opened for them, a room cleaned, a meal spread with a white cloth, bread, wine, a knife, a candle. In the morning, the master breaks any bread left and gives to everyone in his household. Those who provide liberally get large harvests, increased flocks and many children."

A curious custom is to be found at Christmastide in some parts of the Pyrenees. "Wassailing" having tended to come more to be a children's privilege than that of the grown-ups, the boys and girls go to call at the houses where a child has been born during the preceding year. They sing the appropriate chant—beating out the time with their wooden *sabots*—and afterwards demand chestnuts and apples. If anyone is so hardy as to refuse these licensed beggars, they add a stanza to their "poem," wishing the child bad luck—hoping that it will be "twisted like a pig's tail, stupid as a sabot!"

In Béarn, they prepare the tables on New Year's Eve for the dead, in spite of the fact that this un-Christian custom was banned by the Fathers fifteen hundred years ago—and more. The Feast of the Circumcision they celebrate with carnival, another custom that earlier lawgivers tried to stamp out—but with no more success than that attending the effort to put down the feasts of the dead.

They were once ruled by a Huguenot princess, who banned "the insolence and great licentiousness" of the Christmas—and other—festivals, and prohibited "the wearing of masks, dancing in the streets to the tambourin, singing immodest, lascivious and pernicious songs."

But, as Miss Alford remarks, "she could hardly have hoped to succeed where the Church she so hated had failed. As in 1563, so today they dance in the streets to the sound of the tambourin, and sing very surprising songs indeed."

Wassailing the fruit trees—by tapping them with a switch, and putting a large stone in the forks, dragging the Yule log—and beating that too!—acting the old fertility magic in Mummers' Plays of the sort which have almost (but not quite) died out in Britain: all these things they do, and thus remind us of the Ghost of English Christmas Past.

The bear is a creature still to be found in the High Pyrenees, and so Bear is the principal figure in the maskers' plays at the various carnivals. The appearance of the bear—sometimes the leader, sometimes the captive; at once the victim and the sacrificer—is the signal for licence. The bear becomes, as it were, several "bears," who seize on the passers-by, and subject them to cheerfully borne familiarities and indignities, and extract "fines" for the feast which will follow the ritual death of the bear. This mumming is found all over the north of Spain and the south and south-west of France.

Old Christmas Day is remembered in the valley of Roncal by fights between villages, the parties of attackers announcing their approach by ringing bells and waving sticks. But it is pleasant to read that Old Christmas Day is not forgotten in England, either.

Here is a cutting from the London *Evening Standard* under date of 29 December, 1950:

HOLY TREES FABLE

*Midnight Watch*

> Larger-than-ever crowds are expected to visit the famous Holy Thorn trees of Herefordshire on Old Christmas Eve (midnight, 5-6 January). According to legend the trees burst into bloom at midnight, and remain so for an hour. Some people say the trees originated from the staff planted by Joseph of Arimathea to mark the spot where he and his twelve companions landed in England (*sic*) in A.D. 35. Others say they spring from pieces which Joseph took from Christ's crown of thorns at His crucifixion.

A curious feature of Pyrenean Christmas celebrations is the presence of a "Christmas guy" in some places. In the valleys of the Bidassoa and the Baztan, the guy is called Olentzero, and set up in the ingle-nook, a cauldron on his head, a scythe in his hand. After a period of sitting in the chimney-corner, Olentzero is taken out by the village boys, who, with appropriate "wassailing" songs, carry him from house to house.

A Basque version of our own "Christmas stocking" is to be found in Guipuzkoa and Biscay, where the children, on Twelfth Night, put their shoes on the window-ledges, so that the kings may put a gift into them. Shoes are used for this purpose in Holland, on St. Nicholas's Eve. Is it possible that the English nursery-rhyme, which begins, "There was an old woman who lived in a shoe," retains the confused memory of a similar custom in England?

A custom in the province of Alava would seem to bear out the theory that worship of the cat is older than reverence paid to "St. Agatha," for in the town of Oyon the mayor and corporation, dressed in their robes of office, go to church on 22 January, accompanied by a band of music and a paid performer, "the katxi," who is dressed in a parti-coloured uniform of yellow and green, and who wears a pointed hat, and carries a stuffed cat's skin.

Outside the church, before the procession enters, the katxi is, by custom, forced to die a ritual death, and, as the katxi falls to the ground, a village official waves a flag over him, to the sound of music.

The whole town turns out to witness this ceremony, and to see the wheel of fireworks enclosing a puppet matador and bull. That this wheel of fire, in conjunction with the bull which was the chief symbol in ancient Mediterranean religion, perpetuates beliefs far more ancient than Christianity, cannot be doubted, and points to the endurance of tradition among a conservative people.

So ancient, indeed, that, in some of the more curious ceremonies, such as the ritual gelding of the totem horse, the *curé* of the village stays, by old custom, away.

It may sound paradoxical to affirm that the chief characteristics of Spanish popular singing is its rigid traditionalism and its extraordinary freedom of improvisation; but the paradox is more apparent than real. For the improvisation occurs only within the unalterable forms laid down by tradition, rather as there is one (repeated) line in the English song, "For He's A Jolly Good Fellow," which may be altered to suit the company.

There is, alas! insufficient space here to treat of the marvellous diversity of the songs and dances with which the people of northern Spain celebrate their festivals: songs and dances which have proved an inexhaustible mine of treasure for the ethnologist and the folklorist. Some of these customs are exceedingly indecorous, until one remembers that they are ancient fertility rites, and that the coming harvest depends upon their correct performance. Some appear to us to be exceedingly cruel.

There is no space to tell of the trials of strength, which remind one of the similar feats among the Scots, nor to describe the blood-curdling noise that the Basques make, *irrint-zina* or *hilhet*, for if anything were needed to convince people of other lands that the Basques are primitive, this animal screech supplies all the needed proof!

Until the expulsion of the Moors in 1492, the Spanish peninsula was still a congeries of small "Spains," and the title borne by modern Spanish sovereigns, King of the Asturias, had something more than a formal significance. The title once connoted an actual state of affairs: rulership of a scattered kingdom made up of practically autonomous provinces, loosely linked together by allegiance rather to a common religion than to any earthly prince.

Ferdinand and Isabella were, between them, heirs to all the Spains, and with their marriage, and the expulsion of the last Moorish king, Spain was one nation—legally, anyway. It was the ambition of these two extraordinary people to make it so in fact; to break down the dividing provincial jealousies, and to federalize the union of provinces which made up the peninsula. So, from about the year A.D. 1500, there comes a new note into Spanish affairs: a national, as distinguished from a provincial, one.

Madrid is a new city, an artificial construction; built to be a capital, as Washington, Ankara and Canberra have been. Built to be the capital of a new empire, and built where it was built so that no existing petty provincial jealousies should colour the spirit of its outlook and decisions.

Now, so far, we have had no great art—only some chatter—from Canberra, Ankara and Washington. Indeed, no art at all. No painting, no sculpture, no music, no poetry.

Madrid produced much, and, if it was not art of the very highest quality, it was still very far above the level of the worst. It was a polished, rather superficial art, and it could just as well have come from any one of half a dozen other European capitals. We remember that it was Madrid which produced Murillo, but ancient Roman and Visigothic Toledo which produced Domenico Theotocopoulos, nicknamed "Il Greco"—"The Greek"—and we see the essential quality of the Madrileño spirit: manufactured rather than developed, created rather than born—just like Madrid itself, in fact.

All the same, what the art lacked in quality it certainly made

Buying the Christmas turkey in Spain in the nineteenth century.

"Lucia"—the personification of the Spirit of Light. (Her name means "Light.") Pretty Scandinavian maidens, wearing their distinctive coronets of lighted candles, carry round the ritual drinks to celebrate the winter solstice—the ancient Aryan festival of the "unconquerable Sun."

up in quantity, and during that period which coincided with the Spanish imperial expansion—say from A.D. 1500 to 1625—there was a prodigious quantity of Christmas poetry turned out by the foremost Spanish writers, among whom Juan Lopez de Ubeda, Francisco de Ocana and Jose de Valdivielso were the principal. "Their *villancios*," says Miles, "remind one of the paintings of Murillo; they have the same facility, the same tender and graceful sentiment, without much depth. They lack the homely flavour, the quaintness, which make the French and German folk-carols so delightful; they have not the rustic tang, and yet they charm by their simplicity and sweetness."

Of course, it was just to escape that "rustic tang" in their affairs political and artistic, that the Spanish kings built Madrid. It is something that the court poets managed to retain even the "tender and graceful sentiment" to which Miles calls attention. All the same, it is there, the tender and graceful sentiment.

Here is a stanza from Ocana:

*Està entre dos animales,*
*Que le calientan del frio,*
*Quien remedia nuestros males*
*Con su grande poderio:*
*Es su reino y señorio*
*El mundo y el cielo sereno,*
*Y agora duerme en el heno.*

Literally translated:

He lay between two animals,
Who warmed him from the cold,
He who healed our every ill
With his sovereign Power.
He Whose realm and empery
Is all the earth and the boundless sky,
Lies sleeping now in the humble straw.

A more popular carol, preserved by Fernan Caballero, is somewhat, but not very much, more simple in flavour.

*Ha nacido en un portal,*
*Llenito de telaranas,*
*Entre la mula y la buey*
*El Redentor de las almas.*

*En el portal de Belen*
*Hay estrella, sol y luna:*
*La Virgen y San Jose*
*Y el niño que esta en la cuña.*

Here, in a doorway,
Where the spider has spun his web,
Between a mule and an ox,
Is born the Saviour of souls.

In that doorway of Bethlehem,
Are Star, Sun and Moon:
The Virgin and St. Joseph,
And the Little One lying in His crib.

M. J. Quin, writing in 1824, says that, in Madrid, at Christmas, "the evening of the vigil is scarcely dark when numbers of men, women and boys are seen traversing the streets with torches, and many of them are supplied with tambourines, which they strike loudly as they move along in a kind of *Bacchanal* procession. There is a tradition that the shepherds who visited Bethlehem on the day of the Nativity had instruments of this sort upon which they expressed the sentiment of joy that animated them when they received the intelligence that a Saviour had been born." It appears that, after having danced the streets until midnight, the crowds then entered the churches to hear the Midnight Mass, bringing their musical instruments—mostly tambourines and guitars—with them, and provided an amateur accompaniment to the church organ.

As formerly in Wales and the Isle of Man, there are, in Spain more than one Midnight Mass—or, rather, more than one Christmas Night Mass. In addition to the true Midnight Mass, there is the Dawn Mass—such as was until recently celebrated at Tenby, Carmarthen, St. Asaph and other places—and in the Spanish villages at least, a person who misses this Dawn Mass (the Cockerel's Mass, as it is called) is forced by public opinion to attend all three of the services held later on Christmas Day.

In some Spanish churches, at the end of the Midnight Mass, the chief celebrant stoops down, and takes from under the altar an image of the Holy Babe, dressed in all the tinsel finery so dear to Spanish religious taste. This image the priest holds aloft, for the adoration of the people.

In a land where, in spite of the pressure of outside opinion, even the tombstones are to be found cut in the rude likenesses of the men and women lying beneath them, it is not astonishing to find that images of one sort and another have always had a peculiar fascination for the Spanish character—whether of the north or of the south. What I have had to say elsewhere about the relation between images—including the Crib—and drama holds with special force in considering Spain.

The Spaniards have a natural love of play-acting, of "dressing-up," of, in short, drama, and they have taken readily to the opportunity to made material representations of those historical facts which have a deep religious significance. The writer has seen the dress-coated noblemen of Majorca carry the life-sized figure of Christ from His tomb in the cathedral, through the streets of Palma, and so back to the cathedral; and the Christmas images are treated with the same elaborate make-believe.

In her famous book, *The Night of Christmas*, published nearly a century ago, Fernan Caballero well describes the delight of Spanish children in the Christmas Crib.

The same change which affected the early church-dialogues in Italy, France and Britain affected them in Spain, and plays in the vulgar tongue came to entertain the people in Spain just as they did in other Christian lands. Out of the primitive *Stella*, that we have considered elsewhere, came the vernacular Coventry and Towneley Mysteries. Out of it came, too, the fine Spanish *Misterio de los Reyes Magos*, and elsewhere I have described how the "mystery"—though at the end completely removed from all contact with the rustic mind—survived longer in Spain than in any other of the more civilized countries.

I have told how the "mystery" in Spain early became classicized, and that the "mysteries" of the great Spanish poet, Lope de la Vega, are in the highest degree mannered.

The division between the "refined" and the "popular" was too great in Spain for either to have developed along healthy lines. The result of the too wide division was that the "refined" became lifeless and the "popular"—uncorrected by a higher art—became puerile.

The natural end was the expected one: the plays of Lope de la Vega are read only by hapless students of Spanish literature, and the Epiphany play in Madrid had degenerated, by the nineteenth century, into a mere puppet-play, in which the scenes of Christ's birth and infancy were acted by wooden images.

It must not be forgotten that Spanish customs have been exported from the mother country to colonies scattered over America, Asia and Africa, where the customs of the Spaniard have modified the customs of the original inhabitants, and in turn have been modified by them. So that it is not always easy now to know whether or not a certain custom is, say, Aztec or Spanish; Dahomeyan or Spanish; Quiche or Spanish—and to trace the history of Christmas in the vast Spanish empire is a task for which I have not the time or the space.

I recently received a Christmas-card from a friend who lives in Albuquerque, New Mexico. The card bears this information:

LUMINARIOS

Many, many years ago in the early Spanish days, Luminarios (festive lights) were used by the people of the Old Southwest on the Eve of Saints' Days and especially on Christmas Eve.

Luminarios are made by partly filling brown paper bags with sand, with a candle inserted inside, and are placed on the tops of garden walls, roofs and walkways. At night the candles are lighted and the homes are outlined in soft, radiant light.

At Christmas, Luminarios are said to light the way and guide the Christ Child to each home.

New Mexico is now a state of the U.S.A., but the influence of the original Spanish settlers is still strong. The Señora Calderon de la Barca has left us, in her *Life in Mexico*, a deeply interesting account of the manners and customs of a Spanish colony a little more than a century ago. In particular, she mentions a sort of drawing-room dramatic entertainment, or charade, which appears to have been based upon the wanderings of Mary and Joseph in Bethlehem in search of shelter.

The game—for such it was—was called *Posadas* (*posada* being the Spanish for "inn") and it lasted for eight days: a visit to a different *posada* being theatrically enacted on each of the eight days that the game lasted.

"On Christmas Eve, a lighted candle was put into the hand of each lady, and a procession was formed, two by two, which marched all through the house . . . the whole party singing the Litanies . . . a group of little children, dressed as angels, joined the procession. . . . At last the procession drew up before a door, and a shower of fireworks was sent flying over our heads, I suppose to represent the descent of the angels; for a group of ladies appeared, dressed to represent the shepherds. . . . Then voices, supposed to be those of Mary and Joseph, struck up a hymn, in which they begged for admittance, saying that the night was cold and dark, that the wind blew hard, and that they prayed for a night's shelter. A chorus of voices from within refused admittance. Again those without entreated shelter, and at length declared that she at the door, who had thus wandered in the night, and had not where to lay her head, was the Queen of Heaven! At this name the doors were thrown wide open, and the Holy Family entered singing. The scene within was very pretty: a *nacimiento* . . . one of the angels held a waxen baby in her arms . . . a padre took the baby from the angel and placed it in the cradle, and the *posada* was completed. We then returned to the drawing-room—angels, shepherds, and all—and danced till supper-time."

We know from classical writers that the Carthaginians offered gifts to one of their goddesses, the Lady Baalat, in the form of cakes, and the Christmas sweetmeat, eaten by all classes in Spain, and called *turròn*, may be the descendant of some Carthaginian ritual food. But ritual eating—"Take ye and eat!"—is so widespread, that it would be impossible to say with certainty whence the custom of giving and eating *turròn* comes. The Slavs have their Christmas *kolatch* cakes, the Tyrolese peasants their *zelten*, the British their Christmas pudding.

*Turròn* is a sort of nougat or "almond-rock," and it is a point of honour to buy it when it is offered for sale at your door. It comes in varying qualities, at varying prices, and for the poor there is a coarse kind, cheap to buy. But all buy it, and all eat it at Christmas.

Other Christmas delicacies to be found in Spanish homes at Christmas are almond soup, truffled turkey, and chestnuts cooked in every imaginable fashion, for the chestnut grows well in Spain, and its fruit is a favourite with Spanish palates.

Miles suggests that the giving of *turròn* may be a survival of the Roman custom of giving something sweet at the January Kalends, so that the ensuing year might be full of sweetness.

Except among the "internationalized" classes—the cosmopolites who are to be found in the Ritz Hotel in any great capital—it is not the Spanish custom to entertain, at Christmas, any but blood- and marriage-relatives. Christmas, in all Christian countries, is essentially the feast of family reunion, as it is the feast of the Divine Family, but in Spain it is the feast of the family *only*. The Spaniard is a man who has traditionally cultivated the virtues of hospitality, but he does not ask his friends to his house at Christmastide.

There is one truly agreeable custom observed in Spain at the time of the Nativity, that I am glad to see has not been abolished in the sad upheavals through which Spain has passed in recent years: the custom of granting an amnesty to military and political prisoners and convicted criminals.

On or just before *La Noche-buena,* the prison-governors, taking along with them the *defensores* or advocates, visit the prisoners, and, after holding a sort of drumhead judicial examination, liberate all those whose offences seem reasonably pardonable.

It is also the pleasant custom in Spain to visit the sick in hospitals—whether or not they be relatives; and one is conscious, in studying Spanish Christmas customs, that the sense of the Holy Family's essential humanity is always most strongly present in the Spanish mind. "Who is cold and hungry and bewildered on this night when, two thousand years ago, the Saviour was Himself cold and hungry and bewildered?" seems to be a question which forces itself upon the Spanish consciousness, and one whose answer there is no evading.

It has for long been a matter of reproach against the Spaniards that they "have no sense of time." It would be more just to say that they have a sense of the timelessness of eternal things. For the Spanish child, putting out his shoes for gifts, it is not unreasonable to think that, after the Three Kings have visited the Holy Child, they will stop by the little Spanish boy's window-sill, and leave him their gift. It is nothing to the Spaniard that all this happened two thousand years ago: he sees no reason to doubt the natural fact that everything which is good may be repeated for ever. Only in the bad lie the seeds of its own death.

CHAPTER TWENTY-ONE

# ASTROLOGICAL ELEMENTS IN THE CHRISTMAS STORY

"STAR" is one of the few words, dating from ancient times, which are common to the Semitic and the Indo-European—or "Aryan"—languages. It is unlikely that the Semites borrowed it from the Indo-Europeans—the Hittites and the Mitanni were the "Aryans" in closest contact with the Semites of Assyria and Israel—so we shall assume that "star" is a loan-word from the Semitic tongues.

Now loan-words, in any language, imply that the word has been introduced to express an idea not formerly the possession of the people who have borrowed the word to express it. A loan word always means that a new thing has been presented to the attention.

The French have borrowed our word, "riding-coat," and turned it into *redingote*; the Spaniards have borrowed our word "folk-lore" and used it unchanged. We have taken *chauffeur* from the French, and *tobacco* from the Caribs, and *cocoa* from the Aztecs, because all these words represent ideas new to the people who borrowed them. And when the ancient Indo-Europeans, coming into contact with the immeasurably more civilized Semites, borrowed the word "star," the *idea* of the star was a new one to them. Not, of course, that in their wanderings from South-west China to the Mediterranean the "Aryans" had not noticed that there were lights in the sky. Of course they had; but they regarded them as . . . just lights. Probably called them just that: The Lights.

It was not until they came into contact with a complex of peoples of roughly common race—the Semites—that the "Aryans" felt the need to designate the heavenly lights as a particular sort of lights; and borrowed the necessary word from the peoples who had made the *star* an object of peculiar attention.

Who first thought to reduce the casual notice of the heavens to a rigidly disciplined science of observation, we shall never know, but the Chaldeans had the reputation in the ancient world of being the founders of astronomy, as, later, they became famous as the most expert practitioners of the science of astrology. Chaldean soothsayers flocked to Rome, in the height of its imperial glory, and exercised much influence upon affairs and the opinions which govern event.

The evidence of an expert knowledge of astronomy, based upon close observations extending over an immense period of time, is to be found in the siting of buildings and cities in Egypt and Mesopotamia, whose orientation is exact to within inches of true. But there is also the evidence of inscriptions: carved and painted and penned records from Egypt, clay-tablets from Assyria and Babylon.

The Babylonian astronomers calculated the length of the year to near-exactitude, and divided the day-and-night into twenty-four hours (or, to be precise, twelve *beru,* or double hours). They also divided the equator into parts, each of which was subdivided into sixty minutes, and those parts again into sixty seconds. The reason for the division of the day and night into twenty-four parts (or twelve double parts) was that the Babylonians had a duodecimal system: that is, they reckoned in twelves, instead of, as with us, in tens.

Sixty being a "hand count" of twelves, was a favourite number with the Babylonians, and to this day we divide our compass in accordance with Babylonian ideas, and our weights and measures show traces of Babylonian influence, through Roman introduction.

The Ancient Jews were the "backward" cousins of the Assyrians, who owed their intellectual progress to the fact that they had invaded the land of a people of very high culture—the Sumerians. The Sumerians lost their independence and even their identity as a people, but not before they had passed on their culture to their conquerors. "Star" may even have been borrowed from the Sumerians by the Semites, before—ages afterwards—the "Aryans" borrowed it from the Semites.

The Babylonians fought and enslaved certain Jewish tribes, and led them captive to Mesopotamia, where the Babylonians could keep an eye on them, and see that the defeated Jews did not prepare for another revolt. The Jews bewailed their captivity, but it did much—this contact with the Babylonians—for the general intellectual level of Judaea—as the captivity in Egypt did.

By defeat and enslavement, the Jews were civilized far beyond the level of a pastoral people. They returned from captivity with an established culture, and among the many things that the Babylonians taught the Jews was an inordinate interest in the stars—for, by the time of the Babylonian Captivity, the Babylonians had developed astrology out of astronomy, and it was rather an astrological than an astronomical interest in the heavens that the Jews took back with them to Jerusalem.

The Bible is full of references to astrology: or, rather, it is obviously the work of different writers of a people conditioned to a way of astrological thinking. And the majority of these references pass unnoticed without the help of an able commentary. Still, there are certain books of the Bible in which the astrological element is clear enough, even without the help of a commentary. The Book of Job—an early work, dating from a time when the stars were still believed to be living things—is full of wonderfully poetical references to the stars: "Canst thou bind the sweet influences of Pleiades," God asks the whirlwind, "or loose the bands of Orion? Canst thou bring forth Mazzaroth in his season? Or canst thou guide Arcturus with his sons?"

Isaiah, too, and Daniel, are full of star-lore, and what I shall call star-thought; and one of the most significant points in the story of the Nativity of Jesus Christ is the strong astrological element in the story—an element which, so far, seems to have escaped exegetists.

Logically speaking, the Gospel story's account of the Nativity (St. Matthew's for preference) should follow on Isaiah, since the Nativity completes the tale that Isaiah had to tell. Isaiah's "Lo, a Virgin shall conceive, etc.," finds its obvious completion in the actual conception that was prophesied by Isaiah.

Now, whatever later ages may have decided to think of the story of the Annunciation, the early compilers and editors of the New Testament were in no doubt of the astrological significance of the Nativity episode.

In ancient Jewish astrological lore, Gabriel is the angel who governs the Moon; and Virgo, in the original zodiac of the Babylonians, represents the Moon-goddess. Therefore, the astrological bias in the editing of the New Testament would definitely equate the Virgin (Mary) with the Moon (Goddess), since Gabriel, the Angel of the Moon, is the spirit chosen to announce the tidings to Mary. It is significant that Christian art has always shown the Virgin Mary in association with the Moon. Murillo's "Assumption" is a good example.

A word here about the original zodiac. At first it consisted only of six signs: Taurus, Cancer, Virgo, Scorpio, Capricorn and Pisces; and all these signs but one are to be found as important elements in the story of the Virgin, who, let it be remembered, was to "crush the Serpent." There are two of our six original zodiacal signs. Three others used are as obvious. In the first place, the Gnostics and the early Christians (both being under the influence of Jewish mysticism even where they were not Jews themselves) always equated Jesus with the Fish. This was "explained" by showing that the Greek word for "fish," *ichthys*, was formed of the initials of the phrase (in Greek) *I*esous *Ch*ristos *T*heou *H*yios *S*oter: Jesus Christ, Son of God, Saviour. But one may make a dozen anagrams of the letters of *ichthys*, and with meanings the very reverse of "Jesus Christ, etc."

The fact is that the reference to the fish is purely astrological, as also is the insistence upon the Ox (*Taurus*) at the side of the Manger. The presence of this beast at the Nativity, and also the fact that the chief narrator, Matthew, is always symbolized as *Taurus*, has an astrological significance which need not detract from the real importance of the Birth. For, as the Apocrypha says, in *The Book of the Wisdom of Solomon*, "God Himself gave me unerring knowledge of the things which are—the circuits of years and the position of the stars; the thoughts of men, the diversities of plants and the virtues of roots." Thus Solomon ranks astrology equally with other wisdom.

Now "Anne," the mother of "Mary," brought her daughter and the Child to the High Priest. This seems a perfectly natural touch in the narrative, until we remember that the High Priest, as a ritual badge of office, used to wear a breast-plate set with twelve jewels, each engraved with the name of one of the twelve tribes of Israel. And the connexion of these twelve stones with the signs of the Zodiac was a commonly accepted fact among the Jews.

"And for the twelve stones," says Josephus, the great historian of the Jewish people, "whether we understand by them the months, or whether we understand the like number of the signs of that circle that the Greeks call the Zodiac, we shall not be mistaken in their meaning."

It is said, indeed, that the people of Israel, trekking through the wilderness, distinguished the various tribes by banners bearing the sign of the Zodiac appropriate to each clan.

Now here is an important point to consider. What really is the supremely dominant fact in the Nativity story, as St. Matthew tells it—as he sees it, rather? I think that I shall not be mistaken if I suggest that it is the appearance of the Star. The Star, in St. Matthew's narrative, binds every element of the tale together. The Three Kings say: "We have seen His Star, and we are come to to worship Him." Their coming justifies the Star, as much as the Star justifies their coming; and it justifies the Nativity, too, in the sense that the Birth would lack completeness did the heavens not match their signs with those earthly events with which they had connexion.

The Three Kings are astrologically significant, in the light of a certain statement in a version of the Creation Legend found on a Babylonian clay tablet:

*He prepared the mansions of the great gods.*
*He fixed the stars, even the Lumasi to correspond to them.*
*He ordained the year, appointing the signs of the Zodiac.*
*For each of the twelve months* he fixed three stars.

The enormous difficulty in the way of detecting all the astrological significance of the "setting" of the Nativity is our ignorance of the true date of the Birth; 25 December was quite arbitrarily selected by the Church in the fourth century A.D., and no one knows quite when the date should be fixed. If we did know, our comprehension of the symbolism of certain legends would be much more than it is. Perhaps the presence of the Ox, *Taurus,* is a confirmation of an ancient tradition that the Nativity took place in the spring? But what of the Shepherds: those obviously most important characters? Why are *they* so prominent in the story? Well, in ancient Akkad, where the astronomers studied the Moon

(*Virgo* in the original Zodiac) with elaborate care, the name for the haloes which are sometimes seen around the sun and moon were known by words which mean, in Akkadian, "sheep-fold," possibly because the Moon was regarded as being the shepherd of the stars. A Babylonian hymn to the Moon has the line:

"Thy word, O Moon-god, maketh sheep-fold and cattle-pen to flourish!"

The connexion between Shepherds and the Star is made very obvious!

It is in the apocryphal gospels that the old legends may best be studied: they are missing in their completeness from the present authorized New Testament. There, in the apocryphal gospels, may be found the goat (*Capricorn*) who has curiously given place, in popular legend, to the ass who stands with the ox at the Manger—possibly because the goat came later to symbolize the Devil, and was thus felt to be unsuitable as an attendant at the Nativity. Of course, it was astrological symbolism which originally put him there, but when that symbolism was forgotten he was changed to an ass—a completely non-Zodiacal creature.

The sign of *Cancer* seems, indeed, to be missing. He was originally a crab or tortoise, and I confess I cannot find him yet. Perhaps he has been changed into something "nicer," as the goat-fish, Capricorn, has been. Or perhaps there is reason for his absence. He is worth looking for. Our ancestors recognized and were not frightened by the astrological significance of the Nativity. It is worth bearing in mind that the font in the ancient Romney Marsh church of Brookland—that font which is the instrument of spiritual rebirth; the material agency by which the mystical repetition of the Nativity is enacted—bears on its thirteenth-century leaden surface *the twelve signs of the Zodiac*.

# BIBLIOGRAPHY

It is unnecessary to cite every authority drawn upon, but the following is a list of the principal works consulted in the preparation of this book.

I have not mentioned the standard histories of England and other countries, which are available to all readers, such as Green's *Short History of the English People*, Henri Martin's *History of France*, etc.


Alford, Violet: *Pyrenean Festivals*

Anwyl, E.: *Celtic Religion in Pre-Christian Times*

Ashton, John: *A Righte Merrie Christmasse!*

Aubrey, John: *Diary*

à Wood, Anthony: *Athenae Oxonienses*

Beard, Charles R.: *Lucks and Talismans*

Brand, John: *Observations on Popular Antiquities*

Camden Society: Reprints—various

Camden, Sir William: *Annals*

Chamberlaine, John: *Letters*

Chambers, E. K.: *The Medieval Stage*

Chambers, R.: *The Book of Days*

Collier, J. P.: *Annals of the Stage*

Cortet, E.: *Essai sur les Fêtes Réligieuses*

Corti, Count: *A History of Smoking*

Davies, Thomas: *Memoirs of the English Stage*

Dawson, W. F.: *Christmas and its Associations*

D'Israeli, Isaac: *Curiosities of Literature*

Duchesne, L.: *Christian Worship: Its Origin and Evolution*

Dugdale, Sir William: *Origines Juridiciales*

England, George (ed. by): *The Towneley Plays*

Evelyn, John: *Diary*

Fitzgerald, J.: *The Great Migration*

Fosbroke: *Encyclopaedia of Antiquities*

*Folk Lore Record, The*

Frazer, J. G.: *The Golden Bough*

Frazer, J. G.: *The Dying God*

Frazer, J. G.: *The Magic Art and the Evolution of Kingship*

*Gentleman's Magazine*

Gomme, Sir G. L.: *Folk Lore Relics of Early Village Life*

Graham, S.: *A Vagabond in the Caucasus*

Grimm, J.: *Teutonic Mythology*

Halliwell, J. O. (ed. by): *Ludus Coventriae*

*Harleian MSS.*

Harrison, Jane: *Themis: A Study of the Social Origins of Greek Religion*

Harrison, Jane: *Ancient Art and Ritual*

Hastings, J: *Encyclopaedia of Religion and Ethics*

Henderson, G.: *Survivals of Beliefs Among the Celts*

Hole, Christina: *English Customs*

Hone, W.: *The Ancient Mysteries Described*

Hone, W.: *Every-Day Book*

Hone, W.: *Table-Book*
Jones, Charles C.: *Recollections of Royalty*
*Journal of the Archaeological Association*
Kelleher, D. L.: *An Anthology of Christmas Prose and Verse*
Legh, Gerard: *The Accidents of Armory*
*London Magazine, The*
MacCulloch, J. A.: *The Religion of the Ancient Celts*
Machyn, Henry: *Diary*
Martinengo-Cesaresco, Countess: *Essays in the Study of Folk-Songs*
Mead, William Edward: *The English Medieval Feast*
Miles, Clement A.: *Christmas in Ritual and Tradition Christian and Pagan*
Morley, Henry: *English Plays*
News-Sheets and Pamphlets of the seventeenth and eighteenth centuries
*Notes and Queries*
*Oxford Book of English Verse*
*Paston Letters, The* (ed. James Gairdner)
Pearson, Karl: *Woman as Witch*
Pepys, Samuel: *Diary*
Reinach, Salomon: *Cultes, Mythes et Religions*
Renan, Ernest: *The Poetry of the Celtic Races, and Other Studies*
Rhys, Sir John: *Lectures on the Origin and Growth of Religion as Illustrated by Celtic Heathendom*
Rhys, Sir John: *Celtic Folklore: Welsh and Manx*
Rhys, Sir John: *The Welsh People*
Rickert, E.: *Ancient English Carols*
Roth, Cecil: *History of the Jewish People*
Sandys, O. W.: *Christmastide: Its History, Festivities and Carols*
Sandys, W.: *Christmas Carols Ancient and Modern*
Serao, Matilde: *La Madonna e i Santi*
Sharp, T.: *A Dissertation on the Pageants or Dramatic Mysteries Anciently Performed at Coventry*
Sidgwick, F., and Chambers, E. K.: *Early English Lyrics*
Stow: *Survey of London*
Stubbes, Philip: *Anatomie of Abuses*
Swift, Jonathan: *Journal to Stella*
Symonds, J. A.: *The Renaissance in Italy*
Tille, A.: *Die Geschichte der deutschen Weihnacht*
Tille, A.: *Yule and Christmas*
Toulmin Smith, L. (ed. by): *York Plays*
Underhill, Evelyn: *Mysticism: A Study in the Nature and Development of Man's Spiritual Consciousness*
Vaux, J. E.: *Church Folklore*
Waite, A. E.: *The Holy Grail*
Walpole, Horace: *Correspondence*
Walsh, W. S.: *Curiosities of Popular Customs*
Westminster, *Archives* of the City and Liberty of
Weston, Jessie: *From Ritual to Romance*
Whitelocke: *Memorials*
Williams: *Domestic Memoirs of the Royal Family and of the Court of England*
Wright, T. (ed. by): *The Chester Plays*

# INDEX